KT-143-119

AFRICA IN CRISIS

the causes, the cures
of environmental bankruptcy

by
Lloyd Timberlake

edited by Jon Tinker

An Earthscan Paperback

©Earthscan 1985
ISBN No 0-905347-57-9

Published by the International Institute for Environment and
Development, London and Washington, DC.

Typeset by Wetherby Typesetters, Wetherby, UK
Printed by Russell Press, Nottingham, UK

Cover photo: Mark Edwards/Earthscan

This book was edited by Jon Tinker and produced by
Barbara Cheney, with assistance from Rebecca Fowler.

Gerald Foley of Earthscan provided much of the
information on deforestation and energy. Dr John Gulland
of Imperial College, London, supplied details of Africa's
fisheries, while Dr Roger Blench of Cambridge University
(UK) provided data on pastoralism and indigenous plant
species. Renée Sabatier of Earthscan brought together the
research on health.

Phil O'Keefe of Newcastle-upon-Tyne Polytechnic (UK)
and Ben Wisner of Rutgers University (US), gave helpful
advice throughout this project — as did personnel at the
World Bank, the US Agency for International Development,
the Club du Sahel and Britain's Overseas Development
Administration. Professor Ieuan Griffiths of the University
of Sussex (UK), Paul Richards of University College
London, Andrew Millington of Reading University (UK),
Keith Rennie of the International Union for Conservation of
Nature and Natural Resources, and Gerd Meuer of the West
German radio service *Deutsche Welle* all offered helpful
advice on the final test. *But the comments and opinions
expressed remain solely those of the author.*

Earthscan is an editorially independent news and
information service on global development and
environmental issues. Part of the International Institute for
Environment and Development, it is financially supported by
several UN agencies, the European Community, the Nordic
aid agencies (DANIDA, FINNIDA, NORAD and SIDA), the
Netherlands Foreign Ministry, the Swedish Red Cross, the
World Bank and the Fondation de France. However, none
of these agencies are responsible for the opinions expressed
in this book.

Contents

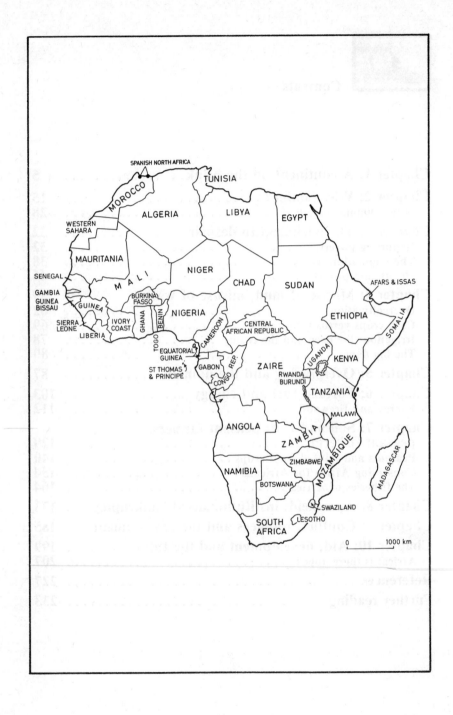

Chapter 1

A continent on the brink

"Starve the city dwellers and they riot; starve the
peasants and they die. If you were a politician,
which would you choose?"
Relief worker in the Sahel

This book was born in May 1984, when I visited Ethiopia some months
before the world became aware of an 'Ethiopian famine'. At that time,
people were just beginning to bring their pain and need into camps and
towns whose names have since become so familiar: Korem, Kobo,
Alamata, Makalle. People were not dying hourly then, as they were in
those camps a few months later. I saw what UN reports later called the
'drought-affected'.

> *The babies were quiet with hunger; the hunger had allowed
> colds and diarrhoea to take hold. Noses and eyes streamed with
> mucus; the mucus attracted flies, which crawled across open
> eyes. Mothers' breasts were flat, empty. Many mothers were
> trying to care both for their children and their own parents,
> men and women probably no more than 40 years old, but as
> decrepit as I remembered my own 95-year-old great-
> grandmother. Women were pre-chewing food for their parents.
> Men had all their possessions in small sacks, and no seeds or
> oxen back home upon which to build a future. The camp
> 'hospital' had the luxury of a tin roof and the smells that only
> hundreds of cases of diarrhoea in a closed room can cause.
> Corpses were left in place for a long time, because it was so
> hard to tell the dead from the merely exhausted.*

A year later, in mid-1985, famine had swept across Africa, from the
Atlantic to the Horn and south to Mozambique and the South African
bantustans. An entire continent was near the brink of collapse: the biggest
disaster to strike the planet since World War Two devastated Europe.

Mark Edwards/Earthscan

A starving woman is fed porridge at Korem relief camp, Wollo Region, Ethiopia. In 1985, such scenes were common in 20 African nations.

It was said that at least 30 million Africans in 20 nations did not have enough food to live on; that 10 million had abandoned their homes and farms in search of food and water; many had abandoned their countries. But these figures were mere guesses. No one knew the numbers of dead and dying, least of all the governments responsible for their welfare.

The African droughts and famines are not sudden natural disasters, nor are they simply caused by a lack of rainfall. They are the end results of a long deterioration in the ability of Africans to feed themselves, a decline caused largely by mistakes and mismanagement — both inside and outside the continent.

Fifteen years ago the Sahel, that strip of nations just south of the Sahara desert, was ravaged by a similar tragedy, and its causes were largely identified by international experts. But the same mistakes have continued almost without change: that catastrophe taught the world little. Now, radical changes must be made, or 'disaster' will become a permanent way of life for many Africans.

Unless policies are altered, "development in Africa will continue to be frustrated, leading to what the Economic Commission for Africa has called a political, social and economic 'nightmare' by the turn of the century", the normally cautious and conservative World Bank said in a 1984 report. The Bank was not talking about the famine, it was talking about the steady decline in living standards and agricultural production which preceded and caused it.

"Many institutions are deteriorating, both in physical capacity and in their technical and financial ability to perform efficiently", said the report. [1] "Although the picture varies from country to country, even those with good records in the 1970s now face serious difficulties. In short, the economic and social transformation of Africa, begun so eagerly and effectively in the early years of independence, could be halted or even reversed."

Africa's plight is unique. The rest of the world is moving 'forward' by most of the normally accepted indicators of progress. Africa is moving backwards. "Features of modern society to which many Africans have been exposed are withering: trucks no longer run because there are no spare parts and roads have become impassable; aeroplanes no longer land at night in some places because there is no electricity to light the runway", according to the World Bank. The continent's living standards have been declining steadily since the 1970s. Its ability to feed itself has been deteriorating since the late 1960s.

The scramble to get emergency food aid into Africa is necessary and may save lives, but it offers no long-term hope for the continent.

The tragedy has had one positive effect: it has started a painful reappraisal among those responsible for Africa's 'development', and brought a new willingness to admit mistakes.

*"It is hard to look at black Africa without feeling that
something has gone terribly wrong. It is not just the spectacle
of suffering that troubles us. It is the sense that we — we of
America and the West who thought we knew how to help these
people — did not know well enough, although we acted as we
did"*, wrote Washington Post *columnist Stephen Rosenfeld. "It
is now broadly recognised, not simply among critics but in the
establishment circles that provide funds and wield power, that
our advice has been deeply flawed."*

Advising Africa has become a major industry, with European and North
American consulting firms charging as much as $180,000 for a year of
an expert's time. At any given moment, sub-Saharan Africa has at least
80,000 expatriates working for public agencies under official aid
programmes. More than half of the $7-8 billion spent yearly by donors
goes to finance these people. Yet in the two and a half decades since
African independence, Africa has plunged from food self-sufficiency to
widespread hunger. Is Africa getting the right advice? This book suggests
it is not.

"We ...have failed in Africa, along with everybody else", admitted
World Bank senior vice president Ernest Stern. "We have not fully
understood the problems. We have not identified the priorities. We have
not always designed our projects to fit..."

Djibril Diallo of Senegal, spokesman of the UN Office for Emergency
Operations in Africa, put it more bluntly:

*"Africa's problem — Africa's biggest problem — is too many
people going around the continent with solutions to problems
they don't understand. Many of these solutions are half-baked.
But this is not to put all the blame on the North. Some
Africans don't understand African problems."*

Other Africans have been using far stronger language. Edem Kodjo,
former secretary-general of the Organisation of African Unity, told a group
of African leaders in 1978: "Africa is dying. If things continue as they
are, only eight or nine of the present countries will survive the next few
years. All other things being equal, absolute poverty, instead of declining,
is likely to gain ground. It is clear that the economy of our continent is
lying in ruins... Our ancient continent ...is now on the brink of disaster."
[2]

And others have called for radical change: "During the Sixties, we
became quite adept at arousing the conscience of our erstwhile colonial
masters", wrote Nigerian journalist Peter Enaharo in the magazine *Africa
Now*. "To put it bluntly, we blackmailed the hell out of the liberalism

then sweeping Western Europe... This became such a ravishing foreign aid earning procedure that, although times have changed, we have not altered our tactics significantly. The time has arrived for Africa to grow up.''

Africa is dying because in its ill-planned, ill-advised attempt to 'modernise' itself it has cut itself in pieces. The cities where the governments live have been torn from the countryside, and development budgets have gone to filling those cities with hotels, factories, universities and cars. This has been paid for by milking the seven out of every 10 Africans who live on the land, by taking much from them in labour and produce and giving back little in money or support. In these policies, Africa has been advised, financed and assisted by Northern governments and aid agencies.

The result? Cities surrounded by shanties, hotels full of Northern development experts, factories either idle or producing goods few can buy, universities producing graduates who can find no work, expensive cars full of civil servants, businessmen, soldiers and policemen. East Africa has a Swahili word for them: the *Wabenzi* — the Mercedes-Benz tribe.

> *"It's the town that's done for the peasants"*, said one elderly *Senegalese farmer. "Twenty years on we've come to realise what Independence really meant. It was just for the towns. One of these days we'll be asking Dakar for a reckoning, you'll see."* [3]

But in taking too much from its farmers, Africa has taken too much from its land as well. It has overdrawn its environmental accounts, and the result for much of Africa has been environmental bankruptcy. The big farm schemes of the Northern experts, and the small efforts to stay alive of the rapidly growing rural populations, have overcultivated, overgrazed and deforested the soil.

As the soil erodes, so do Africa's living standards. Bankrupt environments lead to bankrupt nations — and may ultimately lead to a bankrupt continent.

To describe Africa's crisis as 'environmental' may sound odd. In Europe and North America the environment is often a luxury issue. Is the air more or less hazy? Are there as many birds as there were a decade ago? Are the cities clean? What have environmental concerns to do with the fact that in 1985 the entire Hadendawa people of northeastern Sudan faced extinction due to starvation and dispersal?

The Sudanese government, with the help of Northern aid, World Bank loans and Arab investment, has put vast sugar and cotton plantations on its best land along the Nile. It has ignored rapidly falling yields from smallholder farming in the 1970s. It seems not to have noticed that the land — the 'environment' — upon which eight out of every 10 Sudanese depend for their livelihoods is slowly perishing due to over-use and misuse. It invested little in dryland regions where people like the Hadendawa live. So when drought came, these pastoralists and peasants had no irrigated settlements in which to take temporary refuge, no government agencies to buy their livestock, no sources of drought-resistant sorghum seeds ready for planting when the rains resumed. But neither have the government's investments in cash crops produced money to pay the nation's way through the drought. The result is starvation and debt: Sudan's external debt in 1985 was estimated at $9 billion. President Nimeiri, overthrown in April 1985, has paid a personal price for leading Sudan to environmental bankruptcy.

Soil erosion matches the erosion in farmers' political power, as they are more and more squeezed out of their nations' political and economic life. In democracies where large proportions of the population live off the land, the farming lobby forces governments to put money and attention into the soil. In the 1890s and 1910s, US farming families starved to death in droughts on the Great Plains. But today soil and water conservation programmes, crop insurance, rural credit, agricultural education and advice, forestry services, fish and wildlife services — all these make it possible for rural people in the industrialised world to survive natural disasters such as drought and flood.

Africa is far behind in providing such services and institutions. How can countries such as the Sudan, Mali or Tanzania hope to develop industrially or economically when more than 80% of their populations — the rural people — are growing poorer every year?

> *A Senegalese peasant saw his land being taken to make way for an irrigation project to grow rice which would be so expensive that only city people could afford it. He said: "We know that the government wants larger and larger areas brought under irrigation because that is what the Americans and others are paying for. But this money is given for the sake of politics, not for seeing the peasant improve. Who benefits? Who gets the money? Who gets the land and machinery? All this will serve us nothing."* [4]

If bad policies are the cause of Africa's crisis, environmental bankruptcy is its driving force. The famine "suggests a breakdown in the relationship between people and environmental support systems that could lead Africa into a crisis of historic dimensions — one that goes far beyond short-term emergency food relief", wrote US environmentalist Lester Brown. [5] This breakdown can only be repaired by development which is 'sustainable', which takes from the land only as fast and as much as the land can provide, which puts back into the land as much as it takes from it. And this can

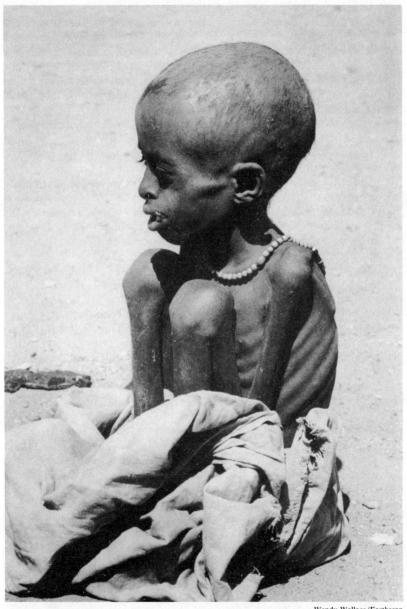

Wendy Wallace/Earthscan

One of 30 million: a child of the Hadendawa people, Eastern Sudan. The Hadendawa faced virtual extinction as a culture due to hunger and dispersal.

only be achieved by bringing the farmers into political and economic life.

As this book makes clear, techniques of reversing environmental degradation are widely known. Each chapter describes ways in which Africa's rural people can and are being mobilised to conserve soil and water, to plant and tend trees and to increase production at the same time.

The answers to environmental bankruptcy are not technical ones. The colonial solution was for the rulers to impose on the ruled a series of regulations and edicts, ignoring the socio-economic factors which forced the people to degrade their environment. This view blamed the victim, saw the African as lazy, ignorant, backward and irrational. The same essentially colonial attitude dominates much environmental thinking today: the stupid peasant must be educated not to cut down trees.

And the purely technical solution also ignores the depressing political and economic realities of modern Africa. Just as the rural peasant exists on a day-to-day, hand-to-mouth basis, so too does his government — beset by low commodity prices, by high oil prices, by high interest rates, by a high-value dollar and by debts which are huge in proportion to foreign exchange earnings (see Chapter Three).

In the short to medium term, the threats to these fragile governments come not from the countryside but from the *Wabenzi* — the disaffected urban elites: the entrepreneurs, civil servants, police and armed forces. Zaire is ruled by a former army sergeant, Burkina Faso (formerly Upper Volta) by a former captain, Liberia by a former master sergeant, Ghana by a former flight lieutenant, Nigeria by a former major general, Libya by a colonel — all of whom seized power in coups. Such leaders see little short-term political gain in paying attention to a rural majority which has no political power — this despite the lesson of the 1968-73 Sahel crisis, during which every government fell, largely because the rural crisis became so severe that it *did* reach the capitals.

The policies of nearly all African governments favour the urban elite, by keeping food prices low, or by seeing to it that profits from major cash-cropping schemes go to urban-based companies and individuals. Governments see little economic motive for investing in the rural hinterland. One of Africa's many vicious cycles is at work here: government policies degrade the rural resource base; degraded farmland produces little of economic value.

Obviously, a government will find it difficult to stay in power if the majority of its people are seen to be starving, although it may well be able to ignore a famine in a remote area where few journalists or foreigners ever go. Obviously, a nation in which the majority of the population plays little part in the cash economy will have difficulties developing economically. But it would require vision and courage for national leaders to see and act on the basis of these realities. Such vision and courage are rare in African governments today.

Mark Edwards/Earthscan

"Features of modern society to which many Africans have been exposed are withering", said the World Bank. This Lagos suburb is slowly being overwhelmed by garbage.

The industrialised nations which aid and advise Africa also lack motivation to change their ways. When money for Africa was plentiful in the 1970s, due to high commodity prices and easy credit, much of the investment and aid went into 'white elephant' projects in the cities, says the World Bank now. "External financial agencies have shared the responsibility for this inadequate discipline over the use of investment resources", it admits. [6] This donor culpability is hardly surprising. When Northern aid agencies lend for the sort of steel and concrete projects which former European development commissioner Edgard Pisani scathingly dubbed "cathedrals in the desert", they do so in the knowledge that Northern goods, equipment and expertise will be used. Northern economies receive a direct economic boost. Were aid agencies to invest in the sort of grassroots, community-participation rural development so badly needed in Africa (see Chapter Ten), there would be little economic kickback. That form of development assistance requires little from Northern construction and manufacturing firms. (The Soviet bloc has been particularly reticent to give Africa any development assistance. In fact, until late 1984 — when embarrassed to do so by Western donations — it had given no money or food for famine relief in its client state of Ethiopia.)

Recently, Britain has cut back on most forms of development assistance. Only one area of the bilateral aid programme was growing substantially:

the Aid-Trade Provision. These projects, suggested by British exporters and designed to help British exporters, grew from 10% of total bilateral project aid spending in 1980, to 25% in 1982. [7]

In the long run, encouraging grassroots rural development would probably do more to make recipient nations good customers for Northern exports than present programmes tying aid to the purchase of goods. It would also help to stabilise a continent whose many small wars and guerrilla uprisings sometimes threaten to escalate outside the continent. But it would require vision and courage for Northern political leaders to see and act on the basis of these realities. Such vision and courage are rare in Northern governments today.

This book explains how famine is not necessarily the result of drought, how people and policies cause drought, how drought reveals the misuse of natural resources and the vulnerability of the rural poor (Chapter Two).

It examines the causes and cures of environmental degradation, and the background against which this degradation has occurred: debts, falling commodity prices, high interest rates, extreme population pressures, inappropriate aid (Chapter Three).

It dissects the roles of overcultivation, overgrazing, deforestation, erosion and the decline of food production.

It examines the fuelwood crisis and the misuse of water resources, and explains how Africa's environmental diseases and loss of wildlife are both a cause of and a symptom of the continent's decline (Chapters Four-Seven).

In each instance, it offers examples of places where Africans are setting things right, proving that the problems are not insoluble.

The book shows the relationships between Africa's environmental bankruptcy, its millions of environmental refugees, and the continent's political and social instability (Chapter Nine). Finally, it shows how development based on the under-used skills and ambitions of small farmers could help Africa build a more stable, famine-free future.

Chapter 2

Why famine?

"These people are dying under the supervision of
the Red Cross and the United Nations."
Relief worker at a famine camp in eastern Sudan

In 1985, 30 million Africans were hungry because of the drought. In a 'normal' year, 100 million Africans are malnourished and severely hungry.

So when do we declare a famine? Do not 100 million severely hungry people make a famine? The UN in late 1984 set up a special office for 'Emergency Operations in Africa', and began to churn out statistics to persuade rich nations to give more food and money.

It said that because of drought in Angola, one third of all children were dying before they reached the age of five. But one-sixth of all Angolan children die before their first birthday in a 'normal' year.

The UN said that 10 million people had "been forced to abandon their homes and lands in search of food and water; up to half of these are overcrowded in temporary shelters and large numbers have fled to urban areas". But in a 'normal' year in Africa, hundreds of thousands of people abandon their homes and move into 'temporary' shanties in the big cities.

None of this is meant to claim there was no drought, no famine in Africa. But there is a temptation on the part of politicians, and indeed almost everyone else, to separate the problems and processes of 'normal' times, from the problems and processes of 'disaster'. There is a 'disaster response', a pouring in of food and money. There is no logical reason for starting or stopping this response at any particular time. Ethiopia's drought began in 1981, but there was no spasm of relief aid until late 1984. Chad has suffered drought for 10 years, Cape Verde for about 15. But the disaster response starts and stops, the timing based more on news reports than on real human needs.

For Africa's hungry in 1985, the drought was not a 'different' struggle.

It was just a time when many more than usual accepted defeat in their long, exhausting struggle to feed themselves. Many surrendered to death; many more abandoned their land.

We can accept that their struggle during normal times is caused by political and economic factors, but when a drought is declared we forget politics and economics. We see the tragedy as 'an act of God', a lack of rain, something off the scale of the normal. But those 30 million drought victims were not 'extra' to the 100 million who normally go hungry, because of the way African governments and the rest of the world run African affairs. They were just the most vulnerable of those 100 million. They were dying and fleeing as much because of politics as because of drought.

Numbers versus human beings

In the North, and even in the capitals of the stricken countries, famine becomes largely a matter of numbers: numbers of people 'affected', of homeless, of dying. The numbers are only the roughest of guesses. To most African governments, peasants go largely uncounted and unnoticed when alive. We should not be surprised that their deaths are not accurately tabulated.

It is almost impossible to get past the numbers, to the misery and pain of the individual victims, and then to multiply that a millionfold to get some idea of the total horror. Mercifully, perhaps, the human mind cannot absorb death and despair by the million or even by the thousand, in Auschwitz or Korem, in Biafra or Kampuchea.

One could document the suffering by taking a camera or notebook into the relief camps, but for every victim in those camps there were tens of thousands suffering in their own villages. Yanguse, a 33-year-old mother of five, lives on the Kobo-Desse road in Ethiopia's central highlands. Her oxen had died; her half-hectare of land was so over-used that even in a 'good' year it gave only a fifth of what it gave a decade ago, and it had ceased to produce anything. Her husband was ill, feverish, and there was no doctor to diagnose or treat his illness. When I visited them in May 1984 he was using borrowed oxen to sow seed which — I know now — never got rain, never grew.

"We have no money, and only a little sorghum from some friends. I may have to turn to relatives — but they have nothing either", said Yanguse.

Outside the villages, among the nomads, there was just as much hunger and exhaustion, but it was spread in flimsier huts across wider areas. In the Borkena Valley of Wollo Region, Ethiopia, trees were straining under the weight of vultures which had come to feed on dead cattle. But there

Barbara Cheney

Borkena Valley, Wollo Region, Ethiopia. Vultures wait their chance to feed on the dying cattle of the Afar nomads. Only a small proportion of Africa's suffering was brought to the famine relief camps; much of it spread across the vast landscape, out of range of television cameras, often out of range of relief efforts.

were people camped beneath those trees as well, the vultures giving their hovels an end-of-the-line feeling that was almost melodramatic.

> *I saw a tiny fraction of the 'drought affected', a few thousand, no more. But I saw the humans behind the statistics, and then for months read about and saw on television their growing numbers. The Ethiopian camps swelling by the thousand, and armed soldiers keeping thousands out of Korem, where I had watched children learning their alphabet in an outside classroom. The hundreds of thousands crossing into the Sudan. The camp at Wad Sherife in eastern Sudan which held 5,000 drought refugees in late 1984 and 35,000 in early 1985; an old man filled an exercise book with numbers of dead: 17 one day, 24 another. The camp at Wad Kawli where 40,000 dug for water in a dry river bed. It was of these camps that a relief worker said: "These people are dying under the supervision of the Red Cross and the United Nations".*

During 1984 and early 1985, these 'drought affected' kept increasing across Africa. But those who had been to the camps, and those who could perceive as real the images they saw on television, could only think of the fly-covered faces, the withered adults, the young bodies that looked like bad stick drawings of children by children.

* *Sudan:* some 4.5 million Sudanese hungry in Darfur, northern Kordofan and Red Sea province, and hundreds of thousands of refugees still coming in from Ethiopia and Chad.
* *Ethiopia:* almost eight million affected, the numbers expected to rise. Speculation on whether or not a million were already dead.
* *Chad:* the 'worst drought' in its history. At least 1.5 million, almost a third of the population, depending for survival on food aid. Some 70,000 new arrivals destitute in the capital N'Djamena; 1,000 dying each month. About 600,000 refugees fled into the Sudan, 40,000 into the Central African Republic and 8,000 into Cameroon.
* *Niger:* the 'worst drought' in the past century; 2.5 million directly affected; 400,000 displaced.
* *Mali:* 'worst and longest drought' ever, with 1.2 million people hungry and 95,000 uprooted. Scorched pastures and decimated herds; dust storms so severe that the sun was invisible for days on end.
* *Mozambique:* 2.5 million hungry, 1.6 million severely undernourished.
* *Mauritania:* 1.1 million out of a population of 1.8 million in need of emergency assistance; accelerated deterioration of rangelands, trees, oasis agriculture and groundwater supplies.

* *Burkina Faso:* 500,000 affected; complete crop failure in the north.
* *Angola:* 500,000 in critical need of assistance; acute malnutrition; large-scale movements to towns, roads and railway lines. To make it worse, far worse, here as in Mozambique, Chad, Sudan and Ethiopia, famine was combined with war.

There were more countries on the 1985 UN list: Botswana, Burundi, Cape Verde, Kenya, Lesotho, Rwanda, Senegal, Somalia, Tanzania, Zambia, Zimbabwe.

The deeper causes

To the average newspaper reader, the causes of Africa's troubles in 1983-85 seemed tediously obvious: there was a shortage of rain, leading to poor harvests, leading to famine. The rains would eventually come again, and the troubles would be over.

But rainfall was not the whole explanation of Africa's hunger. The 'drought' began in the Sahel in 1983, but in 1983-84, five Sahelian countries — Burkina Faso, Mali, Niger, Senegal and Chad — harvested a record 154 million tonnes of cotton fibre (up from 22.7 million tonnes in 1961-62). Cotton is grown largely by small farmers in the region, the same small farmers who could not grow enough food to feed themselves. The Sahel set another record in 1984; it imported a record 1.77 million tonnes of cereals (up from 200,000 tonnes yearly in the early 1960s). The fact that cotton can be grown but grain cannot has more to do with government and aid agency policies than with rainfall. (See Chapter Four for a discussion of these policies.) In fact, Africa's ability to feed itself has been steadily diminishing for more than two decades. When the rains return, Africa's problems will *not* be over. The famines are the hotspots of a more generalised malaise.

A drought is a lack of water, but not necessarily a disaster. Whether or not a drought becomes a disaster depends on how people have been managing their land before the drought.

This realisation is percolating into the upper reaches of the aid and development organisations. "Although Africa faces one of its worst crises in modern history, the famine is not only the result of inadequate rainfall. The effects of the drought, in terms of its impact on agricultural production, on the conditions of national economies and on people, are the result of long-term trends", said World Bank senior vice president Ernest Stern in late 1984.

Independent organisations are more blunt: "The spotlight of public attention focused in late 1984 on emergency food relief; the media regularly attributed the famine to drought. But the drought, though a triggering event, is not the basic cause", said the Washington-based Worldwatch Institute. [8]

When *Newsweek* magazine in early 1985 asked Dawit Wolde- Giorgis, head of Ethiopia's Relief and Rehabilitation Commission, what his nation could do to avoid "suffering from continued drought", he mentioned neither rain nor food relief:

> *"We have to start over again with the forestation programme. We have to start irrigation, soil and water conservation projects. If we had the know-how, the technology and the capability to properly utilise existing water, we would not face shortages in the coming years. But we don't have the technology, the manpower, the money."*

What is a disaster?

Droughts, earthquakes, floods, hurricanes: none of these are necessarily 'disasters'. To become a disaster, such events must kill and injure people and destroy their property. A drought on a desert island is no disaster, nor is a flood in an uninhabited mountain valley.

It is the relationships between humans and these trigger events which determine whether a disaster will occur, and, if so, how big it will be. In 1984, the Swedish Red Cross and Earthscan published a study *(Natural Disasters: Acts of God or Acts of Man?)* which found that the number and severity of so-called 'natural' disasters is increasing, especially in the Third World. It is not that weather patterns are changing to produce more floods and cyclones, nor that earthquakes and volcanic eruptions are more frequent or more violent. But more and more people are *exposed* to the natural trigger events. The poor, the malnourished, the young and the old are disastrously vulnerable to disaster triggers.

Six times more people died from natural disasters each year in the 1970s than in the 1960s. Most of the victims were poor people in poor countries.

In the cases of hurricanes, earthquakes, tsunami (tidal waves) and volcanic eruptions, people are turning these events into disasters by getting in the way of them in larger numbers. The poor live in dangerous housing on dangerous ground. Managua, Nicaragua and San Fernando, California are all *prone* to earthquakes, but Nicaraguans are many times more *vulnerable*.

* In 1972 a quake struck Managua and killed 5,000 people; in 1971 a slightly stronger quake struck San Fernando, and killed only 65 people.

* In 1974, a hurricane hit the deforested hillsides of Honduras, killing 4,000 peasants. A similar hurricane struck Darwin, Australia, that same year, killing 49 people.
* The average Japanese disaster kills 63 people; the average Peruvian disaster kills 2,900.

In the case of floods, people make the disaster itself more likely, by clearing vegetation and compacting the soil so that the land loses its 'sponge effect' — its ability to soak up large quantities of rainwater and release it slowly. Given the rapid rates of world deforestation, it is not surprising that floods are the fastest growing natural disaster: 5.2 million people affected per year in the 1960s, 15.4 million per year in the 1970s.

Like floods, droughts are largely caused and exacerbated by human action. Though apparent opposites, droughts and floods are closely related. Droughts are indeed partly caused by too little rain, and floods by too much, but both are also caused by the land's inability to *absorb* rain.

Given the overcultivation and land misuse forced on many people in the tropical Third World, one would expect drought to be a major disaster worldwide. It is. Droughts already affect more people than any other disaster, and are increasing rapidly in number and intensity. During the 1960s, drought affected 18.5 million people each year; during the 1970s, 24.4 million. And in the one year of 1985, at least 30 million suffered in Africa alone.

Rain in a drought

The people of highland Ethiopia felt the destructive impact of rain on over-used soil during one week in May 1984. I was in Wollo Region then, during the third year of drought, and there were suddenly about four days of unseasonal, unexpected, heavy rainfall.

Throughout the region, farmers harnessed up weak oxen and began to sow what seeds they had left. But Wollo today is a moonscape of treeless hills and valleys. All the land that an ox can climb or a man stand upon has been cultivated. Farmers even suspend themselves by ropes to sow hillsides too steep to stand upon.

The rains of May 1984 bounced off this compacted, vegetation-less watershed soil. The water ran quickly off in flashfloods, carrying away soil and precious seeds towards the lowland deserts to the east, or towards the Nile basin to the west. After a night of rain, I looked out from a hilltop to see massive erosion, hills looking as if they had been dynamited, mud and rocks from the fields of hill farmers strewn over the fields of valley farmers.

On the rangelands, a thin, sickly grass sprang up which bloated the drought-constricted stomachs of the nomads' cattle, killing many of them. Drought-weakened old people and children were wet and cold at night. In the relief camps, rain poured through flimsy huts designed to protect from the sun, and water settled in the depressions that were the hut floors. The death rate increased.

Tragically, the World Food Programme used satellite photos taken after these rains to gauge Ethiopia's need for food relief. Presented with images of light vegetation through the highlands, estimates were far short, leading to greater hunger in the coming months.

In Wollo, the May 1984 rains were a minor catastrophe in the midst of a major catastrophe, doing far more harm than good.

Drought: the differences

Drought is not like most other disasters: it can be seen coming, slowly, from a long way off.

Drought, more than any other disaster, chooses its victims. Although the wealthy usually live well protected from hurricane and earthquake, they are not immune to either, if caught in the wrong place at the wrong time. But the wealthy are *never* killed by drought.

What is true of individuals is true of nations. Drought may strike hard at rich nations with large areas of dryland agriculture, such as the United States and Australia, but (except perhaps in newspaper headlines) it never 'devastates' them. The agricultural systems are protected by soil and water conservation schemes, the farmers themselves by insurance and credit. The United States and Australia both suffered droughts in 1983. Production suffered; maize yields in the US had not recovered by early 1985; farmers lost money, and many who were already in debt went bust. But none starved.

Oxford economist Amartya Sen has described drought and famine as largely crises of 'entitlement'. It is not so much that there is no food, but that large numbers of people are not entitled to what food there is because of their positions in society. [9] On a global scale, this is clearly the case: if the hungry Ethiopians had enough dollars, they could ultimately buy food. But whether this analysis applies in practice to thousands of people starving in a camp is debatable. Nevertheless, some relief agencies have experimented successfully with handing out money, not food, in famines.

Barbara Cheney

Africa on the move. These farmers are walking to a relief camp in Ethiopia's Central Highlands to get their rations of grain. Ten million people across the continent have been uprooted and forced to seek water, food, new shelter.

Ethiopia: the politics of famine

For famine to follow drought, two pre-conditions are required: a vulnerable agricultural system and misplaced political priorities.

A study of the 1972-74 Ethiopian famine by British nutrition experts found that famine was rarely associated with total food shortages. Instead, "when shortages are threatened, prices of staple foods in local markets tend to rise catastrophically, and people cannot afford to buy or transport the food that is available", according to Frances D'Souza of the London-based International Disaster Institute.

Most famines follow a set pattern. As food prices rise, young men move to cities or even other countries to earn money to buy food. Next, farmers in the famine area begin to sell livestock, first expendable sheep and goats, then more important and expensive animals like mules and plough oxen. The market for livestock is flooded, and farmers' purchasing power drops further. Rural households begin to move, often to relatives, or to cities or to other areas where there is thought to be food. This movement increases food demand in neighbouring regions, raising prices.

Thus the 'famine' may move outwards from a centre like ripples from a stone thrown into a pond. The speed of this movement is often the same as the speed at which the youngest, the oldest, the weakest members of exhausted, hungry families can walk.

In countries where governments have little knowledge of what happens in their rural areas, the arrival of hungry people in cities or roadside camps may be the first sign of famine. But this, according to D'Souza, "is a terminal sign of distress, and at this stage it is almost impossible to prevent massive death tolls".

The famine in the highlands of Ethiopia is especially tragic because it came as the Marxist Ethiopian government was beginning to adopt the sort of policies which *can* save soil and water. Since the fall of Emperor Haile Selassie in 1974, the farmers had been increasingly organised into Peasant Associations to plant trees and construct soil terraces.

But by 1984 drought and the population density of the central highlands overwhelmed these efforts. Some 70% of Ethiopia's 42 million people live in these highlands. The vast majority survive by growing rainfed sorghum and a type of millet known as 'teff' *(Eragrostis abyssinica).* The government provides them with little or nothing in terms of agricultural education, advice, inputs or marketing help. Ethiopia has the worst system of rural roads in the world: and there is one area of Wollo where one may walk for 10 days without crossing a road.

The present revolutionary government has little idea of what happens outside the main towns and away from the main roads in the highlands; neither did Haile Selassie's government. Yet both this government and the Northern donor governments had ample warning of the present disaster. The first documented reports of drought came as early as March 1981, after poor rains in 1980, and were accompanied by a UN investigation which recommended a relief and development package. The rains failed again in July and August of that year, and yet again in 1982. People began moving from the countryside of Tigray and Wollo into towns. Rains failed again in 1983; farmers began moving into the Sudan. (From much of Eritrea, the initial movement was to the Sudan, because most of the towns are controlled by the Ethiopian government, against which Eritrean separatists have been fighting for 22 years.) In March 1984, the government requested 900,000 tonnes of emergency food aid; donors pledged 94,000.

In May 1984 Earthscan took 25 European and African journalists to the highlands of Ethiopia. Major Northern newspapers and news agencies were represented. All reported that at least five million people faced starvation. Our reports got little attention.

In October 1984, a BBC TV crew, by chance delayed in Addis Ababa where it was changing planes, went to Wollo and saw children dying of starvation. Their film was shown all over the world. The Western public reacted with a convulsion of concern and donations — a reaction which finally galvanised Western governments.

The response was typical of Western reaction to a well-publicised sudden disaster such as flood, or earthquake: ports, airports and nearby warehouses became jammed with a sudden influx of food; storage, transport and distribution systems became stretched to and beyond the breaking point. But this disaster was already three years old.

Peter Cutler and Rob Stephenson of the International Disaster Institute visited Ethiopia in September 1984 and reported on the many reasons that relief operations were not wholly effective. Among them:

* The government was giving the donors almost no information about the amount and type of food stored in government warehouses. Relief agencies had little confidence in the Ethiopian Relief and Rehabilitation Commission (RRC) because of its lack of efficient commodity accounting.
* There was in Addis Ababa "not a single piece of scientifically credible recent data" on the size and location of populations at the point of destitution and social collapse.
* Coordination meetings among relief agencies were infrequent and conducted at a junior level.
* The government restricted travel and data collection by expatriates outside Addis Ababa.
* Celebrations of the 10th anniversary of the 1974 coup in September consumed a vast amount of government time and money — including a month's practice of "parade and banner-waving exercises" by the staff of the RRC.
* The government's relief strategy disguised the size of the famine problem by keeping victims out of roadside towns.
* "Ethiopia's draconian foreign-exchange policy, [made] her unwilling to purchase extra food on commercial markets. Foreign exchange is instead husbanded to pay for the arms needed to fight the interminable and spreading wars of secession and autonomy."

The list goes on, citing failures of the Ethiopian government and relief agencies alike. The point here is not to apportion blame, but to show how people were dying in Ethiopia as much from a scarcity of effective attention as from a scarcity of rain. The root causes lay not in the bureaucracy, but in the relationship between the highland people and their land. The report concludes:

"With population growth constantly outstripping growth in agricultural production; and with virtually no alternatives to agriculture as a means of livelihood for the vast majority, the agricultural base of the Ethiopian economy becomes ever more vulnerable to the periodic droughts which are an inescapable fact of life in the Horn of Africa, as elsewhere. It can be confidently predicted that the scale of suffering and death will likewise grow."

The Sudan

Sudan's drought seemed to strike more quickly than Ethiopia's. And it was complicated by the streams of hungry Ethiopian refugees. But the famines were similar in terms of disaster mismanagement.

Regular rains failed to come in late 1984 in both the western 'breadbasket' provinces of Kordofan and Darfur, and in the east along the Red Sea and the Ethiopian border. Thousands of rural people poured into the suburbs of the capital and other Nile-side towns. It was a quicker exodus than in Ethiopia, perhaps because the crop failure was more devastating and widespread: one UN estimate holds that only 5% of the normal rainfed harvest was gathered.

Both UN and private relief agency personnel in Khartoum saw the tragedy coming as early as October 1984, and began to issue appeals for food. They got little response, because the Sudanese government did not officially appeal for drought relief until January 1985, insisting that the only people starving were refugees from Ethiopia. Only after the government began asking for relief for its *own* people did it become widely known that the eastern regions had had little rain and disastrous harvests for three years. The UNHCR (UN High Commissioner for Refugees) would not at first appeal for relief for Ethiopian famine victims it knew to be on the way, for fear of being accused of luring refugees out of Ethiopia.

Sudan also masked the severity of drought by discouraging journalists from visiting and writing about the victims camped on the edge of the capital, and by trucking thousands of these victims back to the western provinces where they came from. After having been shipped back, many started walking eastwards toward the city and the Nile once again.

But, as in Ethiopia, the real roots of the famine lay in long- term soil misuse, reflected in falling rainfed food crop yields in Kordofan and Darfur since the 1960s (see Chapter Four). Government agricultural adviser Omer Al Amin admitted in early 1985 that the country faced long-term problems in feeding its people, not only because of drought, but because of soil deterioration.

Peter Charlesworth/Earthscan

A camel carcass, western Sudan. The Sahel's climate may or may not be changing. If it is, governments will need to put more effort into soil and water conservation and land use planning. If it is not, they will need to do exactly the same thing.

Early warning?

How and why does drought become famine? Researchers like John Seaman of the Save the Children Fund, Julius Holt of the International Disaster Institute, and John Rivers and others of the London School of Hygiene and Tropical Medicine have amassed considerable data on how people behave in such crises. Some of the findings are contradictory, but they do offer hope that a famine 'early warning system' could be established.

It is generally agreed that in a famine, food prices are high in the worst hit areas. As famine refugees begin to migrate, 'ripples' of rising food prices move out from those areas, and the volume of livestock sales increases.

> *"It seems that the exact pattern of high prices could be the basis of a reasonably precise 'map' of famine conditions and the likely direction of migration of victims"*, *wrote Peter Cutler in 1984, after reviewing data from the Ethiopian famine.* [10]

Several institutions have been trying to feed the prices of grain and livestock in rural marketplaces into a central computer, programmed to sound the alarm when prices begin to behave oddly. This could provide better early warning than satellite photos, which are expensive, and at present difficult to interpret reliably.

Yet one must wonder about the point of such systems. The signs of the Ethiopian disaster were detected as early as March 1981, but the Ethiopian government, the UN agencies and the Northern governments all responded too little, too late. Famines develop over years; the need is more for early action than early warning.

IS THE CLIMATE CHANGING?

The droughts have concentrated attention on the question of whether or not Africa's climate is changing. This is an important question for meteorologists and climatologists — and perhaps unfortunately for Sahelian leaders.

It is unfortunate, because it tempts leaders into apathy. Many of the district officers, forestry and range management workers I have talked to in the Sahel see themselves and their people as victims of an angry God or of a changing climate. Some Sahelian officials concerned with the countryside tend to throw up their hands and say: "The climate is changing. So what can we do?"

Droughts have been recurring in the Sahel for centuries. Sharon Nicholson has described the Sahelian climate as follows: "Rainfall is low, spotty and highly variable; drought is inherent and dry years are more prevalent than wet ones. Climate must be treated as a variable, not as a constant." [11] But some scientists believe that the Sahel's climate is slowly changing over the long term. Studies after the 1968-73 drought concluded that it probably was not. According to a 1980 World Meteorological Organization report: "Most analyses imply that the droughts of the 1970s, although severe, are normal to the climate, in the sense that they have occurred before, and presumably will occur again". [12]

The trouble is that while weather may be seen to change from day to day, climate needs several decades before any 'change' can be announced. Adequate monitoring stations have not existed in much of the Sahel for that long.

Sharon Nicholson's review found that for sub-Saharan Africa from the southern fringes of the Sahara to the Sudano-Guinea strip below the Sahel proper, there was above average rainfall in the 1950s. (All reference to 'average' and 'normal' in such discussions must be treated with suspicion, as there is no agreement over just what either expression means.) Rainfall began to decline in the early 1960s in the Sahel, and in the late 1960s immediately to the south. Then came the Sahelian drought, followed by a slight recovery in 1974-75, and below 'normal' rainfall in the late 1970s and early 1980s.

The Senegal, Niger and Chari Rivers have all suffered severely reduced flows over the past 15 years. Lake Chad is now about one- third of the size, in terms of surface, and one-fourth the volume it was in 1963. The northern part of the lake now dries up every year.

A study of Sahelian rainfall over 40 years by Michael Dennett of the University of Reading (UK) emphasises that only a small change in overall rainfall can lead to what we call 'drought'. "The Sahel's rainfall from 1974 to 1983 was about 5% less than in the 1931 to 1960 period. We cannot, however, be certain of a trend towards long-term decline, although if dry years continue, the possibility of this being due to chance is quite low."

Meteorologist Derek Winstanley goes much further, and believes firmly that the Sahel's climate is indeed getting drier. He points out that by 1985 the Sahelian drought had essentially lasted for 17 years. If the year-by-year variation was indeed random, he argues, one could expect six consecutive years of below-average rainfall once every 60 or 70 years. But the odds against a drought lasting 17 years are 125,000 to one. With fairly large fluctuations up and down, the rainfall during the June-to-September rainy season has been declining for 200 years, claims Winstanley, now at the US National Oceanic and Atmospheric Administration.

Man-made changes?

The mainstream scientific view is still typified by Canadian climatologist Kenneth Hare, who wrote in 1984 that Africa's recent droughts are aspects of "a natural fluctuation". But he added that "it is conceivable — though still unlikely, in the view of some professionals — that human interference may be prolonging and intensifying the dry spells natural to the climate". [13]

How could this happen? There are three possibilities. First, overcultivation, overgrazing and deforestation all strip soil of vegetation. Bare soil and rock reflect more solar radiation back into the atmosphere than do grass, shrubs and trees. Increased reflectivity (albedo) keeps the atmosphere warmer, disperses cloud and reduces rain. At least, there is less rain in the several large computer models of the late 1970s and early 1980s which show that a sharp rise in the albedo over the fringes of the Sahara should reduce rain. Other computer models have obtained similar results for other tropical deserts. The desert, according to the computers, seems to feed upon itself and grow.

Second, computer models suggest that a general lowering of soil moisture could itself suppress rainfall. Much of the rain in tropical moist forests comes from water evaporated off the vegetation, and not from outside. As humans change the landscape so that it holds less water, they may produce a drier local climate. But while this is almost certainly the case when rainforest is cleared over large areas, it is much less likely to be true for arid zones, where little if any rain may be locally generated from evaporation.

The third and most controversial possible 'feedback mechanism' involves dust. Stripping vegetation from the soil allows the wind to throw more dust into the air. This dust reduces the amount of sunshine reaching the earth's surface, which would have the same rain-reducing effect as bouncing more solar radiation back off the earth's surface. The dust over the Sahel is not something that shows up only on scientific instruments. There was so much dust in the skies over Mali and other parts of the Sahel in early 1985 that the sun was hidden for days on end, and planes often could not land. But the effects on climate, if any, remained unproved.

There is another, global, climatic change that may be affecting the African climate. People in the industrialised North are releasing growing amounts of carbon dioxide into the atmosphere by burning coal and oil. Carbon dioxide in the atmosphere increases every year by almost 0.5%, and sometime next century this is expected to raise tropical temperatures by 2-3 °C. The Earth may be warming already due to this 'greenhouse effect': the blanket of atmospheric carbon dioxide reduces the heat that the planet radiates out into space, without reducing the heat received from the sun.

Researchers at the Climatic Research Unit of the University of East Anglia (UK) reported in 1984 that not only would the greenhouse effect increase average temperatures, but it would also increase the variability of the climate.

Northern weather has indeed recently been extremely variable. In 1984, a team of US National Oceanic and Atmospheric Administration researchers, headed by Thomas Karl, showed that six out of the eight preceding winters were exceptional compared to the years 1938-73. There have also been warmer summers in the North: 1983 was the fourth warmest year on record, and the record itself was set in 1981. This growing variability could be bringing Africa more droughts.

So what?

If the droughts are increasing in Africa, what can be done about it? Climatologists do not believe that high-technology offers any answers if rainfall is declining over large areas. Cloud seeding is unlikely to bring rain, as there are usually no clouds to seed; in any case, the process is too expensive to benefit large areas during a drought. Hare, being a climatologist, calls for more research, and better funding for such research, especially as meteorological and hydrological services have been deteriorating in Africa in recent years, just when they are most needed.

But his main conclusion is that the most useful and obvious step towards lessening the impact of adverse weather — whatever the long-term drift of the climate — "is to control land use": protect land from livestock, plant forest and shrub stands, reduce overcultivation. "Measures taken to control desertification (the human misuse of agricultural land so that it becomes worthless) do not merely restore plant cover and soil conditions; they also repair the microclimate."

> *For drought-stricken Africa, the cry that the climate is changing is ultimately a cop-out, an excuse for political inaction. We do not know if the climate in dryland Africa is really becoming drier, and we do not know how to reverse this change quickly even if it is occurring.*
>
> *But it is certain that bad land management is reducing the use that can be made of the rain that does fall, causing the moisture to evaporate or run off damaged soils rather than seep into the ground to be used by crops and vegetation. Plant roots depend on root-level microclimate rather than climatic averages, and as Chapter Four will show, misuse of the land is widespread, is increasing vulnerability to drought and is reversible. Rainfall patterns cannot at present be either modified or predicted, but human behaviour can and must be changed.*

Chapter 3

The backdrop to despair

"Should we let our people starve so that we can
pay our own debts?"
President Julius Nyerere
of Tanzania, April 1985

Africa's human and environmental crisis is being played out against a
backcloth of world recession, low commodity prices, high interest rates,
expensive energy and misplaced aid.

Mixed with these outside factors are two key internal ones: population
and health. Africans are increasing in numbers faster than the people of
any other continent. At present rates, the world's population is doubling
every 40 years. Africa's population is doubling every 24 years. But Africa's
population growth is not steady; the rate of growth itself is increasing.
Only Africa among the world's major regions will have an increasing rate
of population growth throughout the 1980s, peaking at about 3% in 1990.
Virtually every aspect of environmental bankruptcy is made more acute
by this demographic explosion.

Population growth is intricately related to health. Fifteen in every
hundred African children die before they are five — one of the crucial
reasons why Africans have large families. Environmental degradation will
never be really checked in Africa while five million children die each year.

So before looking in more detail at the growing environmental
bankruptcy of Africa, this chapter examines the internal and external
background.

IMPORTING POVERTY

Africa is poor and getting poorer. No African state has an annual turnover
as large as that of Exxon. Only South Africa, Nigeria, Egypt, Morocco
and the Ivory Coast have GNPs large enough to get them on a list of the
world's 100 largest corporations. [14]

But African poverty, like all things African, is relative. Some 30% of sub-Saharan people live in middle-income, oil-exporting countries such as Nigeria, Gabon, Angola and Congo. Another 10% live in countries with per capita incomes which have grown faster over the past 20 years than in the continent's poorest countries; but these — Ivory Coast, Kenya, Botswana, Malawi, Mauritius — have all run into economic problems recently.

Half of all Africans live in countries like Ghana, Guinea, Liberia, Sierra Leone, Tanzania, Togo, Uganda, Zaire and Zambia, which do have exploitable natural resources but which have suffered from low or falling per capita growth since 1970. Only about 13% of the sub-Saharan population (39 million) live in poor semi-arid countries like the Sahelian nations or in poor nations with difficult environments like Senegal, Rwanda and Burundi. [15]

However, being a citizen of a relatively wealthy state does not guarantee health or prosperity. Oil-rich Gabon's average life-expectancy at birth is only 45; for Angola it is only 42. The average Nigerian lives to 49, but about one in every seven Nigerian babies dies before his or her first birthday.

Many of Africa's economic problems are imported from abroad.

In 1980, Africa produced over three times more commercial energy in the form of oil and coal than it consumed. But the producers sold to the North, to nations which could afford the products. At the beginning of the 1980s, the poor nations were spending large proportions of their export earnings on commercial energy: Burkina Faso 71%, Senegal 77%, Kenya 63%, Tanzania 50%. These proportions are large partly because of oil price hikes during the 1970s, and partly because of declines in export crop production and export crop prices. The only African nations with a favourable trade balance in late 1984 were five oil exporters: Algeria, Libya, Gabon, Congo and Angola.

The oil importers are paying for their oil largely with agricultural commodities such as peanuts, cotton, sugar, tea, coffee, tobacco, cocoa and palm oil, the prices of which have fallen drastically. Prices for primary non-oil commodities fell by 27% between 1980 and 1982.

But the 'real prices' are the price of commodities relative to the price of manufactured goods. On this basis, the prices of the region's 25 most important commodities have been falling on the world market for the past decade. In 1971 the beef from one Sahelian cow could pay for a barrel of oil; in 1981, nine cows were needed. [16]

"Not only has our [cocoa] production level fallen by almost half, but the price our cocoa demands has fallen to one-third of its average price five years ago", said Ghana's President Jerry Rawlings in 1983. "These are the harsh realities of our situation." [17]

Debt

Africa's foreign debts have grown since 1972 faster than those of any other Third World region. But rising debt has not been matched by growth in either exports or foreign currency reserves.

As aid to Africa has stagnated, the composition of national debts has shifted from 'soft loans' (with low or no interest and long pay-back periods) toward commercial loans, credits from suppliers of imports and trade arrears. [18] This change from soft to hard loans has coincided with high international interest rates, little if any growth in export demand, and a rising value of the dollar, the currency in which most debts must be repaid.

How did Africa get so deep into debt? In the 1970s, commodity prices were high and credit was relatively easy to obtain. Burundi and Kenya did well from coffee; Niger experienced a uranium boom; Tanzania made large profits from coffee and sisal; the Gambia found a good market for groundnuts, Malawi for sugar and Ghana for cocoa. Much of the money borrowed during the boom years went to finance "large public investments, many of which contributed little to economic growth or to generating foreign exchange to service the debt", according to the World Bank.

Sub-Saharan Africa was $8 billion in arrears (largely trade transactions) by the end of 1983, $5 billion credited against Nigeria alone. Africa's total of disbursed public and publicly guaranteed medium and long-term debt was estimated at over $48 billion by the year 1982. (Even these figures are matters of dispute, depending on what type of debts are included and which international organisation makes the calculation.) Debt interest and repayments were expected to rise dramatically from $5 billion in 1982 to $9.9 billion in 1984 to an estimated average of $11.6 billion a year in 1985-87. Already, 13 African countries have had to renegotiate debt repayments, some more than once.

"Unless corrective measures are taken, the external resource position of sub-Saharan Africa is likely to become disastrous in the next few years", the World Bank concluded prosaically in 1984. [19]

"Africa's debt burden is now intolerable", said Tanzanian President Julius Nyerere more bluntly in London in early 1985. "We cannot pay. You know it and all our other creditors know it. It is not a rhetorical question when I ask, should we really let our people starve so that we can pay our debts?"

One village

For many small farmers, the oil price rises came at the worst possible time for agricultural development. Consider the village of Shereik which stands on the Nile north of Khartoum.

Farmers had switched in the 1970s from oxen-powered irrigation systems to diesel pumps, so as to irrigate more land. The low price of diesel seemed to assure them profits. But oil prices rose quickly, and the price of cotton, which accounts for 55% of Sudan's exports, fell. Sudan had to ration diesel.

As a result, in 1984 the irrigation pumps were idle for most of the time, hardly watering the area the oxen once watered, but costing much more. Shereik's farmers had sold their oxen to save feed costs, and could not afford to pay the going price of $250- 375 per ox to buy more. The village shops now stocked only a few essentials: tea, noodles, beans, soap; in the 1970s they had sold meat, cheese, wheat flour, canned fruit, syrups and sugar.

Shereik in 1984 only held 800 people; 800 more, mostly young men, had left to find work in Khartoum, Port Sudan and even the Gulf states. It was not easy to leave, because oil rationing had decimated public transport. Child mortality in the village was high, from malaria and malnutrition. About 100 malaria patients reported to the village clinic each month, but there were only enough drugs to treat three of them. The clinic nurse bought medicines for his patients in the larger towns, and sold them at the clinic at cost.

Shereik is a microcosm of Africa in the mid-1980s. The effects of world economic disorder disrupted the lives of farmers in the remotest villages — farmers who had made apparently wise and ambitious economic decisions.

Crisis management

Most African governments are being forced to give low priority to long-term planning, while they manage the day-to-day crisis of debt servicing and import shortages.

It is hard to tell to what extent African crises cause political instability, and to what extent political turmoil and mismangement have caused the crises. By 1985, the 51 independent African states had suffered at least 60 coups; and in 1982, 22 nations had military rulers. For every successful coup, there has been at least one unsuccessful one.

In 1982, the London-based Overseas Development Institute — an organisation with deep sympathies for the continent's struggle to develop — offered this bleak summation: [20] *"In Black Africa as a whole, political instability is reflected in the frequency of abrupt changes of government (often by military coups), the widespread use of political power for individual gain, the abuse of human rights, and in extreme cases either civil war, such as in Chad, or wars between neighbouring states, such as in the Horn of Africa. In many countries there is an increasing incidence of corruption, violent crime and a loss of confidence in government generally. Poor economic performance has contributed to these wider problems, and in turn these difficulties have further weakened the region's economies."*

British geographer Ieuan Griffiths takes a more historical perspective: [21] "Barely viable colonies made chronically poor states. Riches did not flow and maldistribution of wealth remained much as before with black elites simply substituted for white colonial elites. New governments were often profligate with meagre resources, and the cost of the very symbolism of nationhood was frequently excessive. Political power was abused and corruption in high places became a fact of life."

This too is part of the backdrop to the present crisis. In some nations, corruption and abuse of power have been brought under control. More often, both have increased. Failing economies have brought political crises: political crises have disrupted economic development — another of Africa's vicious cycles.

Does aid help?

Africa has had more aid than other parts of the Third World, but seems to have benefited less.

Between 1970 and 1982, the sort of aid known as 'official development assistance' (ODA includes aid to African governments from Northern governments, international banks and UN agencies, but excludes voluntary aid and commercial loans), increased in real terms by 5% a year. In 1982, it amounted to $19 per person for all sub-Saharan countries and $46 per capita for the poor semi-arid nations — compared with $4.8 per capita for South Asia. However, since 1982, ODA has been static in real money terms.

In the first decade of Independence, much foreign aid went to build the symbols of modernity: plants, roads, dams, ports, conference centres, hotels and universities. Then there was a general realisation that such aid was doing little for the majority of Africans, and during the 1970s, priorities shifted — at least on paper and in speeches — to 'basic needs', food self-sufficiency and 'the poorest'.

But basic needs projects did not seem to have the desired, or in some cases any, effect. There were many reasons for this, some of which will be taken up in detail later on. It was genuinely difficult for aid bureaucracies to get aid through to small farmers; aid agencies had little understanding of the real needs of the poorest; many governments were notably unsympathetic to basic needs; unlike dams or roads, aid for basic needs allows little money to be spent back home in the donor nations.

So today, when the poorest in Africa are further away than ever from having their basic needs met, this sort of aid is going out of style. This is happening both because of past failures and because of swings in ideology in such nations as the United States and Britain, which now put more emphasis on private enterprise and the workings of the 'free market'. In many cases, especially during the present crisis, the 1970s rhetoric remains, but USAID (US Agency for International Development) administrator Peter McPherson has said he wants his agency to concentrate on "growth sectors" and to apply the kind of "tough economic analysis which investment bankers, for instance, conduct before making commitments". The African peasant is hardly a growth sector, neither would his or her plight attract the investments of commercial bankers.

So while the budget of the US Bureau for Private Enterprise — meant to encourage private enterprise in the developing world — has grown rapidly during the 1980s, the Africa Bureau of USAID lost 45 positions, or 20% of its total personnel. [22]

It would be unfair to single out the United States just because its documents are more publicly available. Britain is also spending growing amounts of its bilateral aid on projects tied to the sale of British goods. And Canada requires that at least 80% of bilateral aid be spent on Canadian goods and services. [23] In Tanzania, Zambia and the Sudan, for example, Canada appears trapped into spending much of its aid on high-technology wheat farms — projects which cost the recipient nations large amounts of scarce foreign exchange, employ few Africans, produce foods the majority of Africans do not eat and have had disappointing economic returns.

A 1984 study of African debt by Dr Stephany Giffith-Jones and Professor Reginald Herbold Green of the University of Sussex (UK) is purely economic, and makes no pretence toward an interest in the poor. But it concludes that "the current crisis underlines the need to move away from fuel-intensive, import-intensive and capital-intensive patterns of investment towards choices of projects which use relatively more labour and more local imports". [24]

The Sahel

Is such a move likely to take place? Recent history offers a depressing lesson.

After the 1968-73 Sahel drought, both donors and Sahelian governments pledged that their prime goal was to establish 'food self-sufficiency' in the region. Donors had become aware of the links between environmental degradation and the famine, and promised to finance more projects which improved the environmental resource base. USAID was particularly voluble in this concern.

The money rolled into the region: up from $756 million in 1974, the first year after the drought, to $1.97 billion in 1981. How was it spent?

Between 1975 and 1981, about 35% went to food aid of various types, help with balance of payments and to various Sahelian organisations, according to a report by the Gamma Institute of Montreal. [25] Another third went to "infrastructure" such as transport, telecommunications, health, education and water supply —"perhaps necessary but unproductive in themselves". The final third went to investments "productive in principal", such as irrigated and rainfed cash-crop agriculture.

But only 4% of the aid went to growing rainfed food crops. Only 1.5% went to ecological projects such as tree-planting and soil and water conservation, to improve the resource base upon which rainfed agriculture depends. Yet these were, in the words of the report, the sort of projects "essential for the future of the region".

Little changed for the better, then, after the last drought. Will future priorities be different?

THE POPULATION 'CRISIS'

The fact that African nations cannot now feed themselves does not prove that the continent is overpopulated. Many of the world's more successful nations — Switzerland, the Netherlands and Japan — cannot feed themselves by their own agricultural efforts. Africa almost certainly could.

A 1982 UN study [26] looked at the human carrying capacity of land in the developing world. It found that under current low levels of agricultural technology, four Sahelian nations could indeed not be expected to feed themselves. But given the use of mechanisation, improved seeds, appropriate fertilisers and pesticides, soil and water conservation and the right crops, the Sahel as a whole could feed itself easily. The rich soils of Chad alone could ultimately feed the entire Sahel — and export a surplus. (As shown, Africa *has* increased the yields of the crops it *wants* to grow — the cash crops — even during major droughts.)

Chad is unlikely to become the breadbasket of the Sahe
future, but the fact that it has the soils to do so is part of th
many African leaders resent being told that the continent h
people. "We are not over-populated; we are under-organ
funded and under-educated", commented an Ethiopian rel

But it is hard to see how Africa can continue to cope with such high
rates of growth. Kenya had 20 million people in 1985; by the year 2002,
40 million people are expected to occupy a nation where only 20% of the
land is arable. No European or North American nation, no other part
of the Third World, has ever had to cope with such extremely rapid
increases.

Too few people?

Whether or not Africa is *over*-populated, most of it is certainly not *densely*
populated. The average population density of sub- Saharan Africa is only
16 per square kilometre, much less in the rural areas. This compares to
100/sq km in China, and 225/sq km in India. This widely dispersed rural
population hinders agricultural development, often making it both difficult
and uneconomic to gather and market agricultural produce. It is also hard
to spread tools, fertilisers and pesticides, not to mention education and
health care. Bad to non-existent roads make things worse.

There are even large pockets of human infertility and low fertility
throughout interior Central Africa: in Zaire, Congo, Gabon, Central
African Republic, Cameroon and north-eastern Angola. The causes are
still poorly understood, but appear to be associated with sexually
transmitted diseases. [27] In some central African regions, 40% of women
may be sterile as a result, and there are 35-50 cases of miscarriage per
100 pregnancies. This is a personal tragedy for the women affected, in
that many are turned out by their husbands, and have little support or
cash earning opportunities. But it is even demographically bad, in that
it makes for rapid population growth in cities and along the coast, with
underpopulated interiors.

"How can the soil be cultivated with only six inhabitants per square
kilometre?" asks Retel-Laurentin of the National Centre for Scientific
Research in Paris. "How can roads be maintained, how can the economy
and trading be properly developed?"

The problem of knowing

The spread of people over vast areas also makes the monitoring and
planning of development — whether by governments or international

Mark Edwards/Earthscan

Food and spice market in Niger. Much of the food traded in Africa is unrecorded, sold on the 'black market' and even traded 'informally' across national boundaries. Africa offers few reliable statistics on food production, birth rates and mortality rates.

---

agencies — extremely difficult. For instance, until 1984 the Ethiopian government had been basing all of its food aid requests on a population figure of 32 million. But there had never been a national census. Preliminary results of the first such census, in 1984, found about 42 million people — which meant Ethiopia had under-planned in almost every region and sector, and had certainly underestimated the number of mouths to be fed in the drought-stricken highlands.

Nigeria has a national population thought to be somewhere between 80 and 100 million. It is home to about a quarter of sub-Saharan Africa's people, but has not had an undisputed census since 1952, because census results determine regional and tribal political power and resource allocations.

Accurate crop yield figures are even harder to come by, and are usually based on a very few samplings by people not properly trained to take them. Nigeria's 1980 production of cassava was 6.66 million tonnes according to the Nigerian government. The FAO's Production Yearbook for 1981 put it at 9.2 million tonnes. And it was 14.8 million tonnes, according to the US Department of Agriculture.

> *"I would go so far as to suggest that no African government and certainly no development agency, from the World Bank to Oxfam, knows with any real accuracy either the birth rate, the mortality rate or the food production of any African state",* said Brian Walker, president of the International Institute for Environment and Development and former director-general of Oxfam. *"Yet these three fundamental figures are crucial to the success or failure of any programme of development, if it is to be sustainable."*

Food production figures are further complicated because low official prices offered to farmers encourage selling or smuggling on the unofficial, unreported market. In the past, parts of western Tanzania have been regarded as 'food deficient' by the government and by the UN — because farmers there are selling no food to the government. But visitors report that ample food supplies are being exported unofficially across Lake Tanganyika into Zaire.

Such practices are so widespread in Africa that some experienced World Bank officials privately doubt official Bank figures which show rapidly declining food production in many nations. They do not give voice to their doubts, first because they cannot document them, and second because this might discourage food aid.

City versus country

Population pressures in Africa come not only from reproduction, but from migration as well.

African governments live in cities and, not surprisingly, their policies favour the cities. This bias is summed up in a 1984 report from the Overseas Development Institute: [28]

> "It is now generally accepted that policies followed by many African governments have contributed to reduced farmer income and incentives, especially overvalued exchange rates favouring imports, heavy taxation on export crops, inefficient state marketing and other agricultural service organisations, subsidised food imports and food aid. Urban incomes, often indirectly derived from agricultural taxation, are substantially above those of the farmer. Cheap food in the cities, where other social amenities and consumer goods are also concentrated, has contributed to rural-urban migration."

There are economic, as well as political, incentives to feed the cities with imported food, despite farmers' needs to grow and sell a surplus.

Most African capitals were established in the colonial era, when the European powers were concerned primarily with trade. So most capitals are seaports, or on railway lines to seaports. It may be cheaper to import food from abroad than to collect it from the hinterlands, when roads, fuel, transport and storage facilities are all in short supply. Twenty-eight of 51 African capitals are ports, as are all West African capitals of coastal states without exception from Lagos round to Dakar. This colonial habit of putting capitals on the edges of colonies has left the capitals of even landlocked states far from national geographical centres, such as Ndjamena's position in Chad on the extreme southwest border with Cameroon. Tanzania and Nigeria are building new capitals in the centre of the countries to try to change this.

Governments are further encouraged to import food from abroad because Northern governments are eager to get rid of their surpluses — cheap or even free. Of well over $1.2 billion in food aid shipped to the Third World every year, about 70% is sold at subsidised rates to Third World governments, which usually resell it to help balance their budgets. Thus the eating of French-style loaves made of white wheat flour, which cannot be grown economically anywhere in the Sahel, is a habit which has spread outside the region's capitals into many towns and villages.

Cheap imported food benefits the cities and damages the countryside, and this urban development bias is sucking people into African cities, out of the impoverished countryside. French agronomist René Dumont argues that the exodus from rural areas is more the result of people wanting to leave the countryside than being attracted to cities. Both factors are clearly at work, and it is perhaps academic whether the rural push is or is not more powerful than the urban pull. Either way, the flow continues. [29]

In 1950, there was only one city in Africa of over one million people: Cairo. In 1980, there were 19 cities of over a million. By the year 2000, there are expected to be more than 60 such cities.

Between 1950 and 1980, the populations of Nairobi, Dar es Salaam, Lusaka, Lagos and Kinshasa increased more than sevenfold. Most of the new arrivals move into shanties. In 1981, Lusaka had 540,000 people, 250,000 of them in squatter settlements or illegal developments. Three-quarters of the population (about 340,000) of Bangui, Central African Republic, live in 'spontaneous settlements'. Almost 40% of Nairobi's population of about one million live in squatter communities and shanty towns, and the rate of growth in African cities is expected to continue to be faster than anything ever experienced in Europe, North America or Asia. [30]

But despite this influx, until well into the next century most Africans will continue to live in the countryside. In 1980, almost 80% of Africans lived in rural areas or towns with less than 20,000 inhabitants; in the year 2000, if present trends continue, 69% will still live in rural areas and small towns. But all of this means that relatively fewer farmers are available to grow the food for cities, whose populations are growing at 5-10% annually.

In many African nations, the capital is also the only big city, taking the lion's share of industrial and commercial development and economic opportunities. Capitals like Luanda in Angola, Conakry in Guinea, Abidjan in the Ivory Coast and Bamako in Mali are all at least eight times larger than the second city in the nation. Nairobi, for example, contains more than half of the Kenyan wage earners who can be considered to hold non-menial industrial and service jobs; it holds almost 60% of the nation's manufacturing employment and at least two-thirds of its registered industrial plants. But Nairobi holds only 6% of the population. Most African nations lack the regional capitals and intermediate cities which in countries such as India and Brazil provide markets, storage facilities, social amenities and centres of seasonal labour for those who live in the surrounding countryside.

The muscle of the countryside is further weakened by the fact that it is mainly the young and the male who are leaving to seek their livings in the cities. Some 40% of Botswana's rural households have no adult men. Almost half the men have left some provinces of Cameroon. Some 40% of Zambia's rural families are short of labour. "Twenty years ago the farmer had real status in the community. Today farming is an old person's profession, and farmers don't have much status unless they have material possessions to show for their work", comments B.N. Okigbo in Nigeria. [31]

British geographer Phil O'Keefe describes the results of the men's flight from the Kenyan contryside: [32] *"The young men go to town looking for jobs, taking labour out of the countryside. In theory, the men send money home, increasing the income of the peasant household. But the large numbers of men searching for city work depresses wages; saving is hard. Remittances back to rural families are low, infrequent and often cease altogether. Back on the farm, the task of keeping the peasant household together becomes more difficult. Without the men to work and without money to buy better tools and hire labour, women must work harder. They are not only the hewers of wood and drawers of water, they are the main agricultural labour force."*

Family planning

But whatever the precise figures, most of Africa is not feeding itself. In the early 1980s, the population of the Sahel was thought to be increasing at the rate of 2.5% a year, while cereal yields were increasing at the rate of 1% a year.

In these circumstances, reducing population growth is essential for two reasons. First, a quick reversal of declining food yields is difficult if not impossible. Every extra mouth makes food self-reliance more distant. Second, the very high proportion of young people in African populations means that even if the birth rate were reduced *now* to replacement level (about two children per family), the total population would still continue to increase for decades. This phenomenon of *population momentum* is why China is now trying to impose the norm of a one-child family —and will still face a steadily rising population for years to come.

So what is Africa doing about family planning? The World Bank has graded family planning activities in the six countries of black Africa with over 15 million people each. It described the activities of Kenya and Tanzania as 'weak', those of Nigeria, Zaire, Sudan and Ethiopia as 'very weak or none'. Of the six, only Kenya and Sudan had published population data less than 10 years old on fertility, mortality and contraceptive use. [33] Some governments are positively pro-natalist, especially in the Moslem north; the Sudan has announced it intends to encourage larger families.

Of the 19 African nations associated with the International Planned Parenthood Federation (IPPF), only three — Kenya, Ghana and Mauritius — have a specific goal of reducing annual population growth.

Even in areas of low density, there may still be far too many people for present land-use methods. The very dry Sahelo-Saharan strip immediately to the south of the Sahara is mostly rangeland, which can support only 0.3 people per square kilometre. Today it supports two people per sq km. The zone immediately to the south (identified by annual rainfall between 350 and 600 mm) can support 15 people per sq km; today, it supports 20. It is in this region that desertification is most intense and most serious, and in this zone that over-population is most acute. There is an urgent need to encourage the movement of people southwards, into the wetter Sudano-Guinean zone, where rainfall is higher, intensive agriculture is possible, and the land is still under-populated. In some cases, this is possible within countries, in other areas, it would involve trans-boundary movement, as for example from southern Niger into Nigeria. To a considerable extent, movement within tribal areas across such national borders is already occurring, although unrecognised and usually discouraged by governments.

So far, not a single Sahelian government has established any birth control programme, and most of them want more people. Most

Wendy Wallace/Earthscan

Mother and children of the Balanda people in southern Sudan. Some 45% of the continent is under the age of 15. These children will fuel Africa's population growth for decades to come.

government leaders consider the Sahel to be under-populated. So apparently do most women; a 1977 survey showed that the average number of children wanted by Senegalese women was 8.9. [34]

Africa's population pressure can best be demonstrated by a look into the not so long-term future. Today, children younger than 15 make up 45% of the continent's population (compared to 37% in Asia and 40% in Latin America). This high percentage of youth will fuel population growth for some decades to come. On present trends, by the time Nigeria's population reaches a 'stationary' state, it will be 618 million — far more than the population of the whole continent today. Ethiopia's population size is expected to reach a stationary state at 231 million, but that projection was based on a present population of 32 million, while in fact today's figure is around 42 million. [35]

Why it's hard in Africa

Many Africans are Catholic and many are Moslem, faiths which officially disapprove of contraception. Many former French colonies still carry on their statute books a 1920 French law forbidding contraception. Senegal changed this law in 1980. Sterilisation is still illegal in Rwanda and a crime punishable by death in the Ivory Coast.

An IPPF report on Zaire listed the following 'constraints' to family planning programmes: opposition of the Catholic Church; laws governing the use of contraceptives; roads impassable in the rainy season and poor telecommunications; more than 450 local languages; each ethnic group's fear of becoming a 'minority'; the general social importance of motherhood and of having many children; occasional alarming articles on contraception methods; and a lack of understanding of the relationships between family planning and national development. The same list would apply to many African nations.

There are deeper constraints as well. "The African society is a man's society. The status of women is traditionally very low", says Michael Sozi, a Ugandan and Regional Director of IPPF's Africa Region. Alpha Diallo, IPPF Programme Officer in Lomé, goes further, saying that in Africa a woman is only considered a woman if she is able to conceive. Her status in the community depends on how many children she bears, and since polygamy is more the rule than the exception in Africa, women often compete to try to have more children than other wives.

"Whatever his religious beliefs, the African is convinced that children are given by God and that the number of children each woman will have has been determined in advance", says Diallo. Throughout Africa, "large families are considered signs of power, prosperity and holy blessing".

HEALTH AND POVERTY

The high probability that children will not live encourages African parents to have large families, as does the reliance of most rural African families on children for farm labour. About 20% of all babies born in Burkina Faso and Sierra Leone die before their first birthday. Other nations do little better: Gambia, over 19%; Malawi, 17%; Liberia, Benin, Guinea, Mali and Angola, all over 15%. Why? [36]

The industrialised world sees Africa as basically unhealthy because it is full of so many nasty diseases: cholera, malaria, amoebic dysentery, sleeping sickness, snail fever, river blindness, leprosy, yellow fever. But it is gradually becoming clear that Africa's health problems are not caused so much by diseases as by poverty, and that the diseases are not a cause of Africa's slow development, but a symptom of it.

Wealth determines health, and the poorest of all Africans are the children. The rate at which infants die indicates both the health and the wealth of a nation; infant mortality rates correlate closely with national per capita income. Of the world's 36 poorest countries, 29 are south of the Sahara. The percentage of Africans living in 'absolute poverty' rose from 82% in 1974 to 91% in 1982. [37] Africa as a whole has by far the highest rate of child deaths in the world. In many parts of the continent, children under five make up half of all deaths.

On average, 150 out of every 1,000 African children die before their first birthday — 20 times more than die in Canada, Japan or Sweden, and 1.5 times more than die in Asia. In Sierra Leone the infant death rate reaches over 200 per 1,000 births, but even in oil-rich Nigeria, and relatively wealthy Egypt, the rates are 10 times higher than in the United States.

Within individual countries, death also seeks out poverty. Kenya's relatively prosperous Central province has an infant/toddler mortality rate of 67 per 1,000. Nearby Nyanza province, where incomes are lower, has a rate of 174 per 1,000. [38] The link between poverty and infant mortality is best shown in South Africa, where for every white infant that dies, over 10 black babies die.

It is estimated that five million children under five years of age died in Africa in 1984, a number equivalent to 50 major airline disasters per day. What is killing these children?

Poverty, malnutrition and high birth rates are all causes and effects of one another, and all play a part in the carnage. Children rarely 'starve to death' even in a famine; but they do get very hungry and very weak, very vulnerable to a 'minor' illness such as measles. However, the disease is almost an afterthought — a formality for statisticians.

When such a child dies, if a death certificate is filled out, the doctor writes in 'measles' for 'cause of death'. Some health workers argue that not until malnutrition becomes an officially acceptable cause of death will African governments have a clear idea of their health problems.

Large families mean unhealthy mothers. Maternal mortality rates — deaths from pregnancy-related causes — are as low as five per 100,000 live births in Europe, but reach 1,000 per 100,000 in parts of Africa.

Large families are also hard to feed and house. They may live crowded together with no sanitation, unsafe water, inadequate food, and become more prone to communicable diseases spread by air, contaminated water, and faeces. Repeated illness, especially where diarrhoea is involved, is a major cause of malnutrition. And malnourished children are vulnerable to diarrhoea.

Under repeated assaults of diarrhoea and infections, these children often waste away before their mothers' eyes. It is common for children in rural Africa to be ill for 140 days in a year — nearly 40% of the time. The typical pattern is three or four bouts of diarrhoea, four or five respiratory coughs and colds, an attack of measles or malaria, all complicated by internal parasites and inadequate protein and calories.

Many African children are ill nearly all the time, and few have enough healthy intervals to fully recover and catch up on growth, unlike sick children in industrialised countries.

Between 1975 and 1981, 60% of Ethiopian and Tunisian children under five suffered from mild to moderate malnutrition. For Sudan, the figure was 50%; for Egypt, 47%; for Tanzania, 43%; and for Kenya, 30%. Severe malnutrition affected 40% of the under fives in Burkina Faso, 28% of those in the Ivory Coast and 16% of those in Nigeria. [39]

Malnutrition is often hard to spot, and many of the 20 million or more malnourished children in Africa display no pronounced symptoms. A moderately malnourished child may look entirely normal except for its small size. The child receiving only 60% of the necessary calories may give no outward sign of hunger beyond a frequent desire to breast-feed. But resistance to infection will be lowered, and the child's future physical, mental and emotional development will be imperilled.

> *It is the rate of child death which reduces the average life expectancy in sub-Saharan Africa to about 47 years. The African who does manage to survive to the age of five years has a life expectancy only seven or eight years less than the average Swede or Canadian.*
>
> *But even among those survivors of childhood, rural people still have more than their fair share of debilitating, non-fatal disease. They are discriminated against by disease as they are by their governments. And in the countryside it is the women, disadvantaged by social custom, whose burden of ill health is most onerous. In parts of Africa, particularly the north, the female mortality rate is greater than that of men, reversing the pattern found in most of the world.*

Poverty, water and sanitation

In Europe, at least 95 people out of every 100 have piped water; in Africa, 90 people out of every 100 are without it. Over 80% of all illness in the developing world is directly or indirectly associated with a poor water supply and sanitation.

It is estimated that safe drinking water and sanitation could cut infant mortality in half in much of Africa. But the availability of safe drinking water in the poorest parts of Africa is low, even by Third World standards. In Ethiopia only 1% of the population has good water; in Sierra Leone, 2%; in Zaire, 5%; Mozambique, 7%; Congo, 8%; Angola, 10%; Zimbabwe, 10%; Lesotho, 11%; and Kenya, 15%.

Water is not just for drinking. Water scarcity contributes to illness through bad hygiene, and this in turn fosters the spread of infections which affect the eyes, skin and gastro-intestinal tract. Handwashing can cut diarrhoeal diseases dramatically, by 40% in the under-five age group, 20% in the 5-9 age group, and by 10-15% in other age groups, according to one study by the International Diarrhoeal Diseases Research Centre in Bangladesh. Contaminated water carries additional health risks. Those who wash their hands, food, or eating utensils in it risk catching typhoid, cholera, dysentery, gastro-enteritis, polio and hepatitis.

In Northern urban households the average person may use 350-1,000 litres per day. In parts of Kenya, where some women have to walk up to 10 kilometres to fetch water, the consumption per person is as low as 2.5 litres per day — considered the absolute minimum for drinking and cooking. The labour involved is one reason why many African women want large families — in order that daughters can share the burden of water collection.

Lack of water and poor sanitation are intimately linked. In a West Nile village, the mother of a child who had died of diarrhoea was asked whether she had done anything unusual at the time of the illness. She replied that the child became sick during the rainy season. With her child ill and with water lying in pools nearby, she decided to save time by not going all the way to the borehole for it. The village had no latrines, so the child had doubtless been infected by contaminated water. [40]

Cholera is a typical disease of poverty. Crowded conditions plus inadequate water and sanitation are ideal conditions for it. This disease seldom strikes those in upper socio-economic groups, even in regions where it is endemic.

During the droughts, large numbers of people were on the move, searching for waterholes with a trickle left in them. And thousands poured into relief and refugee camps with only the most rudimentary facilities. This combination of large migrations and crowded encampments at waterholes increased the risk of cholera, which in 1984 erupted in Burkina Faso, Cameroon, Ghana, Kenya, Mali, Niger, Nigeria and Tanzania. In just four months, 600 people died and an additional 6,500 cases were reported.

Reports from refugee camps in the Sudan in April 1985 indicated that more than 2,000 people had died in an outbreak of cholera. Cases were also found in Ethiopia. Efforts to stem the tide of the epidemic were hindered by shortages of drugs and fluids used to treat diarrhoeal dehydration.

Buying health

Africa is 'unhealthy' not because Africa is inherently disease-ridden but because few Africans can afford health. The killers in Africa are conditions which are not really diseases (malnutrition), or which in the North are trivial inconveniences (measles, diarrhoea), or which have been virtually eradicated by hygiene or cheap injections (diphtheria, poliomyelitis and tetanus). The same sort of disenfranchisement which keeps rural people poor, keeps them unhealthy.

Traditional health services involve a centrally planned, 'top down' approach, favouring items which can be recorded and counted: hospital beds, drugs, patients, unit expenditures, pieces of equipment. Selective programmes claim to concentrate health resources on the specific diseases or on health risks which strike most frequently and cause the most deaths: smallpox eradication (which has worked); malaria eradication (which has not).

The alternative to this is 'primary health care' (PHC). It tries to get health care out of hospitals and out of the hands of doctors and into communities. It emphasises education and the hardware of health (piped water, protected wells, sanitation systems, safe food storage) rather than the hardware of disease.

Whichever system African countries adopt, their poverty means that hard choices must be made about health care priorities. Every day more than 13,000 African children die. Most of them die in the countryside of conditions which do not require high technology to prevent or to cure. Yet three-quarters of all the health spending of Africa's governments is devoted to providing high technology care to a minority of privileged urban dwellers. Three-quarters of health-oriented foreign aid is spent in the same way. [41]

Health care of all types gets little government money. Sudan devotes 1.4% of GNP to this purpose; Nigeria, 1.8%. Because GNP in most African countries is so small, the absolute figures are absurdly low. Thus Ethiopia, Burkina Faso, Chad, Rwanda, Mozambique, and Zaire spend just $1 per capita per year on health care. The corresponding figures for Sweden, Canada, France and Japan are $550, $457, $370, and $171. [42]

But even in those countries where a higher proportion of the nation's money is spent on health, (Ghana, 7%; Tanzania, 5.5%; Zambia, 6.1%), spending is likely to be directed at cities rather than rural areas. In Ghana, 40% of the national health expenditure is devoted to specialist hospital care for less than 1% of the population, with a further 45% going to another 9% of the population. Only 15% of the budget goes to the remaining 90%. [43]

More than 100 community health workers can be trained and equipped for the cost of educating a single doctor. Worldwide, the cost of training a health worker is between $100 and $500, while training a doctor costs at least $60,000. Concentration on the training of doctors is doubly disadvantageous for developing countries. Not only does it eat up resources which could be spent more efficiently, but it also creates a class of professionals who are highly resistant to changes in the health care system from which they derive so much benefit, and who are liable to look for 'brain drain' jobs in richer regions such as the US, Europe and the Gulf. [44]

In East Africa, there is on average one doctor for every 17,500 people — more than 80% of them are based in cities, where 20% or less of the population lives. [45] The number of people per doctor in rural areas is therefore more like 60,000 to one. If even 50 community health workers were to be trained instead of one doctor, each of them could be responsible for just 1,200 people. But more importantly, the health workers could be based where the people live — in the countryside.

Village-based health workers by themselves cannot secure the World Health Organization's goal of 'health for all' any more than investment in doctors and sophisticated city hospitals. Health cannot be guaranteed by health services alone, as the experiences of many developing countries have demonstrated. Lower child mortality rates and freedom from disease will depend on broad economic development, improved food production and distribution, safe drinking water, better housing, education and anti-poverty measures. Much of Africa is moving away from, rather than toward, these goals.

A few of the world's least developed countries have managed low cost health revolutions. China, Sri Lanka and the state of Kerala in India have all attained 'northern' life expectancies without the northern level of health investment. Their achievements have been explained in part by the high public priority given to food, health and literacy. [46]

In terms of costs and benefits, a number of studies show that African countries can expect the greatest improvement in life expectancies from health investments in maternal and child health services in rural and urban slum areas, costing less than $2 per capita. [47]

Unless things change, it is likely that the continent's mortality rate, which showed slow but steady improvement over the two decades to 1980, will begin to rise again. The effects of the present drought will be felt, not just by those who are now flocking to relief camps, but by the next

Sean Sprague/Earthscan

Measuring up at a mobile clinic near Singida, Tanzania. Growth posters are a cheap way to spot malnourishment in toddlers. The harder job is nourishing the victims.

generation. The babies of famine, born underweight, malnourished during their formative years, are likely to suffer reduced physical and even mental performance for the rest of their lives. An investment in improving their health is an investment in the future of Africa. With the limited resources available, what can be done?

The priorities

UNICEF's programme for maternal and child health, launched in 1982, aims in the next decade to cut by half the rate of death in children under five and in women of child-bearing age. As it does not tackle the poverty and political disadvantage behind Africa's ill health, it may not have the dramatic effects for which UNICEF hopes. But then health programmes seldom attack those deeper problems, and it would be hard to insist on a withholding of health care until the African peasant has a higher annual income and more political power.

The UNICEF approach is founded on the notion that improved conditions for women are essential for better community health. Among the basic elements of the programme are growth charts, breast-feeding, sugar-and-salt drinks to treat diarrhoea, and immunisation against six killer diseases.

* *Growth monitoring:* Growth is a measure of health, yet slow growth is frequently not visible. The use of a growth chart, plotting weight gain and height against age, can make visible the slowing down of normal growth which takes place up to a year before a child's malnourishment is visibly obvious. Mothers can prevent most malnutrition, which results not so much from too little food as from the wrong types of food and from diarrhoeal nutrient loss. Growth charts cost between 3 and 33 US cents, and each can be used for one child for up to five years. Illiterate mothers in Ghana had no trouble understanding how to use them.
* *Return to breast-feeding:* Bottle feeding of infants increases their mortality risk; a Cairo study found the increase to be as much as 30%. Substitute formulas are attractive to busy mothers. The already large families and continuous hard work of African women can make breast-feeding difficult. Giving the baby to an older child to bottle feed may allow the mother to complete other essential tasks. But breastmilk substitutes are nutritionally inferior, and do not pass on to children the mother's resistance to disease. Contamination and over-dilution of baby formulas lead to infection and malnutrition.
* *Oral Rehydration Therapy (ORT):* Diarrhoea kills by destroying the body's ability to absorb water and salts; children simply dry up. Small amounts of sugar and salt mixed with ordinary water get that water through the gut lining. About 90% of all acute diarrhoeal patients, including cholera patients, can be treated with ORT alone. A

Gambian study showed that even when the water used to make the mixture contains bacteria, the solution still rehydrates the victim and has a therapeutic effect. A senior USAID official calls ORT "the most idiotically simple piece of health technology ever invented".

Pre-packaged ORT mixes cost only a few cents. Even so, Gambian health authorities decided that they would be too expensive for many of the country's mothers and opted for a mass radio education campaign to teach mothers how to make up their own ORT solutions. The widely available bottle from a local soft drink was chosen as the 'measuring cup' to be used to get the right proportions of salt, sugar and water. Within two years, 65% of mothers knew how to make the solution, and 40% were using it.

* *Immunisation:* For as little as $5, a child can be immunised against six killer childhood diseases: diphtheria, measles, poliomyelitis, tetanus, tuberculosis, and whooping cough. Tetanus, measles, whooping cough and diphtheria annually kill 352,000 children in Nigeria, 85,000 in Zaire, 61,000 in Kenya and Egypt, 60,000 in South Africa and 45,000 in Algeria. The immunisation of children during their first year of life is one of the cheaper health care improvements which can be made. The most serious obstacles to mass immunisation programmes in African countries are lack of money, lack of trained health workers and the need to educate mothers. Extension workers need to be trained in handling and administering vaccines. Mothers must understand the necessity of returning for 'booster' shots when required. Successful programmes have been carried out in Lesotho (where half of the children are now protected against the six main diseases), Gambia (80% of children now immunised) and Zimbabwe (52% now immunised).

Primary health care in Africa

While African governments give enthusiastic verbal support to primary health care (PHC), their political support and their pocketbooks are directed towards curative rather than preventive medicine. Tanzania, which of all African countries has made the most strenuous efforts to involve its people in discussing, planning and implementing their development, still has a lopsided, urban-biased health system. Despite considerable progress towards the goal of providing a health centre within 10 kilometres of every person, rural areas still have poor health services. Only one-third of the country's 8,153 villages has a health centre, dispensary or first-aid post. The remaining two-thirds have no health facilities at all. [48]

> *Tanzania's urban hospital network still sucks money away from the rural dispensaries. Once built, these hospitals generate recurrent costs which become a permanent drain on the health budget. This drain means that even the rural health centres already in existence are likely to be inadequately equipped and poorly maintained. A 1979 survey of rural dispensaries found that only 30% had child growth cards; only 33% had measles vaccine in store; and only 37% had an adequate supply of basic drugs.* [49]

Nevertheless, Tanzania still plans to build two major consultant referral hospitals and several regional and district hospitals in the near future. What pressures generate such decisions in a country in which the commitment to PHC is very strong? President Nyerere's 1980 election manifesto justifies this type of expenditure by noting that the urban base is crucial to the country's economic advancement and must be developed.

In 1978, Ghana reassessed its health system. According to a government Health Planning Unit report, the emphasis on sophisticated treatment facilities had created a spiral of 'false needs'. Each village without a health post began to believe it should have one; communities with a health post wanted an expanded health centre; and towns with health centres wanted surgeons and operating theatres. Satisfying these demands sucked resources upwards, leaving a vacuum at the bottom of the pyramid, where the real health needs of the nation were multiplying. [50] The bottom of the pyramid consisted of the 90% of Ghanaians who, working in rural areas, produced the country's principal exports and source of wealth.

During the 18 years after Independence, Ghana had trebled the number of its doctors and doubled the number of hospitals — amenities from which only the top 20% of the population received any benefit. In the 10 years to 1978, there had been no improvement in infant or maternal mortality rates, nor in the communicable disease rates. Yaws and cholera had increased dramatically.

So Ghana adopted a new health strategy aimed at providing basic health care for 80% of the population. A PHC programme would attack the disease problems that caused the vast majority of unnecessary death and disability. The country's top 10 health problems were judged to be malaria, measles, child pneumonia, sickle-cell anaemia, severe malnutrition, premature birth, birth injury, accidental injury, gastroenteritis and tuberculosis.

Though Ghana was producing a large number of health workers, less than one-quarter of them were trained for anything other than hospital work. One-third of all nursing graduates, for example, were specialising in institutional psychiatric care. The government's Health Planning Unit decided that midwifery had a much higher priority, and aimed to deploy 6,000 trained nurse/midwives by 1990.

It was not clear in 1985 what results Ghana's reordered public health system would achieve. For the government, the chief attraction of PHC is that it is cheaper than hospital-based curative medicine — a virtue which was only noticed as the world recession began to bite. Having promoted 'high-tech' medicine for so long, the government now has a propaganda job to do. It must persuade the people that PHC is not a 'second class option' for the poor, but an effective way of bringing health to all.

Statistically, Zimbabwe is one of Africa's healthiest countries, yet severe inadequacies still remain. Its relatively low infant mortality rate (70 per 1,000), relatively high life expectancy (55 years), and high literacy rate (65%), place it much closer to Latin America than to the rest of Africa. What the figures conceal is that in Zimbabwe today, malnutrition is extensive.

Despite its lower mortality rate, Zimbabwe's population growth rate has remained high. Most tables put it at about 3.4% per year, which means that the population of 8.3 million would double in 20 years. But the World Bank, having analysed census data, estimates the growth rate at 4% per year, equal to Kenya's and the highest in the world. Another World Bank survey of 1982 indicated that 20% of Zimbabwean children suffered from moderate to severe malnutrition, with 30% of children showing stunted growth. The Bank identified poverty as the main cause, and rural people as the main victims. [51]

At Independence in 1980, the health services of Zimbabwe were largely urban-based, and oriented toward the cure of disease after it struck. Rural areas, where most of the population lives, were neglected. The new government has adopted the PHC approach, to be based on a village health worker for every 50 to 100 families, a rural health centre for every 10,000 people, 55 small district hospitals, eight larger provincial hospitals and four national referral centres.

PHC efforts are presently targeted at Zimbabwe's poorest groups — the families who labour on commercial or communal farms — who suffer more malnutrition and have less access to health care than any other sector of the population. They do not have enough money to buy food: a 1981 study found that an average family on commercial farms had a monthly income of $35, while the poverty line for a family of five was estimated at $116 per month. Another study found that the average wage packet was supporting nearly 10 other people.

Food prices in Zimbabwe today are among the lowest in Africa.
Heavy subsidies are justified by their expected benefit to the

*malnourished rural poor. But the poor really benefit only from
subsidies on maize meal. Richer city dwellers buy up the
subsidised meat, milk and bread. Poor urban households are
estimated to receive only 36% of the beef subsidy, 23% of the
milk subsidy, and 59% of the bread subsidy, though they
constitute the overwhelming majority of the urban population.*

Getting PHC to the people

Primary health care faces formidable obstacles in Africa, not least the
continent's vast and rugged terrain. How does the Sudan provide accessible
health care for all the inhabitants of its 2.5 million square kilometre area?
Much of it must be done on bicycle and on foot. A nomadic tribe in western
Sudan, the Kabbabish, provided each health worker in their territory with
a camel, and the Baggara to the south supplied donkeys.

PHC programmes ask people to change their way of life. A villager,
whose main concern is day-to-day survival, is suddenly confronted by an
enthusiastic, often young, government-trained health worker, who tells
the villager that she must clean up the house, build a latrine, use precious
water for washing, feed the children several times a day, give them milk
or eggs, keep a growth chart for each of them and perhaps not have any
more children. It is then announced that the village must find some way
to pay for this unwanted advice.

Health care is simply a low priority for most rural people. To be
successful, PHC programmes must be able to communicate that today's
investment in health will make survival easier tomorrow.

In the Kakamega district of western Kenya, public opinion on health
matters is sounded out and decisions made at the traditional 'baraza', or
public meeting. The barazas have been instrumental in gaining widespread
approval for local health workers. Recalcitrant families, of whom there
are still a good number, are likely to receive visits from the local headman
or even from a representative of the district chief (a district comprises some
60,000 people). The health workers, mainly women who are paid just $6
per month, tackle entrenched views firmly but cautiously. Many people
in the district believe that giving eggs to children prevents them from
learning to talk. Women who want fewer children fear their husbands,
who disapprove of family planning. The benefits of changes which bring
health must be graphically demonstrated before the villager is persuaded
to accept the cost which has to be paid, in time, labour or cash.

Widespread publicity can help. In 1982, Juba in southern Sudan
discovered that only 8% of the city's children were immunised. Public
health officials launched a concerted campaign involving sports groups,
youth groups, clubs and local government. Extension workers were trained

in low-cost communication: storytelling, drama and group discussion. Newspaper, radio and loudspeaker cars all advertised the advantages of immunisation, and house-to-house visits were conducted. The aim was to reach all of Juba's 'urban villagers'. By early 1985, more than 40% of children were immunised.

Persuasion can come from many sources. In Nigeria, 230,000 primary school teachers now promote ORT and immunisation to millions of children and their parents. The New Naam movement in Burkina Faso is training village volunteers in health extension work. The Organisation of Angolan Women promotes ORT, as do the Ethiopian Women's Association and the Botswana Council of Women.

In Zambia, a national network of voluntary nutrition groups runs a variety of self-funded food supplement and nutrition education programmes. Many of the groups began as traditional village welfare arrangements, and did not receive official legal recognition until 1975. Now they run market gardens, make loans to farmers and fishermen and improve food production techniques.

Children themselves can be a powerful influence. The children of the Sahelian drought have taken the lead in health education in the Tambacounda region of Senegal. Seven school health groups are organised by the children themselves, and through discussion meetings and short plays they explain the reasons for keeping water clean, for disposing of waste and disinfecting latrines. The children have made sure that the food sold in schools is safe — boycotting itinerant food vendors who refused to produce a local authority health certificate. One school group has its own orchard and plans a hen house, while another reopened a village health post which had closed because of arguments between the adults who ran it.

But on a continental scale, the development of PHC in Africa is hampered by the fact that its people are on the move. There are the 10 million said to be uprooted by the drought, the traditional nomads, the war refugees, and the environmental refugees seeking better land or seeking their fortunes in the cities. Successful PHC is founded on community participation. Yet most of Africa's poorest and sickest people exist outside the framework of established communities. They live in temporary settlements — relief camps, government decreed 'homelands' or resettlement areas, urban slums, or just beside the road that might lead them to water.

Chapter 4

Misuse of land, misuse of water

"The Tanzanian ruling class ...had no experience of large-scale
agriculture, and little faith in small-scale agriculture... Most of
its leaders and their parents had sacrificed to get their children
into schools precisely in order to remove them from the necessity of hard work for little reward on the land."
Andrew Coulson —*Tanzania: a Political Economy*

"About 80% of the [Tanzanian] population live
and work on the land."
Barbara Dinham and Colin Hines
-*Agribusiness in Africa*

The 1968-73 Sahel drought popularised an ugly new word for an ugly old
phenomenon: 'desertification'. The word became so respectable so quickly
that by 1977 the United Nations held 'The UN Conference on
Desertification' (UNCOD) in Nairobi.

Perhaps it is now time for the word to be dropped. Its use has never
been particularly rigorous. Firstly, it is used to describe the primarily
climatic phenomenon by which what is now the Sahara desert dried out
over many hundreds of years, although strictly speaking the right word
for this is 'desertisation'. Secondly, it is also used, more accurately, to
describe the conversion of productive land into wasteland by human
mismanagement. Croplands are overcultivated; rangelands are overgrazed;
forests are cut; irrigation projects turn good cropland into salty, barren
fields.

Good land becomes bad. Soil bakes into near-rock, or becomes sand
or salt-crusted dirt.

This second definition emerged from UNCOD and describes what is
happening to so much African agricultural land. But the word is still
associated in people's minds with the spread of deserts. In fact,
desertification in UNCOD's sense is happening in the United States, in
Australia, in India and Pakistan, in Chile, Argentina, Peru and Mexico,
and in many African nations far from real deserts. Only in very special
cases, such as in parts of the Sudan and the Sahelian countries, does the
desert appear to be 'moving in' on rangeland and cropland. But even here
the culprit is more Man than climate. A Niger forestry official put it better

than any scientist, when he told me: "The Sahara is not moving south; we are pulling it south".

Desertification is not about spreading deserts. It is a rash which breaks out in patches wherever the planet's skin is mistreated.

'Desertification' is also an unfortunate word in that it has come to be seen as describing a *cause* of poor agricultural development and declining yields. In fact, desertification is more often a *symptom* of agricultural neglect and mismanagement.

Seeing desertification as a cause has led to a proliferation of 'anti-desertification projects' — dune fixation, irrigation, shelter belts against wind erosion. Such schemes can be helpful where local people have a good reason for maintaining them. But farmers have little motive for increasing agricultural yields without reasonable prices for their produce or transport to market. So they also have little reason for indulging in the backbreaking work involved in anti-desertification projects.

Trying to improve agricultural yields by *only* attacking desertification is like trying to treat leprosy with skin cream.

An unfortunate result of making desertification a separate issue outside agriculture and development is that responsibility for its control was not given to the UN organisations dealing with agriculture (FAO) and development (UN Development Programme). The job was handed instead to the UN Environment Programme (UNEP), headquartered in Nairobi.

In 1977, this seemed a good move. At UNCOD, UNEP mounted one of the best UN conferences ever in terms of scientific data and explication of an issue.

But UNEP is an under-funded, understaffed agency. It has little political clout, because the governments which finance it are not as concerned with environmental problems as they are with the issues under the control of the other UN agencies, such as health, development and agriculture. FAO and UNDP do run anti-desertification projects and programmes, but coordination between them and UNEP is poor, and overall the UN's anti-desertification work has been ineffective.

In May 1984, when UNEP called a special meeting to look at seven years of 'progress' against desertification, it was forced to admit that UNCOD's 'Plan of Action' had been an almost total failure. Virtually nothing agreed to in 1977 by representatives of 95 nations, 50 UN bodies and 65 non-governmental bodies had been done.

By mid-1984, of the 100 nations affected by desertification, only two had prepared the national desertification strategies deemed essential by UNCOD. These two, Sudan and Afghanistan, were in 1985 being savaged by internal war and agricultural failure. Only three countries had followed another UNCOD recommendation and designated national agencies to deal with the problem. In 1984 only one of these agencies was "currently effective", and it was a section within a ministry rather than a nationwide coordinating agency.

To prepare for its special reassessment session, UNEP had sent out questionnaires to all affected nations. It then was forced to hire consultants to help many governments fill in the forms. Even so, the data in the responses of those countries which did bother to respond was so poor that UNEP found them virtually unusable. Governments, even those rapidly losing good land, simply do not know the extent of the problem within their own boundaries.

Nor do they particularly care, according to Harold Dregne, who helped UNEP with its reassessment: [52]

> "Governments do not see desertification as a high priority item. Rangeland deterioration, accelerated soil erosion, and salinisation and waterlogging do not command attention until they become crisis items. Lip service is paid to combating desertification but the political will is directed elsewhere. There seems to be little appreciation that a major goal of many developing nations, that of food self-sufficiency, cannot be attained if soil and plant resources are allowed to deteriorate."

This reflects a more general lack of concern for agriculture by African governments. A 1983 FAO report measured trends in government spending on agriculture per head of a nation's agricultural population between 1978 and 1982. Spending rose in Latin America, in the Near East, and in the Far East — in the latter by over 7% per year. But in the 17 African countries studied, it fell by 0.1% per year. In Gambia and Ghana it fell by over 10% per year. [53]

This lack of concern is surprising considering the scale of the threat. UNEP reckons that 35% of the planet's land surface is at risk from desertification, as are the livelihoods of 850 million people who live on the land directly threatened. Nearly 75% of the world's drylands are already affected, an area larger than Canada, China and the United States put together.

Africa is the continent most at risk. Some 6.9 million sq km of sub-Saharan Africa — an area more than twice as big as India — are under *direct threat* of desertification. Half of the world's people most menaced by desertification live in the Sahel.

UNEP's reassessment found that nowhere in Africa is the situation improving. For most land types in most regions, things are getting worse. In the Sudano-Sahelian region, desertification of rainfed croplands and dry forest woodlands is accelerating, and of rangelands and irrigated lands is accelerating or simply continuing. In Africa south of that region, desertification of rangelands, rainfed croplands and forest woodlands is accelerating; in irrigated areas, it is either continuing or unchanged.

OVERCULTIVATION

Desertification has four main causes: overcultivation, overgrazing, deforestation, and poor irrigation.

Of these, overcultivation is by far the most important cause in Africa. There are two reasons. First, ploughing and sowing disturbs the soil far more radically than stock rearing, leading more directly to rapid erosion. Second, many more Africans get their living from croplands than from rangelands or forests.

In Africa south of the Sudano-Sahelian countries, severe desertification (production down to less than half) affects 4.5 million people on rangelands compared to 20 million people on rainfed croplands. Only 15% of the world's drylands are croplands, but these hold 85% of the drylands' rural population. [54]

The temperate bias

There are few topics more boring than soil science to those who are not soil scientists. The jargon of 'luvisols' and 'xerosols' has made virtually no impact upon public consciousness.

Unfortunately for Africa, the subject has also tended to bore first colonial administrators, and then the government ministers and expatriate planners who have had responsibility for the continent's agriculture since independence. A high proportion of those deciding and advising upon the direction of Africa's agricultural development were trained in agricultural universities — if they had any agricultural training at all — in temperate Northern nations with deep, fertile topsoils and regular, year-round rainfall. Or they were trained by people trained in such universities.

"For the outsider who enters Africa, the governing dream has always been to change the place", wrote Patrick Marnham, a British journalist and author. "The models for such change have been drawn from the North, that is, from the nations of Europe, Asia and America that lie between the 35th and 60th parallels — where the corn comes from... As the North penetrated Africa, it has proved less and less capable of learning from experience." [55] What is true of Northern outsiders has proved equally true of modern African leaders.

It is hard to overestimate the effect of this temperate bias.
Twenty-first century historians may well be forced to write that

it did more to hold back African development than colonialism, war and world trade patterns put together.

Planners laugh today at mistakes such as the British groundnut (peanut) scheme in Tanganyika during the late 1940s, which failed spectacularly over 10 years at a cost of £35 million. Its political impact on the British Labour government is one of the rare examples of a development failure damaging a government domestically. The best Northern agriculturalists of the day tried to plant peanuts on 1.2 million hectares of land which did not get enough rain for peanuts, and which turned cement-hard in the dry seasons.

The result was three very large patches of partially-cleared bush. The groundnut 'experts' made the most elementary agricultural errors, yet such large-scale failures continue today throughout Africa, perpetrated by African policy-makers, Northern advisers and commercial firms alike. During the 1970s, a vast rice cultivation programme got underway on the banks of the Niger in the Mopti region of Mali. By October 1984, rice could be harvested in only 10% of the area because the flow of the river was too strong. [56] Peasant groups demanded that the scheme's promoters let them plant other crops to cut their risks. The promoters refused and threatened the peasants with exclusion from the programme. Result: 70,000 to 80,000 peasants faced with financial disaster.

In 1970, the Canadian government committed $7 million to a project to grow most of the wheat needed by Tanzania. By 1983, Canada had committed $44 million to this effort — a sum being matched by a Tanzanian government desperately short of foreign exchange. Using mechanised equipment purchased from Canada and run on expensive imported petrol, 24,000 hectares were ploughed up on the Hanang Plains southwest of Arusha. This provided only about 250 skilled jobs for Tanzanians and recruited only 100 local men as casual labour at less than $1 a day. The Barbaig pastoralists who had used the land were squeezed onto poorer ranges, which their cattle rapidly overgrazed.

The soil is fertile and able to hold water because of a high clay content, but it is very sticky when wet and shrinks and cracks when dry. "Severe erosion threatens to turn the whole wheat-growing area into a dust bowl within a decade", wrote Derek Warren of Oxfam. Canadians admit water erosion is developing and that laying the fields out in big blocks was a mistake. One Canadian expert wrote in defence of the programme that "in a sense the wheat project is an experiment in using these soils for crop production".

Canadian officials have admitted that there is no possibility of Tanzanians taking over the project in the foreseeable future, and that it is costing Tanzania $3.6 million a year in hard currency. But they claim that by producing one-third of the nation's wheat it saves $11.4 million per year — a figure based on Tanzania's 'demand' for wheat, which comes almost entirely from the better-off city dwellers and the tourist, as maize is a staple for eight out of 10 Tanzanians.

The Hanang project is not (yet) as unmitigated a disaster as was the peanut scheme, but this 'experiment' may not be the best way for either Tanzania or Canada to spend millions in hard currency each year. Do Tanzanians, as claimed by a Canadian government report, really "thank God — and Canadians" for the wheat project?

Africa's soil cannot be bullied into submission by Northern technology.

The soil

The following continent-wide description of soil types is misleading, because what matters to the peasant farmer are local conditions: the rainfall patterns on a hillside, or the depth of the water table in a valley. Nevertheless, the generalisations demonstrate how fragile and difficult are African soils over vast areas.

Geographer Ieuan Griffiths compares Africa's soil, rainfall and sunlight patterns to layers of onion skin. The core of the onion is the Zaire (Congo) basin. Wrapped around this core are similar 'skin layers' to the north and to the south. [57]

The onion skin pattern starts in the Zaire basin and in much of the rainforest lands of Guinea, Sierra Leone and Liberia. Here, the heavy rainfall has washed nutrients downwards through the soil and left them below the root levels of most crops. It has also washed metal oxides downwards. In places this has left subsurface 'hard pans' (largely impervious layers) which can interfere with water flow and make cropping difficult. Many of these soils are lateritic — that is, they bake pavement-hard when exposed to the sun.

North and south of the onion's core, stretching through many of the West African states and the southern Sahel, are regions with less rain and well-developed soils, locally rich in plant nutrients, but often containing iron oxide hard pans which make cultivation difficult. Right across Africa from coast to coast in the Sahel belt, and in the south stretching through Botswana, Namibia, western Zambia, Angola and into Zaire, are sandy soils, low in humus and not very fertile.

The next skin, north and south, is desert sands, in the Sahara and the Kalahari. And at the far north and far south of the continent, in the Cape and the Maghreb, is the thin skin of Mediterranean soils.

There are also areas of exceptional soil fertility: in southern Nigeria, around Lake Chad, in the Nile Valley of Egypt, in the Sudan and Ethiopia, in parts of the Ethiopian and Kenyan highlands, and in the volcanic

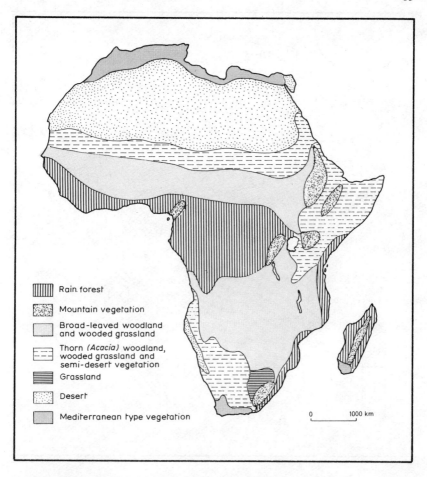

Rain forest

Mountain vegetation

Broad-leaved woodland and wooded grassland

Thorn *(Acacia)* woodland, wooded grassland and semi-desert vegetation

Grassland

Desert

Mediterranean type vegetation

0   1000 km

highlands of Rwanda and Burundi. But the soils of many of these areas have spawned high population densities, and are also being over-used — spectacularly so in the case of the Ethiopian highlands.

As regards rainfall, the tropical moist forest core of the Zaire basin gets 1,500-2,500 mm per year. North and south of that core is a region which gets 1,000-1,500 mm per year. North and south of that skin is a layer which gets 600-1,000 mm per year. Deserts dominate much of the north and southwest. And as annual rainfall decreases, its variability increases. In the Zaire basin, percentage variation from the mean is less than 10%; in much of the Sahel and the arid southwest, it is above 30%.

The point of this quick overview is that the great majority of Africa's soils are difficult to manage — certainly by techniques developed in North

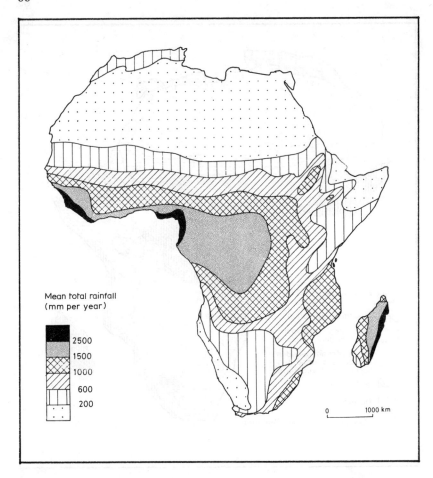

Mean total rainfall
(mm per year)

2500
1500
1000
600
200

0   1000 km

America and Europe. The problem is not just in the soil, but the combination of soil and climate. Most of Africa, outside the rainforests, receives very little rain for most of the year, and long stretches of very hard rain during a few months. Sokoto, in northern Nigeria gets 100 mm more rain per year on average than London, but gets almost all of it in July, August and September.

These heavy rainstorms carry nutrients down below the plant roots, creating soils of low natural fertility. Warm weather breaks down organic matter quickly when water is present, so in areas of short rainy seasons and long dry seasons, there may be a quick but short-term release of nutrients as the rains begin. [58] Many of these problems cannot be cured simply by additions of chemical fertiliser, because there is little or no humus to hold the chemicals and to keep them from being leached out of the root zone.

The climate does more obvious physical damage. Heavy rainfall blasts away the lighter, more fertile humus; the wind blows it away, leaving heavier sand behind; the sun dries it out.

All of this explains why traditional systems of African agriculture show much more concern for the *physical* properties of the soil than for *fertility*. Peasants discovered that fertility was quickly used up and could be replaced only by replenishing humus and soil nutrients; the important trick was to use the soil in such a way that it was not physically destroyed — made too sandy, lateritic, or eroded to bedrock. Thus they developed *shifting cultivation,* where an area is cleared, planted and harvested for a few years, and then left to regenerate while farmers plant elsewhere, or *rotational fallow cultivation,* where people stay in the same village but plant fields in rotation with years of fallow in between — from a few to 20 or more — to allow for regeneration of fertility. Europeans have been slow to learn the subtlety and soundness of these techniques — and even slower to improve upon them.

A map of the traditional cultivation systems of Africa shows only very few, very tiny pockets of permanent cultivation, in river valleys or on volcanic highlands. The rest of the continent is dominated by either shifting or rotational cultivation. Griffiths states flatly that "in large parts of Africa, permanent cultivation is not possible because of rapid soil impoverishment once the natural vegetation cover has been removed. Shifting cultivation is a response to environmental conditions."

Population pressure on the land

But shifting and rotational cultivation require much land and relatively few people. These conditions no longer exist in many parts of Africa.

In the agricultural provinces of western Sudan, the rotational cultivation began to break down in the 1960s. Between 1965 and 1977, farmland productivity fell to between one-half and one-eighth of previous yields. Maize yields per hectare in Kordofan in 1973 were 46% of those in 1961; 1973 yields of the food crop millet were 13% of 1961 yields. By 1977, they had fallen further. But in this region, yields per hectare do not include the vast areas left in fallow, areas which have now been abandoned permanently because the soil was over-used. [59]

Farmers in Kordofan traditionally earned a cash income by collecting gum arabic from the thorn tree *Acacia senegal,* a tree which grows on poor soil in low rainfall (250-450mm/year) areas. The trees are tapped for 6-10 years; they die; the land is burned off; food crops are planted; soil nutrients are used up and the land abandoned; it is left to regenerate

Wendy Wallace/Earthscan

A cotton picker on Sudan's vast Gezira Scheme, the world's largest farm. This woman, who came all the way from West Africa seeking work, has not found her fortune in cotton. But then neither has the Sudan.

for about eight years, while new young self-sown *Acacia senegal* trees reach tapping age.

But "under pressure of a growing population, the cultivation period is extended by several years and the soil becomes too impoverished to recover", reported Jon Tinker, director of Earthscan, in 1977. [60] Population pressure assures overgrazing of the land and the cutting of gum trees for fuelwood. More and more in Kordofan, gum trees do not return; their place is taken by economically worthless thorn trees such as *Acacia tortilis.*

Population pressure is so extreme in the Ethiopian highlands that the government has mounted a massive transmigration scheme to move people to the fertile Nile lowlands. The programme is fraught with complications: charges that the government is moving people against their will from rebellious Tigray and Eritrea, or that the politically-dominant Amharic speakers are colonising regions of other languages. There are diseases in the lowlands, such as malaria, to which the new arrivals have no resistance. The cost is high — estimated by one UN official at $5,000 per person — because the new areas have few or no roads, water supplies, markets, health centres or sources of agricultural equipment. But there may be no alternative to massive emigration for other over-populated and badly-degraded regions of Africa. Ethiopia is perhaps fortunate that it has underpopulated land within its borders. For the over-populated south of Niger, the nearest under-used land is south across the border in Nigeria.

CASH CROPS VERSUS FOOD CROPS

Nowhere in Africa is land degradation simply a matter of population pressure. The widespread planting of cash crops can also cause desertification. First, in situations where croppers are borrowing temperate agricultural practices for large cash crop monocultures — without making due allowance for the realities of Africa's soil and climate — then the schemes themselves can overburden the land. Second, planting the best land in cash crops — which almost invariably use less labour than food crops — can push large numbers of subsistence farmers and herders onto more marginal land, resulting in desertification.

The issue of cash crops or food crops sometimes dominates debates over African development — the debaters often choosing sides for ideological reasons. Those to the left see cash crops as naked capitalism, continuing to exploit independent Africa as it did colonial Africa, severely exploiting the majority of rural peasants. Those to the right see cash crops as the only way Africa can enter the world marketplace and earn the foreign exchange which it so desperately needs to improve the health, education and nutrition of its people.

But the main drawback to cash crops is that over the past decade they have produced less and less cash.

Growing them requires more and more hard currency for imported pesticides, fertilisers, energy and equipment. In 1984, no African nation whose economy was based on agricultural commodities had a favourable balance of trade. Nor is there any indication that crop commodities will begin turning a profit in the foreseeable future. Tentative economic recoveries by industrial countries in 1983 hinted at a recovery of commodity prices, but these dropped again in 1984. By mid-July the dollar commodity price index had fallen by 3% from a year earlier and by 17% from 1980 levels. [61]

Over the past decade, real income from cash crops has declined; production of cash crops has declined; African shares in world markets of most commodities have declined; governments' balances of trade have worsened, and most African countries are sinking deeper into debt. Yet between 1974-76 and 1982, the area devoted to major export crops such as coffee, cocoa, tea, sugar, cotton, tobacco and hard fibres grew by 11.4%, according to FAO figures quoted by The Economist Intelligence Unit (UK).

African governments feel the need to grow more cash crops in much the same way African peasants feel the need to have more children. If children are dying, more — not less — children are needed. And if crop prices are falling, more — not less — cash crops are needed.

By the end of the 1970s, the economies of many African nations were firmly tied to cash crops. Today, nine African countries are dependent on just one crop for over 70% of their income. [62] Over 90% of Burundi's export earnings came from coffee, which provided over 70% of Rwanda's earnings and almost 70% of Ethiopia's. Peanuts provided 90% of Gambia's export earnings, 60% of Guinea Bissau's and almost 40% of Senegal's.

Other nations over 50% reliant on one single crop included Mauritius (sugar), Uganda (coffee), Chad (cotton), Sudan (cotton), Ghana (cocoa), Kenya (coffee) and Mali (cotton). More countries are heavily dependent on mixes of cash crops, such as Malawi (tobacco and tea), Burkina Faso (cotton, karite nuts and livestock), Ivory Coast (coffee, cocoa, timber, cotton, bananas and palm oil).

Africa's share of the world commodity markets fell during the 1970s and has continued to fall. Africa produced 34% of the world's coffee in 1970, but only 23% in 1979. It produced 57% of the world's palm products in 1970, but only 29% in 1979 (largely because one company, Unilever, decided to shift investments from West Africa to Malaysia).

As Africa has invested more heavily in cash crops, per capita food production has declined. But there is great controversy over whether the latter was a result of the former. The record cotton harvest in the Sahel in 1983-84, coinciding with record grain imports (see Chapter Two), suggests that scarce resources are going to cash crops and not to food crops, and food crops are suffering as a result. Africa was producing enough food to feed itself as recently as 1970. By 1982, the equivalent of the continent's entire urban population was being fed on imported grain. [63] And in 1984, some 140 million Africans — out of a total of 531 million — were fed with grain from abroad, according to the Washington-based Worldwatch Institute, which predicted that "in the years ahead, the continent's dependence on imported grain will almost certainly be greater than ever". [64]

For the 24 sub-Saharan African countries most affected by drought, grain production fell from over 150 kilogrammes per person in 1970 to below 100 kg (estimated) in 1984, according to the World Bank.

In the other Third World regions, per capita production was increasing. Based on a 1961-65 average production index of 100, food production per person has risen in both Asia and Latin America from 100 to 115. In Africa it has fallen from 100 to 80.

The World Bank view

The World Bank argues that cash crops are the only way to get money into the subsistence economy and to improve yields of food crops.

This argument is best set out in the 1981 Bank report, *Accelerated Development in Sub-Saharan Africa: an Agenda for Action,* which argued that encouraging *peasants* to grow cash crops for exports (as opposed to basing export crop production on large plantations) need not, and in most cases does not, lead to declines in yields in food production.

It claims that "countries which have been doing well in cash crop production have also been most successful in expanding food production". It went on to point out ways in which cash crop production can get money and equipment to smallholders and increase their food yields:

"Export crops are the nucleus around which extension, input supply and marketing services are built; these also benefit food producers."

"Food production directly benefits from after effects of fertiliser expended on the commercial lead crop."

"The existence of a commercial crop facilitates the propagation of productivity-increasing equipment."

"Where individual farmers undertake cash crops to such an extent that they develop a food deficit, ...cash crop production creates a local market for food crop producers that is often more secure and stable than distant urban markets."

In effect, the Bank argues that encouraging cash crops is the best way of getting cash into the farm, and without cash the farmer cannot buy the inputs which will enable him to grow more food. It is a good argument in theory — but does it work, in Africa, in practice?

The Bank itself seems to be becoming less convinced. The optimistic "cash crops is good for food crops" argument is conspicuous by its absence in the Bank's 1984 report, *Toward Sustained Development in Sub-Saharan Africa: a Joint Programme of Action*. Why?

The cash crop squeeze

The relations between cash and food crops remain complex, and vary with crops, land-use and labour patterns. But we are less concerned here with the 'food versus cash' debate than with seeing how unplanned expansion of both cash *and* food crops can encourage desertification.

First, though such crops as sugar cane and pineapples may be grown on vast plantations, much of Africa's cash crops are grown by smallholders, and many smallholders have done well financially through them. Tea and coffee do use good land, because they will only grow on well-drained, highland soils. But a farmer on such soils can often grow a considerable amount of subsistence food on a small quantity of land. More important, the spurts of intense labour required in growing tea and coffee come at different times than the peak labour periods for food crops. There is little labour competition.

In the drylands, the picture is completely different. First, population density is lower, so labour is generally in shorter supply. The cash crops of the Sahel are peanuts and cotton. The planting times for these are about the same as for sorghum and millet. The same sort of tasks — planting, weeding and harvesting —must be completed within the same few months, from June-July to October-November. The World Bank's 1981 *Accelerated Development* report itself admits that the peanut region of Senegal may be an example of where cash crops have squeezed food crops.

On the Mumias sugar project in western Kenya, where smallholders now grow sugar on a contract basis for the Booker McConnell company, the squeeze is of a slightly different character.

Many of these farmers had planted most of their land in sugar and had less than a hectare to grow food, in an area where families averaged over 10 people. As they earned less than 3,000 Kenyan shillings ($200) a year from sugar production, families could not long survive a crop failure or deteriorating terms of trade. Yet terms of trade have been deteriorating and there have been several droughts in the region. The food cropping area tends to get overcultivated and production falls; hunger and desertification result.

In the Sahel, the land squeeze works not just on an individual's plot, but on national levels. The cash crops tend to get irrigated land along the rivers in the south (the Senegal, the Niger). Since they need less labour per hectare than subsistence farming, this squeezes food croppers northwards into areas of lower rainfall and poorer soils which cannot stand cropping year after year.

> Being pushed onto marginal land forces farmers to bring into production even more marginal land. Yields both per hectare and per farmer fall. In Niger, grain yields fell from 500 kg/ha in 1920, to 350 in 1978 and were expected to fall to 250 kg/ha by the year 2000. Per capita grain production fell by 44% between 1951 and 1974. [65]

On the rich soils near the Nile, the Sudan's Mechanised Farming Corporation rents vast tracts, usually in 4,000 hectare units, to private entrepreneurs at nominal rents. This has led to 'agricultural strip mining' or 'suitcase farming': the growing of crops for a few years, running down the soil and moving on, often before the corporation has even registered the lease.

According to Martin Upton, an agricultural economist at the University of Reading (UK): "Such projects have generally been badly planned and encouraged investors to mine the soil, take a few quick crops and get out. The government doesn't give investors any security of tenure, so there is little incentive for them to take any long-term interest in the land." [66] One study shows that 89% of private profits from one rural area of the Sudan were invested in cities, and only 11% in the rural sector. [67]

Cash crops can combine with population growth to encourage farmers to overcultivate the declining areas reserved for food, or to cultivate them poorly and at the wrong time, or to neglect them. All these factors can result in land degradation — and hunger.

Priorities of attention

If food crops got proper attention from marketing boards and extension workers, and drew better prices in the marketplace, farmers would use improved varieties where available and fertiliser on food crops. Less land could grow more food, and farmers would be encouraged to take care of that land.

But food crops suffer not only from land and labour squeezes, but from an 'attention squeeze' as well. The World Bank suggested in its 1981 report that cash crops also draw the attention of extension workers and marketing boards to food crops. This *might* happen, but in practice it does not. The efficient extension workers and marketing boards specialise in cash crops. Food crops tend to be left to either inefficient and underfunded marketing boards, or to private traders, who take advantage of monopolies on storage and transport facilities to maximise profits at the expense of the farmers.

Cash crops get far more help, advice and credit than food crops not only from governments, but from development agencies and development banks as well. They get more research towards improving yields, and towards developing varieties resistant to drought, salt, pests and disease.

Kenya's peasant coffee growers, backed up by the Coffee Board of Kenya, get help with loans, advice on pesticides and fertilisers and crop care, and efficient marketing backup. But farmers complain that the boards dealing with food crops are far less efficient, and less prompt in collecting the harvest, than the Coffee Board. The need for large Kenyan maize imports in 1980, for example, was partly due to the fact that the purchasing bodies had not been able to collect and store big harvests of previous years; farmers, stuck with surpluses, had reduced planted areas. [68]

The southwest of Burkina Faso is fertile but sparsely populated because of diseases such as river blindness. The centre of the nation is more densely settled, but soils are poor and productivity low. When there are good harvests in the southwest, farmers cannot market their food crops effectively. Farmers with a huge millet harvest in the south of the country told Oxfam field staff that they intended to grow more cotton in place of this food crop the following year, because it would be collected by the state at harvest time instead of sitting in their granaries waiting for a buyer. Additionally, they would receive a guaranteed price for their cotton from the state. [69] In fact, according to the Club du Sahel, they have planted 70% of their land in cotton and now produce 90% of the nation's output, leaving only 30% of their land under sorghum, maize, rice and peanuts.

Thus when food harvests are good in the southwest, there is no one to buy the surplus, and people in the overfarmed and desertified centre of the country may go hungry. This odd situation has led donor nations such as West Germany, the United States and the Netherlands to experiment with what they call 'triangular operations', giving money to the government to buy food in the southwest of its own country and transfer it to the centre.

In theory and in speeches, socialist Tanzania has since Independence backed the 'self-reliance' of the peasants. In fact, in 1983, agriculture was receiving only 12.5% of Tanzania's total development investment, down from 15% in the previous five-year plan. But some 80% of this went to large-scale farming projects, increasing dependency on foreign inputs. Only 2% of the development budget was going to peasants.

Loans from the Tanzanian Rural Development Bank to farmers for small-scale domestic food production *shrank* from 6.7% of the total in 1971-72 to 5.1% in 1979-80; over the same period loans to parastatals and companies grew from 6.4% to 70.7%. [70]

In 1978-79, of money loaned by the Tanzanian Rural Development Bank for agricultural inputs, 61% went to tobacco. Smallholder tobacco-growing hammers the environment by quickly depleting soil fertility, and by deforesting large areas to obtain fuelwood to cure the tobacco. So even a country where there is a deep political commitment to peasant agriculture has failed to put such a policy into effect.

Large food production projects tend to be surprisingly similar to the plantations of the bad old days of the later colonial period. They take up a great deal of land and rely more on inputs of capital and labour-saving equipment from abroad than on the abundant labour of local people.

Benin, Ethiopia, Ghana, Kenya, Nigeria, Mozambique, Sudan, Togo and Zambia have all tried such experiments. Most are inefficient, because they are directed by unmotivated bureaucrats with little knowledge of agriculture. French agronomist René Dumont predicted that Zambia's plans in the early 1980s to embark on a 10-year, $500 million food production programme would end in state farms which would be "bureaucratic, corrupt and inefficient".

Part of the attention squeeze derives from the fact that cash crops also tend to be grown in areas with the best lines of communication. Intensive peanut production in Senegal and cotton production in Uganda have been mainly concentrated in areas close to railway lines, and agricultural production around Kano, Lagos, Nairobi, Kampala and other urban centres is extremely intensive compared to other parts of these countries. [71]

UK economist Robert Chambers points out that when roads are built, land values rise and the wealthier and more influential move in, displacing local farmers. The resulting 'elite roadside ecology' gives a false impression of development in a given area. But roads also tend to produce an ecology based on cash crops. The 'tarmac bias' of marketing and extension services and of visiting experts also attracts the most attention to the wealthier cash crop growers along the roadside. [72]

Price Fixes

Farmers farm when they can make a living from farming. Many who cannot, leave for the city. Others who cannot may stay on the land, but lack the money, the labour or the incentives to protect and improve their farms. Thus pricing policies which work against the farmer may also speed environmental degradation.

Much has been written about how government policies deliberately keep food prices low, so as to favour the urban elite upon which governments depend. And the World Bank, USAID, the European Community and other donors have tried hard to encourage African governments to increase the prices paid to farmers for food crops.

Nigel Twose, a British development writer, suggests that in some places this is a small part of the problem and a small part of the solution. Writing about the Sahel, he said:

> "Unlike export crops which are bought by the state or directly by a multinational company, most food crops in Africa are sold on the open market to private traders or to the consumer. This makes official government prices for food mostly irrelevant. And for countries faced with a heavy debt burden, it has been simply impossible to encourage the production of food rather than a crop which will earn foreign exchange." [73]

In much of the Sahel, the only efficient marketing operation is run by private traders, who know where harvests are good and get to them long before any government marketing board. At the time of harvest, farmers have just managed to get through the long dry months, and then the planting and growing season, without any money coming in. They need cash to pay debts and expenses, and are often forced to sell grain which they know perfectly well they will need in the coming dry season. (Poor farm and village storage facilities also encourage quick sales.) In Burkina Faso in 1982, traders were able to buy the harvest for 30 francs a kilo and sell it seven months later in the dry season for 120 francs, according to Twose. But at the height of the dry season, few farmers had the cash to buy much grain at those prices. [74]

This 'efficient' working of the private traders should be kept in mind by those calling for widespread 'privatisation' of African food purchases in the interests of efficiency. In 1984 and 1985, USAID and the World Bank have put heavy pressure on a number of African governments to abandon inefficient parastatal marketing organisations, and allow more private trading and higher farm-gate prices. This pressure has been at least partly successful even in some countries with avowedly socialist economies, such as Ethiopia and Somalia.

Government grain buyers are not always irrelevant. Paul Vallely described in *The Times* of London how government grain purchasing agents 'ambushed' peasants bringing their grain to the market town of Areka in the southern region of Sidamo in Ethiopia:

> "There was almost a riot in Areka that day. The officials from the Agricultural Marketing Corporation waited until most of the peasants had brought their teff [an Ethiopian millet] into the dusty marketplace and then made themselves known. They announced the official price they had decided on and told the farmers the AMC would buy their entire stocks. The price was ludicrously low. The peasants protested. Some even began to gather up their grain, saying they would rather not sell it at such a price. The AMC men then announced that no one would be allowed to withdraw his produce. The farmers began to shout and drag their grain away. The AMC men were jostled. Then the government heavies moved in and the peasants knew they had no choice but to comply." [75]

Among the ways in which urban populations draw incomes from the rural population, Robert Chambers lists "monopoly marketing of cash crops which allows the surplus to be creamed off, to benefit the bureaucracy of the parasital which manages marketing, as notoriously with some West and East African marketing boards". Chambers deliberately substitutes his own invented word 'parasital' for 'parastatal'.

The Kenyan magazine *Weekly Review* ran in early 1985 a cartoon which must have touched the hearts of many of its farming subscribers. In it, a farmer receives with great joy a letter from his marketing cooperative. With mounting horror, he reads the list of the co-op's 'overheads' — entertainment fees, expanded staff, retirement benefits etc. Finally, prone on the floor, he reads that he *owes* his co-op 25 cents for every kilo he sold them. The cash crop farmer "is all too often relieved of an excessive proportion of the product of his labours by government agencies", comments The Economist Intelligence Unit. [76] In no year between 1966 and 1982 did the Cameroon cocoa farmer receive more than 58.3% of the international daily price for cocoa. In 1977, for example, a year when the daily price averaged a record $5,789/tonne, he received only 18.6% of that amount. The Brazilian farmer, by contrast, received 80.8% of the high 1977 price and never received less than 49% of the price between 1966 and 1982.

Where export cash crops are grown on mixed small farms, and where adequate marketing and extension support is also given to food crops for home consumption, cash cropping probably does benefit food production. But where cash crops are grown as monocultures; where they force subsistence farmers onto more marginal land; and where investment in export crops means the almost total neglect of peasant food crops, they can contribute to environmental bankruptcy. And there is little doubt that in many parts of sub-Saharan Africa since Independence, an over- reliance on export cash crops has undermined rather than supported food production.

IRRIGATION: THE NEED AND THE REALITY

Africa has a great *need* for efficient irrigation. Rainfall, even when sufficient in terms of yearly amounts, tends to come during only a few months. And parts of the continent have great irrigation *potential.* There are 12 major river basins shared by four or more nations: the Niger flows through 10 states; the Nile and Congo through nine each; the Zambezi through eight; and Lake Chad and the Volta each drain six. Some of these rivers, notably the Nile and the Niger, flow through otherwise arid areas.

But large-scale irrigation is a difficult undertaking anywhere, requiring careful planning, surveying, design and construction. The project managers need extensive technical training; the farmers who will use the systems need training and supervision and the ability to communicate among themselves and with the managers. The state, or the scheme's promoters, need to find the money and expertise not only to build the necessary dams and canals and drains, but to maintain them.

In Africa, many of these necessities are lacking. Comments Larry Dash, former director of USAID's Sahel programme: "Even in the US West, with all our educated farmers, it took 25-30 years to get irrigation right". Africa now has less land under irrigation than any other continent besides Australia; Egypt, South Africa and the Sudan are the only African countries with more than one million irrigated hectares each.

The funds required to keep large irrigation projects going once they are built come under the heading of 'recurring costs' — money hard to raise from donors and hard to find in the budget of the recipient government. It is difficult to get well-trained engineers, technicians, agronomists and health workers to live in the isolated rural areas where such projects are usually located.

So big irrigation projects often go wrong quickly. Canals leak and even break open. Upstream farmers use too much water, depriving their neighbours downstream. The drains necessary to take irrigation water from the fields once it has done its job are left out altogether, or too few are built, or they fall into disrepair. The result can be a form of desertification: the soil becomes saturated either with water or with salt brought up through the soil by the rising water table. Productive fields become wet deserts or salty deserts.

D. Deriaz/WHO

An ancient manual irrigation system in Burkina Faso, with help from plastic sheeting. Africa desperately needs more irrigation, but has often tried to go too far too fast, and spent thousands of dollars per hectare ruining productive land.

In the Sahel during the late 1970s and early 1980s, 5,000 new hectares were coming under irrigation every year. But every year another 5,000 hectares of irrigated land were going out of production due to waterlogging and salinisation, according to the donors' Club du Sahel. In 1979, Mali had about 17,000 hectares of irrigated land in need of rehabilitation, while Senegal had 5,000 hectares. [77]

Bad irrigation is the least serious cause of desertification in terms of area, but one of the most serious in terms of opportunity and money lost. In the Sahel in 1982, one-sixth of all project aid was going to the development of irrigated agriculture, and new schemes were costing as much as $17,000 per hectare.

Irrigation often displaces quite large numbers of people, forcing them onto more marginal lands, which they are then forced to overcultivate. If the irrigation project in question is effective, the displacement may be a necessary trade-off. If the project itself spoils the land, then ripples of desertification due to overcultivation and overgrazing may move outwards from a core of wet desert.

The governments of Senegal, Mali and Mauritania have been cooperating in a scheme to irrigate over 375,000 hectares on the Senegal River Basin with the construction of two dams: the Diama near the coast, both to irrigate and to stop salt water from coming upriver during the dry season, and the Manantali 1,000 km upstream. Officially, according to British environmentalists Edward Goldsmith and Nicholas Hildyard, the scheme is meant to promote "communal rural development", by setting up small-scale village farms on which farmers will grow traditional crops by traditional methods. But in fact, such villages will have use of a maximum of only 7% of the irrigated land, and the establishment of such farms will cease by 1987. "In effect, the decision has been made to favour large-scale mechanised agriculture — with its imports of fertilisers and pesticides in order to produce crops for export — at the expense of the individual smallholder", according to Frédérick Mounier of the aid organisation 'Frères des Hommes '. [78]

Even worse, the soil near the coast is already high in salts, and French experts fear that the Diama Dam will raise the water table enough to bring these salts to the surface. The Manantali will displace herders and disrupt traditional migration routes, and result in overgrazing. It is also expected to kill off 42,900 hectares of open woodland.

As with cash crops, there is nothing wrong with irrigation as such. In fact, Africa needs more irrigation on a scale which farmers can manage and repair. But the way large-scale irrigation is often carried out in Africa can contribute to environmental bankruptcy. Some of the continent's huge dams have had a particularly unfortunate history.

THE BIG DAM

Has the 'big dam' now finally gone out of style? Officials at the World Bank say privately that they want nothing to do with such projects any longer. And the Arab Bank for African Development says the same, condemning many of Africa's large dams as 'white elephants'. But white elephants can have a momentum of their own.

Despite the great need for irrigation, the first big dams of Africa were devoted to producing electricity, and other uses and consequences were ignored. [79] However, this did not apply on the Nile, where the irrigation purposes of Egypt's Aswan Dam have always been seen as more important than its electricity production. And dams were erected early in Sudan on the White Nile (Jebel Aulyia) and Blue Nile (Sennar, begun in 1918) purely for irrigation.

Much of Africa's hydro-electricity remains under-used, or at least oddly used. The Akosombo Dam on the Volta River, which created Africa's largest man-made lake, was built to help make Ghana one of the world's major aluminium producers. The dam produces some of the world's cheapest electricity — not in real terms but on the basis of the contract between the government and the multinational Kaiser Aluminium Company. Yet Kaiser does not now use Ghana's bauxite to produce aluminium. Instead, it imports bauxite ore from Jamaica, produces alumina in Ghana with Akosombo's cheap electricity, then ships the alumina to the United States and converts it into aluminium there. From this are made such things as pots and window frames, some of which Ghana doubtless imports at great expense.

The Akosombo was completed in 1966, the year Ghana's first president, Kwame Nkrumah, was overthrown — a fact which British geographer Ieuan Griffiths maintains was no coincidence, as the high cost of the dam helped precipitate his fall. Ghana has yet to realise the 'secondary effects' that were to accompany the dam: accelerated industrialisation, improved transport to the interior along the 300-kilometre-long lake, and a general spreading of development. [80]

The motives behind some of Africa's major dams have sometimes been rather peculiar, says Griffiths:

"Not surprisingly, decisions to build dams often have been highly political and controversial. The Kariba Dam was a symbol of federation between the Rhodesias because it straddled the boundary between them, and so the technically superior Kafue site, nearer the copperbelt consumers, was passed over. Cabora Bassa, built in Portuguese Mozambique, was a manifestation of South Africa's outward-looking foreign policy. Completion of the project coincided with the independence of Mozambique, but electricity has flowed along the transmission lines to Pretoria with few interruptions."

In fact, in the early 1980s South Africa became virtually self-sufficient in electricity, and could discard the contribution from Cabora Bassa. Not perhaps coincidentally, at about the same time, the South African-backed 'Mozambique National Resistance' (MNR) in Mozambique escalated attacks on the power lines and blew them up five times. South Africa then began to sell electricity to Mozambique, which lacks the grid system to effectively use Cabora Bassa itself.

"We must domesticate this white elephant — Cabora Bassa", commented Mozambique's president Samora Machel. "The elephant's 'ivory' — electricity and irrigation — should go to our agriculture and industry."

Peyton Johnson/WFP

*The Akosombo Dam on the Volta River in Ghana. The dam has yet to
accelerate Ghana's industry, spread development and improve transportation.
It did, however, displace 78,000 people.*

"Dams are beloved of politicians, national plan-makers, financiers and
aid donors alike. They are potent symbols of economic virility and political
prestige; they are clearly visible, concrete and finite projects, demonstrably
a basis for future economic and social development", writes Griffiths.
[81]

They are also the epitome of the sort of capital-intensive projects which
require goods and expertise from the donor countries, putting money back
into the economies of those countries. They allow local government
officials and entrepreneurs to make profits through local contracts, and
often to obtain newly irrigated land for themselves.

The Talata-Mafara dam and irrigation project in northern Nigeria
involved moving 60,000 peasants during three years of construction work,
with no compensation. [82] As they could earn no money during the period,
many had to mortgage their land to the bankers, civil servants and
businessmen of Kano. The elite of Kano also benefited from the Kadawa

irrigation project, as farmers had to rent their lands to those who had the money necessary to invest in irrigation.

Moving the people

Big dams make big reservoirs. The waters behind Akosombo cover 8,482 square kilometres, an area more than three times larger than Luxembourg. Large reservoirs often displace large numbers of people. Akosombo uprooted 1% of the national population: 78,000 people in 700 towns and villages; the Aswan High Dam displaced 120,000; Kariba, 50,000; Lake Kainji in Nigeria, 50,000. [83]

Before and while dams are being built, governments and planners explain how the dam will improve the lives, farming potential, and incomes of the displaced people. This has rarely been the case. The construction and management of a large dam so stretches the planning and administrative ability of most African governments that promises to displaced people are almost never kept. Those displaced by Akosombo were promised new houses on cleared land. The house building and land clearing fell far behind schedule, the houses were unacceptable, and within 10 years, 60% of the resettled people had left the homes and land assigned them.

The effects of displacement can be far-reaching, involving social breakup if lifestyles are disrupted. Many of the Gwemba Tonga tribe of Zambia were displaced by the Kariba Dam and had to change from agriculture based on river flooding to dryland agriculture. The immediate results were an increase in malnutrition and disease, accompanied by increases in alcoholism, divorce and accusations of witchcraft.

But many farmers learned to cope; some got wealthy, and others abandoned the land. The area began to take on an aura of prosperity. However, when Professor T. Scudder studied the Tonga of the middle Zambezi valley in 1981-82, he described it as a "most depressing experience". "Within the villages, diets were worse. Infant mortality probably had increased, with measles once again a major killer of children. The incidence of tuberculosis and of malnutrition had also risen, according to medical personnel familiar with the valley. Housing had also deteriorated, as had household furnishings and local means of transport."

There were more beer halls and men were spending more time drinking in them, financed by cotton income, leaving the training of oxen and the ploughing to inexperienced youths, and the picking and weeding to women and children. Most of the men had also given up growing cereals. Even their drinking did not benefit the women financially, for tastes had shifted to a government-brewed beer and away from the village beer which the women once made and sold.

Dams can bring disease

One of the most widespread environmental diseases in Africa is schistosomiasis (bilharzia), caused by a flatworm which lives part of its life-cycle in water snails and the other part in people. The adult worms settle in the bladder or the intestine, laying eggs with sharp hooks which irritate the affected organ. Sometimes the victim shakes off the disease before serious damage is done, but often he or she becomes debilitated and lethargic, passing blood in the urine or stools. This generally poor condition increases vulnerability to other diseases. Malaria often accompanies schistosomiasis (also known as snail fever), not for any medical reason, but because irrigation schemes create the stagnant water in which malaria-carrying mosquitoes can breed, and the sluggish canals preferred by the schistosome-bearing snail.

The rate at which irrigation schemes spread schistosomiasis among farmers and field workers is depressingly well-documented.

Egypt: rates of schistosomiasis among the population increased in some areas from 21% to 75% after the Aswan Low Dam was completed; the High Dam pushed rates up to 100% in some communities.

Sudan: general infection rate on the 900,000 hectare Gezira scheme of 60-70%, with rates above 90% among schoolchildren. Kenya: almost all schoolchildren affected in irrigated areas around Lake Victoria.

Transvaal, South Africa: infection rate of 68.5% among blacks working on white farms (mostly irrigated), 33.5% among those in 'homelands' (little irrigation).

The disease has been difficult to treat, with many of the medicines providing side-effects more disturbing than the disease. But recent research has led to three drugs which appear effective, all taken by mouth and all with few side-effects. There has been considerable success in reducing it in the Gezira in the Sudan; the snails can also be killed in the canals, and people can reduce their contact with water.

A key problem with the Gezira is that every year it attracts thousands of seasonal agricultural workers at harvest time. Many of these are pastoralists from western Sudan, who take schistosomiasis home with them. Nomads get little medical treatment anyway, but the few clinics of the western Sudan are not equipped to deal with this water-related disease.

WHO claims that "diagnosis is simple and inexpensive", explaining that all that is required are microscopes, trained microscopists, syringes, filter paper and wire or nylon screens. Given that WHO also says that there are 200 million people in the rural world with the disease and 500-600 million more at risk, one may wonder how many generations will pass before 700-800 million rural Third World people are routinely bringing their urine and faeces to the attention of trained microscopists — and getting treatment.

Other problems with large dams include disruptions to fisheries, loss of forests and wildlife, siltation due to erosion, loss of fertility downstream due to impounding of silt, excessive water losses due to evaporation, and even an increase in earth tremors.

The Akosombo, for example, decreased the Volta River's silt load, so that eastward-flowing ocean currents washing Togo's shores carry less silt to replace shorelines washed away by waves. The result has been coastal erosion so rapid that the coastal road has had to be rebuilt twice, and the very existence of the port of Lomé is threatened. The effects are expected to reach as far east as Lagos.

Environmental impact assessments might have turned up some of these problems ahead of time, and plans could have been altered accordingly. But in many cases no such assessments were made, and in others they were made only after construction work began.

Many of Africa's big dams are already in need of major physical rehabilitation, according to a 1981 World Bank report. But the money is not there. Yet major new water schemes are still being planned, and in some cases executed: the Diama and Manantali dams on the Senegal River, for example; development of the Kagera Basin shared by Tanzania, Uganda and Rwanda; the Jonglei Canal under construction in southern Sudan to speed Nile water through the Sudd, the world's largest swamp; development of the 'inland delta' of the Niger and the talked-of diversion of central African rivers into Lake Chad are all projects — real or imagined — far larger than the largest standing African dams. The possible consequences of the latter two particularly have not been fully studied.

More dams!

Despite all the problems with big dams, Africa badly needs hundreds of thousands of new dams and water control projects to get water to the right place at the right time. But the dams required are *small* ones — not because small is beautiful, but because small is manageable. Systems can be changed and rebuilt as change and repair become necessary, by groups of farmers rather than by outside contractors and expensive machinery.

Despite the spectacular dams of the American West, the water projects which make agriculture so successful there are the small dams on streams and the small 'tanks' (rainfall reservoirs) on individual farms.

The same applies in South Africa, which despite its many rivers, is a water-poor country. It has some large dams, but its agriculture is based more on the fact that it has half a million dams, most of them small, most for irrigation rather than electricity.

Africans have been slow to 'manage' their streams and rivers in this way because African agriculture has traditionally been 'extensive'. Land was abundant, and it was easier to expand onto new land than to work to divert water to agricultural purposes. Where water has been abundant and land rich but scarce, African traditional societies adopted sophisticated water management techniques.

The job now is to spread such 'appropriate' techniques around the continent and to borrow more from other arid and semi-arid regions: micro-catchments, contour-damming, water-spreading.

In some cases, it is entirely possible that 'appropriate' might mean big. The Aswan High Dam was completed in 1970. It has spread disease, increased soil salinity in places, increased erosion along the Nile's banks, destroyed Egypt's sardine fishery, and displaced thousands of people. But in this time of frequent and severe drought it is being hailed as the saviour of Egypt. History has yet to judge it completely, but the High Dam "has proved throughout the years that it has carried out its role in protecting Egypt against drought", said Egyptian president Hosni Mubarak recently.

But where 'appropriate' does mean big, the builders will have a wealth of data from all around Africa (and the rest of the world) on how unplanned bigness has radically changed peoples' lives and peoples' environments, without delivering the promised benefits. They will have an encyclopaedia of mistakes to plan against.

Chapter 5

Overgrazing and the nomads

Tenant
farmer: "The heat of your grazing land has bowed your legs.
           And here you are, bundled in a heavy robe, with
           nothing above your head but the Judgement Day, pull-
           ing buckets from the well and working in mud with
           your bare hands."

Nomad: "I sort the bigger sheep, which I drive to the grazing
           land, and then take a long nap myself. As for you,
           go on waiting for your money which is always
           delayed."
                     (popular song/poem from the Sudan,
                 in which a farmer and nomad argue lifestyles)

The problems of nomads, and the way in which they are forced to overgraze the rangelands, is a distinct and separate component in Africa's growing environmental bankruptcy.

In Ethiopia, the Awash River — the only major river which runs eastwards out of the highlands, eventually to disappear into the sands of the dry northern lowlands — was developed in the 1960s to provide irrigation for Dutch, Israeli, Italian and British firms (and for very wealthy Ethiopians) to grow sugar and cotton. The Italian firm MAESCO was producing alfalfa to feed animals in Japan.

This development stopped the August flooding which covered the basin with rich soil and which provided grazing lands for the Afar people. The tribe was forced into less fertile parts of the valley, which became seriously overgrazed. When drought struck Wollo Region in 1972, 25-30% of the Afars died.

In 1984, I watched the Afar starving again. Some of the tribe had brought hundreds of thousands of their cattle up into the large, dead-end Borkena Valley in the Wollo highlands. The cattle had grazed the pasture to bare ground, and were dying. Armed clashes were breaking out between the Afar and the settled farmers.

The traditional agricultural and environmental safety valves had been destroyed by development. The result was starvation and conflict.

In the African drylands — the Sudano-Sahelian strip, large areas of Botswana and South Africa, and the drier areas of Kenya, Tanzania and Zimbabwe — live some 15-24 million people who have animal-based economies. Most of them are pastoralists, people who derive most of their livelihood from domestic livestock fed on natural forage rather than cultivated fodders and pastures. [84]

In theory, pastoralists can be divided into transhumants and nomads. Transhumants tend to live in one place, usually cultivating a crop, and take or send their herds off to the same distant pastures for part of each year. Nomadic herders spend all their time with their herds and follow no set yearly pattern. In practice, the two types of pastoralism are hard to separate, for even the most widely-travelling nomads often follow a fairly standard yearly route and occasionally grow crops.

Africa's drylands are resource-scarce. Pastoralism provides people with a technique for moving through these scarce resources, using their animals to gather and store the grass and rain in a usable form; animals have the added advantage of being able to transport the resources over large distances. This is important given the erratic rainfall in the dry rangeland areas, erratic both in time and place.

It may rain during the drier periods where it has not rained for 10 years, and will not again for 10 more years. Heavy rain may produce lush grass over a few square kilometres, while the surrounding area remains dry and barren.

Nomads are skilled at getting their cattle, camels, sheep and goats quickly onto the new grass which is more than twice as digestible as dry grass. In much of the dry rangelands, livestock rearing may be the most efficient and productive use of the land. Indeed, it may be the *only* productive use of the land. Pastoralism depends on flexibility, and anything which reduces this flexible response to resources limited in time and space threatens the viability of pastoralism.

As livestock are the major resource base of pastoralists, they have taken on a social importance far beyond mere calories. Animals are money; they are symbols cementing relationships within and between families, clans and tribes. The social importance of animals has repeatedly frustrated plans by outsiders, who see herds in terms of beef on the hoof to make herds more 'productive' in terms of meat and milk for outside consumers.

To be efficient, pastoralism requires mobility and large areas of land, even in good years. In drought years, even more is needed. Many of the herds which the Mauritanian government lists as 'Mauritanian' migrate seasonally into Mali and Senegal. Many of these herds remain *out* of the country longer than they do inside it, especially in years of low rainfall.

Mark Edwards/Earthscan

Nomads' herds near Tahoua, southwest Niger. Pastoral systems may be the most efficient way — may, in fact, be one of the only ways — of getting a living and getting protein from Africa's drylands.

Some 'Mauritanian' herds spent the entire 1968-73 drought out of the country. [85]

Herds of controversy

Just as agricultural 'experts' tend to regard the African peasant as stupid, so have many outsiders looked at Sahelian pastoralism. Since herders regard animals as money (so this view goes) they stupidly maximise herd size. As more and more land is taken up by cash crops and subsistence crops (due to population growth and the increased cultivation of marginal land), and as more wells and better veterinary services allow more animals to survive, then bigger and bigger herds are being squeezed onto smaller and smaller ranges. The herds overgraze this land, reducing it to desert.

The view that desertification of the rangelands is entirely due to overstocking with animals was at its height during the 1968-73 Sahelian drought, when one often read that goats alone were advancing the Sahara southwards 15 km a year over a broad front. The pastoralists' bad name goes back to a Victorian theory that pastoralism was a stage of human development, more 'modern' than hunting and gathering but not as modern as settled farming. Anthropologist M.J. Herskovits argued in 1926 that East African herders were locked into elaborate social and political systems — the 'cattle complex' — which forced them to maximise herds, no matter what the cost to the environment.

Today, ecologists are increasingly critical of this view, arguing that pastoralism is a perfectly rational way of using scarce resources. They argue that there is no convincing definition of 'desertification' in the dry rangelands, that grasslands can recover more quickly than suspected, and that herding keeps many areas from relapsing into unproductive bush. Eminent experts disagree by factors of four or five over the 'correct' stocking rate of a given range; for most dry areas no one knows, within a margin of 30-40%, what the present livestock population in fact is. This point should be kept in mind when examining any figures on African livestock.

While there is little evidence that herds *permanently* degrade the dry Sahelian grasslands, there is considerable evidence that overgrazing damages it at least temporarily over vast areas, so that carrying capacity drops quickly and animals die of hunger rather than thirst.

The 1968-73 Sahel drought, for example, killed hundreds of thousands of grazing animals. But it had no real effect on rising livestock population trends. According to World Bank figures, cattle numbers in sub-Saharan Africa in 1980 were 31% *up* on 1961-65 levels, and sheep and goats had increased by 60%.

French rangeland expert Michel Baumer warned after the last drought that "the situation has become extremely precarious in the Sudan as in all the countries in the region, and is today much more delicate than in the late 1960s. The next serious drought might well entail more severe consequences than the last one." He seems to have been right.

But most of the examples of overgrazing in the drylands come from local observation around wells, around cities, or in places where nomads have been encouraged to settle. Studies in the early 1980s by the USAID-funded Niger Range and Livestock Project suggested that pastoralists had too *few* cattle to sustain their lifestyles — rather than too many — and needed credit to rebuild herds.

Desertification by herds is more obvious in mountainous grasslands such as those of West Central Africa, Ethiopia and some of the South African 'homelands'. French geographer J. Hurault, in a 1975 study of the mountain rangelands of Cameroon and Nigeria, showed how trampling of the grass in the uplands led to sheet erosion and the disappearance of perennial grasses, while in river valleys it led to gulley erosion and landslips.
[86]

Mark Edwards/Earthscan

A FulBe herder and his animals near the Niger River, Niger. Despite the proximity of the river and the relatively 'lush' vegetation, the animals still show the effects of drought.

A profound ignorance

In 1982, I was with 25 European and African environmental journalists on an Earthscan field trip studying desertification in the Sahel. In Niamey we met several young British and American researchers who had been living and travelling for months at a time with pastoralists of the wide-ranging FulBe (Fulani) people.

The researchers were enthusiastic about their work and their results. Their Niger Range and Livestock Project was trying to find out how the FulBe conducted their business of livestock-rearing: when and why they moved their herds; when and why they sold, loaned and borrowed animals; how they cooperated and bartered with settled farmers; why and if they needed money; what sort of mixes they tried to achieve among cows, goats and sheep. The researchers claimed that for the first time ever good data was being gathered on all of this, that such things had not been understood before by outsiders.

For the journalists, this meeting was highly instructive. For a week they had been briefed on all the 'management schemes' which had been and were being tried in the Sahel and elsewhere in Africa to make livestock rearing more 'productive': wells had been dug; grazing fees had been imposed; rangelands had been divided into blocks to be alternatively used and left fallow; group ranches had been organised. The UNCOD Plan of Action had called for a vast Sahel-wide project called SOLAR (Stratification of Livestock in Arid Regions) in which calves were to be reared by nomadic herdsmen in the traditional manner in the arid north, moved south for fattening either on farms or in feedlots, and finally their beef marketed in the big cities and high-population areas of the West African coast.

Yet, according to the researchers in Niamey all these schemes to 'improve' pastoralism had been tried without the devisers having any clear idea of how the pastoralists operated.

Given the profound ignorance of what pastoralists are up to, it is not surprising that attempts to manage their activities have almost universally failed. Alan Grainger collected testimony of such failure in 1982: [87]

"There have been many livestock projects since the drought [1968-73], but few positive results. Things go wrong in implementation. Planners don't have an overall view of the problem." — Dr Ibrahim Touré, UNESCO range management expert based in Dakar.

There is an "almost unblemished record of project non-success in the Sahelian livestock sector." — Michael Horowitz, State University of New York.

"The picture that emerges is one of almost unrelieved failure." — Walter Goldschmidt, University of California.

The main reason these projects have failed is because they have been imposed without an understanding of pastoralist societies, and imposed to achieve objectives which have little to do with the objectives of those societies. Given the incredible lack of basic data, why have African governments and aid and development agencies been so willing to put so much time and money into large livestock projects?

The answers are complex, and probably as much psychological and political as agricultural. To understand them, it must be realised that even African decision-makers are as much outsiders in terms of pastoralism as are northern 'experts'. According to Horowitz, speaking of the Sudano-Sahelian region, "with the exception of Mauritania in the Sahel and Somalia in East Africa, the ruling elites in these states are drawn from groups which are not only not pastoral, but which have historically viewed pastoral people with ambivalence at best, and often outright hostility".

These leaders see pastoralists, wandering across national boundaries, as large bodies of armed, unruly, uncontrolled and untaxed citizens.

Pastoralists often are a threat to peace, in that many go armed and have strong traditions of cattle raiding. Like most Africans, pastoralists indeed have more loyalty to their own tribe or clan than to a central government. The Niger government, for example, is especially suspicious of FulBe nationalism.

Pastoralists are also seen as being in charge of a major resource in the form of high-protein beef, a potential earner of large sums of foreign exchange. In this view, African governments are joined by the Northern experts, with images of the levels of production achieved by US and Australian cattle ranches and of the large and growing Northern beef markets. During the brief enthusiasm for SOLAR, the Sahelian leaders talked of exporting beef all over the world.

All of this has led to deep confusion as to what livestock projects are supposed to accomplish. Horowitz summed up USAID goals in 1979:

> "Livestock projects have been supposed, simultaneously, to increase productivity, reverse the ecological deterioration of the range, shift production from a dairy to a beef orientation, improve producer income and quality of life, and maintain a regular supply of cheap meat for the internal market, and increase the supply of high-quality meat to the export market."

'Rationalised' destruction

Africa is littered with examples of arrogant and failed attempts to 'rationalise' pastoralism, which have often caused desertification and bloodshed, as well as wasted considerable amounts of money.

Sedentarisation — the forced or encouraged settling of nomads — can be the most environmentally destructive process. In the dry years of the late 1970s, for example, the government had encouraged northern Kenyan pastoralists to settle, via the UNESCO 'Integrated Project on Arid Lands' (IPAL). The project appeared to combine the worst of both the modern and the traditional. It included permanent settlements, as well as food aid and veterinary and well-digging services. But the traditional desire to maximise herds for long-term security was not replaced with any other coping strategy. The result was overgrazing around settlements and a tendency to keep the valuable milk-giving animals on these overgrazed ranges while the men braved the well-armed cattle raiders of the region to take unproductive animals to distant fields. So IPAL hired a public relations team to encourage the Rendille, Gabra, Samburu and Boran people to sell stock for cash. [88]

IPAL succeeded in generating a greater understanding of pastoralism, but after seven years of work its main conclusion was that "it will only be possible to increase human welfare of pastoralists and to stop desertification if the mobility and dispersion of livestock can again be increased considerably, and if overall numbers of livestock can be better controlled through a greatly improved marketing system". [89]

Things have worked out somewhat better for some of the Sudanese pastoralists encouraged to take up irrigated cotton and peanut cropping, according to Norwegian anthropologist Gunnar Sorbo. The pastoralists ignored the management's rules and combined herding with irrigated cropping. Their animals gave them the independence to refuse to grow peanuts and cotton when it did not suit them. But they used their added income to buy more livestock, "encouraging a considerable overstocking of the surrounding grazing zone".

In a review of sedentarisation policies worldwide, one expert concludes that "where settlement has been imposed on nomads compulsorily by government decree or in other ways, the results have been disastrous..." [90]

Wells

Wells and other watering points have a bleak record in the history of African rangeland management. In theory, they can 'open up' ranges which have ample grass but too little water. Mauritania has 55 million hectares of usable rangelands, but only 39 million are used, largely because of water shortages. [91]

If water can be provided, by hand-dug wells, machine-drilled boreholes, dams, cisterns or even delivery by tankers or lorries (as occasionally happens in drought years in Ethiopia and Somalia), then livestock can have access to more resources.

> *African governments and foreign aid agencies have been enthusiastic in digging wells. It is the easiest form of pastoral 'development' and it produces physical things which can be listed in reports. To an outsider, it is self-evident that in an arid region where water is scarce, providing more water is bound to help. But well-digging has largely failed to help pastoralists and pastoralism.*

Most are dug without consulting the pastoralists, and without fitting the new water sources into pastoralist routes and strategies. Many are dug along main roads and tracks to markets, which leads to overcrowding, and the trampling effect of thousands of hooves is one of the most potent factors for local desertification. Many provide too much water, which encourages nomads to keep herds around them, rather than moving from

Mark Edwards/Earthscan

A well in western Sudan. Mixed herds — camels, sheep, goats and cows — spread risks and use rangelands more efficiently. But the complexities of the nomads' coping strategies are often far beyond the government 'advisers' who deal with them.

well to well. Aid agencies have competed in digging new wells and boreholes, and have not consulted among themselves.

For all of these reasons, watering points tend to be over-used and often contribute more to desertification than to the opening of new ranges.

Wells also tend to break down.

* In northeast Kenya only 14 of 54 boreholes drilled since 1969 were working in 1979.
* In Botswana 40% of boreholes never function.
* In Tanzanian Maasailand most of the former permanent water supplies were either broken down, clogged up, working at reduced capacity or in need of spare parts. [92]

These findings indicate the unreality of elaborate schemes to control the use of watering points by turning pumps on and off to encourage nomads to move along — a practice which has sometimes so angered nomads that they have deliberately destroyed pump equipment. And it takes a brave (or foolhardy) government official to turn off a borehole surrounded by thirsty livestock and armed nomads.

*Yet unplanned wells continue to be dug. "Planners do not learn
from their mistakes. To see governments plan to make elaborate
installations of waterholes or to launch stock-reduction
programmes after these have been repeatedly branded as failures
makes one wonder why writing was ever invented", concluded
one exasperated expert.* [93]

Ranching

If the objectives of settling nomads include either increasing land carrying
capacity or protecting the land, ranching does not seem to be a way of
accomplishing either.

Ranching has been the commonest livestock development strategy
proposed by aid agencies. Walter Goldschmidt of the University of
California feels that this is because it "accords with Euro-American notions
of landholding, farming and business operations and appears as simply
being the right way to do things. That it is destructive to the native way
of life is at best viewed as irrelevant, at worst as desirable." [94]

Ranches are owned by individuals, the government, or groups.
Individual commercial ranches were first begun in Kenya early this century,
and Kenya is the only African nation which has had any success with high-
yielding European beef and dairy cattle, perhaps because it had a good
supply of European farmers familiar with such cattle, and possessed high
grasslands free of the diseases and pests which have decimated such breeds
elsewhere in Africa. Today Kenyan farmers run sophisticated livestock
operations.

Government ranches are found in almost all nations with pastoral zones.
In 1984, government ranches in Niger sold off cattle in an attempt to warn
pastoralists to do the same as the drought was beginning to take its toll
of forage. But in many countries such ranches are put under the control
of minor civil servants from cities who have little knowledge of stock-
rearing and little desire to spend hours on the rangelands.

'Group ranching' is a general term for any system which vests ownership
in a number of individuals or families: it has been tried in 18 African
countries, without any examples of unqualified success. [95] A key problem
is that group ownership rarely approximates closely enough to the complex
ownership and holding patterns of the traditional system. Maasai in
Tanzania have refused to take cattle donated by the government to the
Maasai group ranches the government was trying to initiate, because they
were suspicious concerning the government's rights over and plans for
those cattle.

Ranching seems only to have worked in Africa under a specific set of
conditions: the ranches must be owned by private individuals managing

them for profit and assured of a market for beef and dairy products — conditions which now exist only in Kenya and Botswana.

'Game ranching' — the control and systematic harvesting of large African antelope and buffalo — offers great theoretical promise because these animals are largely resistant to local disease, adapted to the environment and faster-growing than domestic livestock. Impala and wildebeest, for instance, reach maturity in one year, while African cattle take over 30 months. All the antelopes have more protein and less fat as a proportion of live weight than African cattle. Yet game ranching, perhaps because it has been little studied, little tried and under-capitalised, has yet to prove itself.

Recent studies by ecologist David Western in southern Kenya suggest that pastoral systems are a more efficient way of exploiting the nutrients available in arid savannas: [96]

"Contrary to commonly held views, the results do not show natural wildlife ecosystems to be more efficient than pastoralist-dominated systems; quite the opposite in fact. Both appear more efficient than commercial systems."

Governments should perhaps take note of this finding as they consider projects to settle or limit the wanderings of pastoralists.

Cattle and tsetse flies

Wildlife, soil and forests have been protected in large areas of Africa by the tsetse fly, the bite of which can give both humans and animals the disease trypanosomiasis — called sleeping sickness in humans. Wildlife are largely immune, but may harbour the trypanosomes — the animal microbes — which cause the disease.

Some 10 million sq km of Africa — an area larger than the United States — is dominated by the fly, and for generations planners have dreamed of opening it up for cattle rearing and mixed farming. The tsetse belt coincides roughly with the humid and sub-humid tropics, but extends down into Zambia, Zimbabwe, Malawi and Mozambique: the present front line of the tsetse war. Past eradication campaigns have involved shooting more than a million large wild animals thought to harbour the disease, and more recently large-scale deforestation. Today the campaign is waged largely with insecticides such as DDT, dieldrin and endosulfan. All have caused controversy, and conservationists are aghast at these chemicals being broadcast widely in the wildlife rich areas of south-central Africa. Experiments are now being conducted with 'tsetse traps', screens baited to smell like animal breath, where the attracted flies are killed with contact insecticides which do not get loose in the environment.

Environmentalists' concern about the whole tsetse campaign is that it could open vast areas of fragile soils and low or erratic rainfall to an unplanned land scramble, perhaps spending millions of dollars to desertify much of central Africa. Dick Pitman of the Zambezi Society of Zimbabwe claims that this would wreck schemes which have evolved in Zimbabwe to get the financial benefits of tourism and wildlife culling to local people. British conservationist Marcus Linear fears it will wipe out wildlife before game farming has had a chance to prove itself. [97]

Since 1979, both FAO and the International Livestock Centre for Africa (ILCA) have begun studies on cattle varieties resistant to trypanosomiasis. The ndama cattle of far western Africa and the muturu of coastal western Africa appear to have natural resistance, but are smaller than the usual African zebu breeds. However, crosses between the zebu and the muturu exist in both Nigeria and Benin which combine zebu size with natural resistance. Improving and spreading these resistant breeds would seem a safer way forward than massive spraying of chemicals, the long-term effects of which are little known in Africa.

The adaptive nomad

Pastoral nomads are not, in fact, locked into a destructive land-livestock relationship. Nor are they romantic independents, living in perfect harmony with Nature. The nomads are highly skilled and knowledgeable herdsmen, with a long tradition of making the best of a tough environment. Many are able to adapt quickly to changing circumstances, to take advantage of new opportunities or to save themselves in time of drought.

Neither is the pastoralist always the adversary of the farmers. In fact, across Africa many pastoralists exist in symbiotic harmony with settled farmers. They swap animals, meat, dairy products and hides for grain and other farm produce, and often hire themselves out to one another. This has worked well, for example, in the Bagamoyo region of Tanzania, where in the dry season farmwork is slack and the farmers hire themselves out to help the pastoralists draw water. Again, the FulBe hired the settled Samba in eastern Nigeria to herd their excess cattle, paying them in livestock. The Samba began to amass herds, and now sometimes hire FulBe to tend Samba herds.

During the 1970-71 drought in Kenya, the nomads proved highly adaptive. Many Turkana became fishermen on Lake Turkana. Some Rendille began farming the damper areas of Mount Marsabit's forests. The Boran and other tribes participated in irrigation schemes, while Somalis in eastern Kenya established an irrigation scheme on their own with no outside help or encouragement.

Governments have not been very successful at encouraging nomads to sell cattle, but economic forces can do so. Philip Burnham describes how on the Adamawa plateau in Cameroon the price of steers doubled between 1970 and 1980 in terms of the amount of manioc flour that the price of one steer could buy. Thus FulBe herders have found they can get by, and even thrive, with smaller herds, selling cattle to buy grain and saving labour costs as well.

In parts of Nigeria, the opposite has happened. There the price of grain has risen several hundredfold in relation to the price of milk since the early 1970s. This forces herders to sell more and more animals to meet their family's grain needs. One response to this has been the evolution of a group of 'farming nomads' — *FulBe na'i* —whose herds cannot support this high offtake. So they produce enough grain to feed their families through agriculture. But the large amounts of cheap cattle have encouraged the farming Samba people to invest in livestock. Thus the farming of both peoples has become more 'mixed'. [98]

The pastoralist's readiness to adapt to changing circumstances does not always result in a better life. Africa's nomads were being periodically killed by drought and ruined by diseases such as rinderpest long before newspapers began covering such disasters. Today's land squeezes, caused by rising populations and by land deterioration, are putting more and more pastoralists on the margin of existence, and are causing increased conflicts between farmers and nomads, as both invade each other's 'traditional' lands.

In the Sahel especially, population pressures are pushing farmers north of the line above which less than 300 mm of rain falls each year. Land this dry cannot support permanent cropping, and was traditionally left to nomads. (Indeed, colonial laws making cultivation illegal north of a certain point remain in several Sahelian countries, though they are rarely enforced.) Desperation is now forcing farmers to move beyond the point where cultivation is sustainable, into the pastoralists' best grazing land.

Drought hits herders especially hard, as it can wipe out their capital and the basis of their social organisation. The 1968-73 drought forced many pastoralists to give up herding permanently, many settling in poverty in the towns. Others turned to farming, often crossing national borders to find good farmland. FulBe from the arid zone appear to have been migrating across borders since the mid-1970s, although, since the process must be clandestine in the political climate of modern West Africa, it would be difficult to prove.

Another process documented by Jeremy Swift and the Niger Range and Livestock Project in Niger is the creation of cattle-less herders. The WoDaaBe of Niger cannot simply settle down and farm during dry spells, because they tend to live outside the arable region, and population densities are high in the farming regions to the south. The drought forced many to sell cattle; the cattle were bought by townspeople who loaned them back to the herders to be cared for.

These contracts are essentially similar to the debt-traps created in certain types of landholding in South America: the debtor can never accumulate enough capital to escape. In this case the pastoralist can never build up a large enough surplus, because of his dwindling capital base, to free himself from his contracts.

"A growing proportion of the 5% of Africa's rural population who are pastoralists appear to have no animals, which is the equivalent of landlessness. The result is very low per capita incomes for those involved and the need for large migratory movements, either seasonal or semi-permanent, as wage labourers", according to Barbara Dinham and Colin Hines. [99]

While pastoralism may be the most effective use of land resources given adequate grazing land, the land squeeze will inevitably force growing numbers of pastoralists to change their ways. Most such changes have been dictated by disaster or by outside agencies, with the result that the pastoralists, the land and the nations involved have rarely benefited.

As pastoralists continue to adjust to the realities of Africa's growing environmental bankruptcy, the result will be that growing numbers of poor, perhaps cattle-less, herders will be isolated in increasingly drought-prone arid regions, while competition will grow fiercer in regions where herders already compete with farmers.

Both developments will serve to provide decreasing amounts of animal protein for Africa. Before the 1968-73 Sahel drought, livestock accounted for half the total exports of some Sahelian nations. In the early 1980s, despite the fact that herd sizes had almost recovered to pre-drought sizes, the Sahel was still exporting meat, but had become a net importer of dairy products. USAID estimated before the 1980s drought that between 1985 and 1990 this region would become a net importer of meat as well as milk — despite some of the largest herds in Africa.

Ways out?

Any attempts to improve pastoralism must have as a starting point the pastoralists themselves. This would seem obvious, but the great majority of attempts to tinker with pastoralism have been based on goals sought by outsiders rather than on the skills and desires of the herders themselves. Nevertheless, there are some pointers to success.

After the 1968-73 drought, an Oxfam worker in Niger started a herd reconstruction project based on traditional FulBe stock-loaning practices. Following an old custom of sharing animals (*habbanaae,* meaning 'tie down the cow'), locally-bought cows were loaned to herders for the period of three calvings, at which time the borrower returned the cow (or the cash equivalent) but kept the three calves and the milk the cow gave over the period. Also, lactating cows were loaned for short terms to especially poor families over the dry season. About 290 families totalling 1,500 people were helped to rebuild viable herds and to resume their normal lives. As the herders paid off their debts, the Oxfam representative began to make a profit, which is said to have created book-keeping problems at the head office in the UK, because it had never happened before. Governments could learn from such examples.

During the 1980s, the ILCA began to emphasise research into ways of working with traditional systems. Its work in Mali, Nigeria, Ethiopia and Botswana has produced a number of interesting suggestions, ranging from new ideas for forage crops and feedstock (including molasses from sugar production) to more efficient butter churns which convert milk into a marketable product. But most of the ideas developed by ILCA remain to be tested with pastoralists. It is a long way from the experimental plot of fodder on the research station to regular use of such crops by herding families.

African societies themselves provide examples of low-cost methods that could be tried elsewhere. In the Guinea highlands local cattle farmers have developed a system of 'live fences' — hedges called *tapades* —which control access to farmland during the growing season, provide green manure for fields and protect fruit trees planted within them. It cannot be automatically assumed that these are applicable elsewhere in Africa, but they might be useful elsewhere in high grasslands where there are conflicts between pastoralists and farmers.

Pastoralists have strong traditions of cooperation among themselves, which can be built upon to develop more formal cooperatives to receive credit and to purchase supplies in bulk. But for this to happen, governments may have to yield some central authority. The Niger Range and Livestock Project had some small-scale success with such cooperatives, but these have reportedly encountered government opposition.

Livestock extension workers and vets from within the pastoralist societies are also needed. Few of the government vets and advisers working with the FulBe people of Nigeria even speak the FulBe language.

Finally, any scheme to improve pastoralism must be part of a total land-use scheme. Government officials with responsibility for livestock marketing, well-digging, veterinary services, arable farming and forestry will have to start communicating with one another and stop competing for funds.

"You cannot ignore what livestock means in the Sahel", said Niger President Seyni Kountché. "They are not just an economic resource; they are a measure of social good, a sensitive barometer of moral health in the Sahelian people. Raising cattle is a way of life for a great many of my fellow citizens.''

A few African leaders and outside experts now know this. They must now develop policies which reflect and build upon this reality.

Chapter 6

Forests, fuel and energy

"There is an advertisement on television in New
York which says, 'Our peanuts are fresh from the
jungle'. The joke is that peanuts don't come from
the jungle; you have to *cut down* trees to plant
peanuts. Then you get the peanuts —
and desertification."
Djibril Diallo, (Senegalese) UN Office for
Emergency Operations in Africa

How can African countries use their forests and the lands on which they
stand in the most effective ways possible? And what is the role of
deforestation in environmental bankruptcy?

Logging for export, clearing for agriculture, and cutting for fuelwood
all consume trees for human benefit. But these uses are often short-term,
foreclosing on the larger benefits forests can offer, foreclosing even on
future national development options. Africa cannot afford to conserve
untouched all its vast areas of forest. But Africa can afford even less to
squander the economic and social benefits which proper forest and
woodland management can bring. Mismanagement often results in
wastelands unable to produce timber, fuelwood or crops.

This is not to take up the cry of some Northern conservationists that
tropical forests and woodlands should never be touched, because they
contain millions of plant species unstudied by science which offer future
generations new medicines, pesticides, crop varieties and industrial
chemicals. It is true that such genetic resources exist in Africa's forests.
But the benefits of these varieties and chemicals tend to go to the North,
or to other parts of the Third World. Until the nations which make the
profits are willing to invest seriously in the conservation of these
woodlands, African governments will remain under tremendous pressure
to clear them for short-term gains.

Indonesian Vice President Adam Malik has summed up the Third World
view: "How much land for the hungry of today? And how much for
genetic resources to be preserved for tomorrow? In the past, we have
neither received a fair share of the benefits, nor have we received a fair
share of assistance — other than inexpensive advice and even more
inexpensive criticism — in the efforts to save the common global natural

heritage. Unless such responsibilities are equally shared, all our good intentions will only lead to global environmental destruction." [100]

A more compelling argument for protecting forests and trees is that they often protect the soil and water regimes upon which the agriculture of agricultural nations is based. They prevent desertification.

Rwanda is Africa's most densely populated nation. It has 220 people per square kilometre, and 95% of them living by subsistence agriculture. On the Zaire border in the Virunga mountains is the 12,000 hectare Parc des Volcans, the densely-forested home of a few hundred endangered mountain gorillas.

Naturally, there is tremendous pressure to clear the park for agricultural land. In 1969, about 40% of the country's national parks were cleared for farming. In 1978, the Rwanda government and foreign conservation groups began cooperating on a project to save the mountain gorilla. A key part of these efforts involved convincing Rwandans of the role the forested mountains played in their agricultural survival, by catching rainwater and slowly releasing a constant supply of water throughout the year. The park brings in tourist revenue — $6.3 million in 1981. But this pales besides the benefits it brings to many in this nation of farmers in terms of soil and water conservation. If the mountains were cleared, there would be floods in the rainy season, and springs would run dry in the dry season. More important, the cleared land would support a human population equal to only two month's worth of the nation's rapid population growth.

Lack of data

We know remarkably little about what is actually happening in African forests. Norman Myers, in a 1980 study of tropical deforestation for the US National Academy of Sciences, said that figures were often simply estimated rather than based on surveys. The best estimate he could find for Zaire, said to have well over half Africa's tropical moist forests, was no more accurate than "within 40% either way". [101] The FAO/UNEP *Tropical Forest Resources Assessment* study in 1981 went some way to fill the information gap, and concluded that Africa was losing forests at the rate of 1.3 million hectares per year — an area about half the size of Rwanda. But despite such efforts, we still have only a patchy and incomplete picture of what is happening.

Deforestation means different things to different people. For some it is the total clearing of trees; for others it is any activity which disrupts the natural ecology of the virgin forest. Change can range from patchy slash-and-burn cultivation, followed by partial regeneration, to complete clear-felling over large areas. In lumping together all activities which disturb the primary forest, and condemning them as deforestation or forest destruction, there is a real danger of obscuring the real issues.

The enthusiastic publicisation of the issue of deforestation "has frequently been blundering and over-passionate with the result that the debate has become confused and there is a risk of jeopardising the success of the crusade", according to Jean-Paul Lanly of FAO. [102]

Tropical moist forest

The tropical moist forests (TMF) of Africa are mainly concentrated in a large block centred on the equator, stretching inland as far as the mountains and highlands on the eastern boundary of the Zaire/Congo basin. Moist forests are also found in most of the countries on the northern coast of the Gulf of Guinea, with smaller amounts in some of the East African countries, mainly Tanzania, Uganda and the island of Malagasy (Madagascar); but these are mostly monsoon forests, with pronounced dry seasons. The total area of moist forest is estimated to be about 1.6 million sq km, of which about one million sq km are in Zaire. TMF includes a wide variety of sub-climates and forest types. The areas of true rainforest — wet jungle — are more or less confined to the coastal plains and the lowlands of the Zaire Basin. In these areas, the climate does not vary greatly throughout the year. The average temperature is around 27°C, and there is no marked dry season. The forests are tall and evergreen, rich in plant and animal life. In Gabon, 122 species of trees and bushes have been identified in a patch of ground of just 0.8 hectare.

Moving inward from the coast, and north or south from the basin, the dry season becomes more pronounced, and the character of the forest changes and shades into the dry tropical forests and savannas of the interior.

Over the whole TMF area, one of the most important factors determining the ultimate effect of deforestation is the soil type. In many of the moist forest areas, the soils are poor. TMF is lush not because of soil fertility but because of the rapidity with which decomposition and recycling takes place. Most of the nutrients in a tropical forest system are contained in the living vegetation and the thick layer of decomposing matter on the forest floor.

If the trees and humus are removed, the nutrients on which the system depends are heavily depleted — much more so than in a temperate forest system, where a far higher proportion of the nutrients are in the ground. It is usually difficult to replenish these nutrients with artificial fertilisers: the high levels of iron and aluminium in many tropical forest soils tend to 'lock-up' phosphate fertiliser in a chemical form which plants cannot use.

Removing trees leaves only a thin layer of useful soil, which is quickly eroded by rainfall or depleted by farming. Where the soils are lateritic they turn hard and brick-like when cleared and exposed to the sun. Tropical rainstorms can be extremely heavy, typically reaching 25 mm in half an hour: up to 40 times the amount in a typical temperate shower. In Ghana, rainfall of up to 200 mm in an hour has been recorded. [103] Normally, the leaves break the impact of the rain so that it penetrates in the form of fine spray, or runs down the trunks of the trees. As long as the forest is relatively intact, there is little if any erosion. But once the trees are removed, erosion can be both rapid and spectacular.

Conventional farming is not impossible on all tropical forest soils once their trees have been removed, as the long-term plantations of rubber and oil palm demonstrate. But it can often be an extremely difficult exercise, requiring heavy investments of money, care and skill.

Logging

Timber is an important moneymaker for a number of West African countries, providing foreign exchange as well as a considerable amount of employment. For countries with few other natural resources and low manufacturing capabilities, timber exports have become essential to their development strategies. Often, only a small proportion of the tree species are commercially valuable, so that large areas can be disturbed or destroyed for relatively small results.

How fast are Africa's forests disappearing? Liberia, for example, obtained about $84 million from wood exports in 1980, just over 11% of its total export earnings. About 80,000 hectares of forest were being logged per year out of its remaining 900,000 hectares of primary forest — a rate which would completely remove the nation's forests in 11 years.

Cameroon, by contrast, where logging of primary forest was also about 80,000 hectares per year in 1980, has about seven million hectares of forest, so this rate could be maintained for nearly 90 years. But there were plans to double the rate of logging as soon as possible.

The Ivory Coast is the biggest timber exporter in Africa, and its foreign exchange earnings from timber amounted to over $300 million in 1980. Ivory Coast's area of closed forest declined by two-thirds in 20 years, from 12 million hectares in 1956 to four million in 1977. However, agriculture destroyed 4.5 times as much forest as logging, a ratio which may be similar in other parts of Africa. Ivory Coast's timber exports are expected to begin to fall within the present decade.

In Nigeria, most of the exploitable forests have already been logged. Once a major timber exporter, Nigeria has banned exports and may soon have to import wood for its own needs. In Ghana, too, the country's forest resources, outside the relatively small area of reserved forests, are rapidly reaching a state where they can only provide a minimal output of commercial timber.

Gabon, whose timber exports earned about $65 million in 1980, is still so richly endowed with primary forest that current logging rates are having little overall impact. Roughly the same appears to be true in Zaire, where logging for export is still a small-scale enterprise.

The estimated total area of replanting in Africa's closed moist forests is about 100,000 hectares per year — far below the rate at which forests are being logged. A tropical moist rainforest cannot be recreated; it can only be replaced with far less rich and varied plantations or secondary forest.

Shifting cultivation

When forests are completely cleared, it is usually to get at the land under them rather than the timber growing on them.

It is important to distinguish between the different types of farming carried out in forest areas. Farmers who move into forest lands all tend to be described as *shifting cultivators,* but it is misleading to group them all under the same heading.

The oldest technique is *forest fallow.* First, the small trees and shrubs are cut, stacked and burned at the bases of the large trees to kill them, though some commercially valuable trees may be left. The burning of the vegetation releases its nutrients, and is equivalent to a liberal application of fertiliser to the soil.

Crops such as cassava, maize, and yams are then grown in the semi-cleared area. The methods used are often quite sophisticated, with the crop varying year by year so as to minimise the problems caused by weeds, according to P. Sanchez:

"....The cultivation system is well adapted to temporary weed control. Crops with successively higher canopies are planted (cereals, cassava, plantains). Thus the least competitive crop, the cereal, is grown when weed infestations are the least intensive right after burning. As the taller crops grow, they permit the regrowth of woody, shade-tolerant species that will start a secondary forest." [104]

After a few years, the accessible soil nutrients are exhausted and crop yields fall. The farmer then leaves the area fallow. The forest plants recolonise the land and a secondary forest begins to grow. Often this is deliberately seeded with fruit or timber trees so that it will be useful even in fallow. Slowly, soil nutrients are replenished and nitrogen is fixed by bacteria or leguminous plants. After a period which may vary from five to 20 years, the regrown vegetation can be cut and burned to refertilise the ground, and the farming cycle repeated. Although less ecologically varied than virgin forest, the regenerated woodland protects the soil and watersheds.

When Africa's populations were smaller, and farmers were able to leave their plots fallow for long enough, there was an equilibrium between forest and farming. The land consisted of a chequerboard of patches of land under cultivation and forest in various states of regrowth. This technique "has given man his livelihood in the tropics for centuries and is significant even now, when after a quarter of a century of experiment in tropical Africa we have failed to introduce to the forest regions any method of food production superior to the natural fallow system", according to one expert. [105]

But in some areas, population growth has made farmers what US environmentalist Erik Eckholm calls "enemies of the forest". [106] Because there is no longer sufficient land, the fallow periods are being reduced, and trees and shrubs have less time to regenerate. Farmers from outside the forests, not familiar with the complex management techniques required, crop the land more intensively and for longer periods before abandoning it. This destroys tree roots and seeds left in the soil when it is cleared. As a result, neither soil fertility nor forests return, and the land may become permanently covered in weeds and grasses. The land is lost both as forest and as farmland.

An FAO report describes the colonisation of West African forests, once logging roads are built, as a "...rush of alien populations using these roads to penetrate the forest, each family settling a few hundred metres from its neighbours in order to secure the largest extension possible from the first clearing." [107]

In the worst cases, the soil over large areas is farmed until it is permanently ruined, and the farming families then move on to another area, "leaving behind them a mosaic of degraded croplands and brush growth where there is no hope of a secondary forest re-establishing itself" writes Norman Myers. [108]

There is almost no hard information on how much land is being destroyed in this way. But farming has certainly made enormous inroads into the forests of a number of countries. Internal population growth plays its part, as does migration into the coastal forest states from the poorer Sahelian countries. An estimated five million hectares of forest were converted to agriculture in the Ivory Coast between 1966 and 1980; farmers destroyed some 300 million cubic metres of saleable timber, far more than was exported during the same period.

Other nations are more fortunate. Gabon is one of the few tropical countries in the world whose forest resources are not seriously menaced by clearing for agriculture, according to FAO. In Zaire, the Congo and Cameroon, losses to agriculture appear relatively small in relation to the total forest area. Large parts of the Zaire Basin are flooded every year, which may protect them from farming (and logging) for some time to come.

Tropical forests do also provide fuelwood, although low population densities mean that fuelwood gathering is hardly a threat to these forests. But around cities, fuelwood cutting can be a major cause of deforestation, particularly in poorly protected forest fringes or where trees grow on common land accessible to all.

The savannas and drier forests

Outside the equatorial TMF zone, Africa is a dry continent. About three-quarters of the vegetated area has an arid or semi-arid climate.

These dry regions support a range of vegetation types, often loosely referred to as savannas. The savannas range from grassland plains with a few scattered trees, through scrub and open woodlands, to dense and complex systems of trees, bushes, and grasses. In many areas, the savanna merges into a true forest in which there are several levels of trees, often described as broad-leaved woodland or wooded grassland.

The savannas and dry forests stretch in a broad band across the whole of the continent south of the Sahara, from the Atlantic to the highlands of Ethiopia. Further huge areas are found in Angola, southern Zaire, Zambia, Zimbabwe, Kenya, Tanzania, Mozambique and northern Botswana.

Large areas of savanna woodland and dry tropical forest are being cleared every year to make way for cash crops. Guinea Bissau loses 20,000-35,000 hectares of forest each year to peanuts and other commercial crops; Burkina Faso loses 85,000 hectares a year. Pressure of land shortage in the peanut basin of Senegal is causing about 50,000 hectares per year of savanna woodland to be cleared to provide farmland.

Tobacco growing also consumes forests. In Tanzania, for example, some 6,000 villages containing 260,000 people rely on tobacco as a cash crop, while the nation relies on it as a key export. These peasant cultivators usually must abandon the growing area after only two years because of the build-up of pests in the soil; tobacco growing is thus practised on a shifting cultivation basis. Moreover, curing tobacco requires large quantities of woodfuel; typically, the annual yield of one hectare of tobacco requires all the trees on a hectare of open woodland. And one hectare of tobacco will need a new hectare of woodland every year, year after year. Farmers plant as close to woodlands as possible to save transport costs, so from the air one can see the tobacco fields eating their way into forests.

Visiting experts have advised Tanzania to charge farmers for cutting trees or to require them to plant fuelwood stands. Farmers resist this because tree-planting time coincides with tobacco planting. Besides, the trees would not be of use for 10 years, and many tobacco growers are farmers who move into tobacco regions for only a few seasons. Officials of the Tobacco Authority of Tanzania fear that such controls would force many farmers to give up tobacco-growing altogether, and tobacco is one of Tanzania's biggest foreign exchange earners.

In Ghana, the government's Operation Feed Yourself "has led to the systematic and indiscriminate destruction of large tracts of bush land which were converted into farmlands. Paddy rice cultivation has made devastating inroads into large areas of natural vegetation and reduced thousands of hectares of bushland into virtually treeless plains", according to FAO. [109] The annual total loss of woodlands is estimated to be about 50,000 hectares.

Throughout savanna Africa, there are reports of farmers encroaching further into the remaining woodlands. In Benin, virtually the whole of the arable land of the country is now occupied by farmers using a fallow system; there is no natural forest left. In the rangelands of Kenya, about 740,000 subsistence farmers are cultivating about 760,000 hectares, according to FAO.

In February 1985, Paul Ngei, Kenya's minister for the environment and natural resources, announced that 17,000 hectares of Kenya's natural forests in 10 districts would be cut to make way for government tea plantations. Kenya already has severe fuelwood deficits, and only 3% of the nation is still under natural forest. [110] The scheme called for deforesting some of the slopes of Mount Kenya, raising fears among foresters of severe erosion and reduced groundwater in the highlands.

Traditional fallow periods in dry woodland range from five up to 20 or more years. The savanna has a reasonably good capacity to regenerate: as soon as the farming is stopped, new tree shoots sprout from roots remaining in the ground. Thus the general effect of cultivation on the savanna is less drastic than in the moist forest. [111]

But increasingly farmers' room for manoeuvre is being reduced. Population pressure and even laws are shortening fallow periods: Senegal in 1964 passed a law which took away ownership of land which was not cultivated within a three-year period. The result is a reduction in the capacity of the soil to regenerate its fertility.

In Kondoa Province, Tanzania, the soils are too fragile to sustain the intensive agricultural and grazing use to which they are put. Some 150,000 hectares are so badly damaged by gully erosion that not only is agriculture impossible, there is little hope of being able to reforest it either, according to Dr E.M. Mnzava, head of the Tanzania Forest Service.

Domestic grazing animals can also destroy woodland. Under natural conditions, there is usually a complex equilibrium between the wildlife and plants. Some wildlife *browse,* eating tender shoots, leaves and twigs from trees and shrubs. Others *graze,* on grass and non-woody plants. But there is considerable specialisation, which allows different species to live off the same grasslands without directly competing. For instance, the small Thomson's gazelle prefers short grass; Grant's gazelle grazes and browses; wildebeest have strong preferences for oat grass. Natural wildlife communities of wild browsers and grazers thus use different levels of an ecosystem: from giraffes, which browse high in the trees, to Burchell's zebra, which graze close to the ground and will even dig down for buried grass stems.

Cattle or sheep can upset this balance. Desertification caused by livestock is covered in the previous chapter; but intensive herds of cattle and sheep which graze, and camels and goats, which browse, are hard on both trees and grass. Goats eat tree seedlings as soon as they sprout, and in times of drought, herders cut down branches or whole trees so goats can get to the foliage.

As a result of all these pressures, there is an almost universal decline in woodland throughout dry tropical Africa. The overall annual loss of open forest in the continent is estimated at 2.3 million hectares. Norwegian geographer Turi Hamer reported that around many of the villages in western Sudan, the acacia trees have all disapppeared, replaced by stands of the poisonous Dead Sea Apple (Calotropis procera), which no animal will eat.

Outside the forest

It is even more difficult to keep track of the destruction of trees outside forests than in them. Yet the loss of such trees, rarely recorded in forestry statistics, may be more important to rural people and rural ecology than loss of forests. [112]

These trees — on farm plots, on communal grazing areas and dotted about the countryside — are usually a more important source of woodfuel than the forests, which are usually too far away from where people live. In the state of Kano in Nigeria, population density is high, and the true forests have virtually disappeared. It is estimated that 94% of the woodfuel needs of the local people are met from trees on farms or fallow land. Out-of-forest trees also help protect watersheds, slowing rain runoff and replenishing groundwater, and controlling water and wind erosion.

Trees outside the forest provide building poles, handles for hoes and ploughs, furniture and baskets, as well as the fibre for ropes, mats and wall coverings. Trees provide a range of food products too: leaves and pods, fruit, honey, nuts, insects and game. The leaves and pods of dryland trees such as the various species of acacia, a rich source of animal fodder, can contain up to 15% crude protein.

There is no 'correct' number of trees for a particular area. Places where the climate is benign and the soils are stable have less need of the protection of trees than where the weather is harsh and the soils are thin and fragile. Where artificial fertilisers can be bought, the role of trees in maintaining the fertility of the soil is less vital. People who can afford to buy fossil fuels can switch away from woodfuels when they become scarce.

But for subsistence farmers, trees are often the only source of some of the necessities of life. As the trees disappear, these essential products become scarcer, the landscape becomes more vulnerable to wind and water erosion, and the fertility of the soil declines. Over much of Africa, the capacity of people to obtain a living from the land they inhabit is being increasingly undermined as a result of tree loss.

Yet many foresters have called the scrubland in which these important trees are found 'useless bush'. In measuring productivity of scrubland, many have not even counted timber less than 25 cm in diameter, though the preferred size for firewood is about 10 cm. When this 'useless bush' is cleared for farming or afforestation, women must walk farther for firewood, fodder, roofing grass, fruit, nuts, bark for dyes and fibres for baskets — or do without.

ENERGY AND FIREWOOD

Trees supply well over 90% of the total energy used in poorer nations, so deforestation and tree loss is crucial to meeting Africa's energy needs.

Africa needs energy for development, to fuel its transport, industry, agriculture and cities. Without oil, coal, gas and hydro-electricity, it cannot progress. But it also needs energy for survival: the wood and charcoal on which the majority of people rely for cooking their food and heating their homes. Environmental bankruptcy is hitting hard at these supplies, making the energy crisis a real and immediate one for millions of rural and urban Africans. Before returning to how more woodfuel can be supplied, by growing more trees, it is worth examining Africa's overall energy needs and supplies.

Conventional energy consumption in Africa varies enormously. South

Africa consumes the most per person — 2,400 'kilogrammes of oil equivalent' (kgoe) per year — but industry, mines and whites use the vast majority of this. Countries like Zimbabwe, Liberia, and Zambia have annual consumptions of 400-500 kgoe per head, but their mining industries grossly inflate the figures; most people burn wood and charcoal.

Most Africans use less than 100 kgoe per year of conventional energy; in many Sahelian countries, less than 30 kgoe. (Europeans use 5,000-6,000 kgoe, up to 200 times as much.)

In 1983, Africa used about 190 million tonnes of oil equivalent; South Africa accounted for a quarter of this. Oil and gas provided half; coal, mainly in South Africa, a third; and slightly less than 10% came in the form of hydro-electricity. Excluding South Africa, Africans make up just over 10% of the world population and consume just 2% of the world's conventional energy.

But even if the continent uses little energy, it is relatively rich in conventional energy resources, and the vast areas still unexplored will probably offer a great deal more. Africa holds about 8% of the world's proven oil reserves: nearly a third in Nigeria, two-thirds in Algeria, Egypt, Libya, and Tunisia, and a much smaller amount in Angola.

There are substantial coal reserves, too. But South Africa owns 43 billion of the continent's estimated 50 billion tonnes of technically and economically recoverable reserves, and coal is a major source of its economic strength. In fact, coal provides 78% of South Africa's total conventional energy consumption, and its coal reserves are sufficient for 550 years at present consumption. South Africa also makes oil and gas from its coal — the only country in the world to do so commercially.

After South Africa, Zimbabwe is the only African nation to use coal on a significant scale: about two million tonnes per year. But substantial reserves are known to exist in Botswana and Swaziland, and lesser reserves in perhaps a dozen other countries, notably Tanzania, Angola and Cameroon. Though small by the standards of major coal countries, these resources could contribute greatly to these nations' energy needs.

Africa consumes little electricity by world standards. The average Ethiopian uses just 18 kwh (kilowatt-hours) per year; the average Briton consumes about 1,500 kwh. In most African countries, the use of electricity is largely confined to industry and to the richer people in the urban areas. Most of the continent's electricity comes from large dams.

Although nuclear power is unlikely to provide much energy in Africa in the coming decades, the continent has a number of important uranium deposits. Total production in 1983 was about 14,000 tonnes, almost half from South Africa, a quarter from Namibia and the rest from Niger and Gabon.

New and renewables

As oil prices climbed during the 1970s, renewable energy sources such as solar energy, wind-power, and biogas seemed to offer the developing world ways out of the oil market.

These technologies have generated much intellectual excitement, but little energy. Both technical and economic problems have prevented most renewable sources from becoming established worldwide in the face of competition from conventional fuels. But their failure in Africa is also rooted in the poverty and shortage of technical resources of most African countries. [113] Energy from renewable sources may appear free, but the technology involved in using them is not. Windmills, solar collectors, solar pumps, biogas digesters, wood gasifiers and other items from the renewable energy catalogue all cost money — in some cases, a lot of money. The installation of a small solar-powered pump can cost $10,000 or more.

Renewable energies have their best chance of being adopted where conventional energy technologies are already in use, but where a renewable can show significant cash savings and reliability. The cause of renewable energy has been seriously set back in many areas because the devices which people tried did not meet acceptable standards of performance.

Solar water heaters for domestic and commercial use offer promise in cities. These are widely installed in Israel, and are increasingly being incorporated into new houses for the well-off in Kenya. There is no technical reason why they cannot be used in other sunny areas. In fact, the main obstacle is often a lack of skilled plumbers and maintenance mechanics in African cities to install and maintain them.

Windmills for water-pumping are finding a renewed role in Kenya. A local firm called Bobs Harries Engineering Ltd, in collaboration with the Intermediate Technology Development Group (UK), has developed a local windmill called the Kijito which has proven itself in field trials and is now going into commercial production. This use of windmills, particularly in association with irrigation or land drainage, is well established in many parts of the world. The limiting factor is not technical; it is the fact that there is very little money available for investment in irrigated agriculture in most of Africa.

Solar crop drying may turn out to be competitive with the use of oil-fired driers. Such techniques were pioneered in Zimbabwe when (as Rhodesia) it suffered an oil embargo; they are still in wide use there. Gasifiers which turn wood into a combustible gas able to power a diesel engine — the same technology as was used to power European vehicles during the oil scarcities of World War Two — have shown considerable promise in Brazil and the Philippines. They may find uses in connection with forest industries in some of Africa's wood-rich countries. [114] In short, where there are existing uses of conventional energy, certain renewable technologies may prove economically competitive and technically feasible.

> *But where people live by subsistence farming, there is little chance of renewable energy playing a significant role in the near future. Most farming in sub-Saharan Africa is done by manual labour; even animal power is scarcely used. There is little money to invest in energy, whether conventional or renewable.*
> *Renewable energy technologies are just as far out of the reach of the majority of small farmers and pastoralists as are tractors.*

Many of the 'renewable energy' aid projects run by Northern countries have much more to do with the donors' need to experiment than with what the recipients need or can afford. USAID has a 'two-phase' renewable energy project in Mali. During 'Phase I', four photo-voltaic pumps and 55 woodstoves were installed in villages; stove dissemination activities were begun; a photo-voltaic refrigerator/freezer and seven lighting systems were installed in village schoolhouses and clinics; wind pumps and electrical generators, a Chinese-style dome biogas digester, solar thermal food driers and water heaters and distillers were all built, according to an official report.

And what was Phase II? A socio-economic survey is under way towards identifying village energy needs! [115]

Overall, new and renewables seem unlikely to contribute significantly to Africa's energy balance in the near future.

The energy future

Energy planning in Africa is more complex than in the developed world, partly because the great majority of energy needs are met at present by woodfuels, most of which are collected and not purchased. So the market forces which dominate European and American energy planning are largely absent.

But the broad outlines of what must be done are becoming reasonably clear, and it is obvious that action is needed in both the realm of conventional fuels and that of traditional woodfuels. Unfortunately, as one European energy development expert put it: "Most African countries may have only four energy planners; and three-and-a-half of them are hydro-electricity specialists".

One way out of the present burden of payments for fuel imports, for some countries at least, is the better development of indigenous fossil energy resources. A French study has identified 16 countries in sub-Saharan

Africa in which there are reasonable prospects of natural gas, and a fairly large gas field has already been discovered off the coast of Tanzania. But oil and gas exploration and development are expensive. Countries need help in arranging the finance, and in creating equitable partnership deals with the oil exploration companies.

There are also prospects for the development of coal. Tanzania, for example, is at present receiving aid from China to develop a coal mine, to provide fuel for a cement factory and a new pulp and paper mill. As well as providing local employment, coal production will save on oil imports.

Hydro-electricity potential exists in many countries, as was described in Chapter Four. Schemes for large dams have for the most part now fallen into disrepute, but that is no reason for ignoring the potential of smaller schemes.

The potential for energy conservation in Africa has scarcely been touched. Most of the transport and industry is extremely inefficient in its energy use because it is old or badly maintained. For the countries concerned, this puts them at a double competitive disadvantage when they are trying to develop their industrial base. Not only are energy imports a heavy burden on their balance of payments; but the fuel supplies they are able to import are used far less efficiently than in the industrial countries. Schemes to improve the energy efficiency of industrial installations and transport fleets would be of immense benefit in many countries.

It also seems inevitable that there will be an increased shift to conventional fuels — kerosene, bottled gas and electricity — in the towns and cities. In some places, these are already cheaper than wood; it is the cost of the stove which keeps poor families from switching away from wood or charcoal.

Wood and charcoal

Virtually the whole population of sub-Saharan Africa now depends on wood for its basic energy needs. In the countryside, wood and charcoal do the cooking and heating and provide the only source of light for many families. And most city people, even in cities like Nairobi, especially the poor, also rely on wood and charcoal.

In poorer countries like Tanzania, Burkina Faso, Rwanda and Chad, wood provides over 90% of total national energy consumption. Even in oil-rich Nigeria, wood supplies about 80% of all energy. (Most statistics on energy consumption confine themselves to 'commercial' energy, a particularly meaningless procedure in Africa, since it excludes all the wood which does not pass through commercial markets.)

D.E. Earl/FAO

An industrial-size charcoal kiln in a Ugandan forest. Such kilns are more efficient than peasants' pits, but they are hard to move, and wood must be transported to them. Charcoal-making in Africa continues to be the occupation of the poorest.

Rural people simply gather what wood they need from the countryside around them: from the open savanna woodlands, from farmland under fallow, from the communal lands around villages, or from poorly guarded forest reserves. They rarely pay for it: the only people buying wood in the countryside tend to be a few salaried people: teachers or government officials living in villages. As a matter of convenience, and perhaps prestige, they may pay someone else to collect the fuelwood they need.

But in the towns and cities, virtually everyone has to pay for woodfuel. It is brought into the towns, either by people who have collected it themselves, or by dealers and middlemen, and sold in wood markets or by the roadside.

Often, the main city fuel is charcoal, made in the countryside by individuals or gangs of charcoal-makers. They work on the savanna and sometimes in the woodlands or even forest reserves, cutting trees and making charcoal in traditional pits or mounds. The charcoal is then sold to urban dealers; charcoal sacks awaiting collection are a common sight on the roads leading into many large African cities.

In some countries, charcoal-makers theoretically need licences from the forestry services and pay a fee for the wood they use. These fees, usually very low, are frequently avoided. In most countries, charcoal-making is largely unregulated and outside official control.

Five or six tonnes of wood are normally used to make one tonne of charcoal. This apparently ridiculous waste of scarce resources has led to suggestions that charcoal-making should be banned.

But the energy equation is not quite what it seems. Charcoal has twice the energy content per unit weight of wood. It is much more efficient to use than wood. Because it burns well, it can be used in small quantities; the fact that a handful of charcoal can be used to prepare a light meal makes it easier to use economically than wood. It is arguable that, overall, burning charcoal can be just as energy efficient as burning wood.

Charcoal has other advantages. Its higher energy content and light weight make it more economical to transport than wood. It is more convenient and cleaner to use: its almost smokeless burning is an important consideration in cramped urban dwellings.

But traditional charcoal-making techniques are wasteful and could be improved. Steel kilns can increase charcoal yields, but they are too expensive for most traditional charcoal-makers. Improved techniques based on the traditional kiln have been developed in the Casamance area of Senegal. The Casamance kiln increases charcoal yields and also permits the recovery of the creosote which is produced when wood breaks down into charcoal. Using this creosote to protect wooden dwellings against termite attack might also help cut down wood consumption.

Trees into fires

Cutting trees for firewood and charcoal-making puts heavy pressure on the wood resources in many areas, although it rarely affects the rainforest. Over the whole of tropical Africa, fuelwood consumption is thought to use up to 15 times more wood than commercial logging. But logging takes place in forests; people cut fuelwood overwhelmingly *outside* of the forests. According to FAO, the annual rate of consumption of fuelwood now exceeds the rate at which tree stocks are being naturally regenerated or planted over large areas of Africa.

In the Sahel, it is estimated that fuelwood is being used 30% faster than it is regrowing in the accessible woodland areas. In Niger, the rate of cutting for fuelwood is thought to be twice that of natural regeneration. Charcoal-makers in the Rift Valley in Ethiopia are converting the acacia forest to semi-desert at the rate of 60,000 hectares per year.

The results of cutting for fuelwood are most easily seen near cities. Treeless ground spreads outwards from virtually all African cities. This does not mean that there are no trees left; there may still be plenty in well-guarded forest reserves or on private property. But trees growing on common lands, or areas from which they can easily be taken, tend to disappear completely.

As nearby sources are used, dealers travel further, and scarcities — often accompanied by erosion and soil degradation — spread in an expanding ring around the city. Much of the 100,000 tonnes of charcoal used annually in Dakar, Senegal, now comes from the Casamance region in the extreme south of the country, a truck journey of over 300 kilometres.

Kano in northern Nigeria illustrates another way that cutting trees for urban needs can spread its effects deep into the countryside. Farmers once lopped branches off the trees on their land, and brought them into the town on their donkeys for sale. They picked up dung and sweepings from the town streets, which the donkeys carried back for use as fertilisers on the fields. This system has now almost completely broken down. The land within 40 kilometres of Kano has now been largely stripped of trees, and urban dung no longer reaches the fields.

Niger's drought and the Kennedy Bridge

Paradoxically, although drought reduces supplies of food and money, it can increase supplies of fuelwood.

The modern Kennedy Bridge spans the Niger River at Niamey. Every morning, strings of camels loaded with wood amble slowly across. But over the past several years, more and more wood has been brought in by trucks. All the easily available wood near the city had been cut, and remaining available supplies were out of easy camel range. As fuelwood prices rose, politicians, entrepreneurs and religious leaders bought trucks and went into the wood business: the *grands patrons des bois,* or firewood barons.

But in 1984-5, as Niger's worst drought of the century began to bite, more and more camels were crossing the bridge again, from farms within walking distance of Niamey. In the drought, the farmers could make little money from their crops; their trees were all they had to sell. So trees on farms, missed by the first wave of expansion in the wood collection business, were being cut in a second, drought-related wave. Collection from this new source will doubtless expand outwards from Niamey as long as the drought lasts. And after the drought, the soil on the farms will be more vulnerable to wind and water erosion, and farmers themselves may suffer wood scarcities.

The same process was going on all across the Sahel. This is the ratchet effect: each climatic crisis tightens the grip of environmental degradation, pulling the ecosystem a few more notches towards bankruptcy.

Why don't people plant trees?

Drought or no drought, the Sahel is the worst hit area in Africa in terms of fuelwood depletion. Trying to grow trees for fuel in the Sahel has become an international obsession over the past decade.

But most of these attempts have ended in failure. According to US forester Fred Weber in 1982, some $160 million had been spent to produce a total of about 25,000 hectares of fuelwood plantation, much of which was growing poorly. [116] The encouraging side of what would otherwise be a totally depressing story is that it is now clear where the mistakes were being made.

The fact that wood is generally scarce in an area does not mean that everyone is suffering from the shortage to the same extent.

Farmers with land can grow trees for fuel. But they are most unlikely to choose to do so. One of the clearest messages which has emerged from studies of why people grow trees is that they want them for fruit, timber, shade and renewal of soil fertility. If they have trees for these purposes, the trimmings and dead branches will go a long way towards meeting their fuel needs. [117] But trying to persuade them to plant trees just for fuel is often a classic case of presenting a solution to a problem which people do not see they have.

Clear land ownership is the exception rather than the rule over much of Africa. In many areas, people do not have permanent possession of land, but are granted rights by village leaders to farm particular patches for a limited period. In some countries, such as Burkina Faso, the land is reallocated every few years, effectively destroying any incentive for farmers to invest in the long-term enterprise of tree growing (or in other soil and water conservation efforts).

In Somalia, FAO reports that the enclosure of land to protect it from communal overgrazing is, ironically, leading to increased rates of destruction. Farmers who are enclosing land feel obliged to invest a certain amount of labour in it, and need to establish their individual ownership. So they clear away most of the trees and cultivate small patches here and there. Since most of the newly-enclosed land is covered with only the thinnest vegetation, the removal of trees and the cultivation causes increased erosion. [118]

US anthropologist Marilyn Hoskins points out that the power to reallocate land is an important source of local influence. If land is taken over for tree growing, it can no longer be allocated on a short-term basis. This may be a reason why village elites sometimes oppose tree growing programmes which might otherwise win popular support. [119]

Tree growing in such societies requires that a consensus be built up among the community on the need to grow fuelwood, on how to share the work of planting and tending the young trees, and how to divide out the wood which is finally produced.

Looking into some communal tree growing programmes in the Sahel, Hoskins found that the people taking part had no real idea of how the ultimate benefits would be shared. Some did not know and were not willing to guess. Others thought the trees would go to the government forestry service, or to the village chief, or even to the foreign project organiser. Such confusion is hardly a basis for enthusiastic local help.

Few African villages or communities have a unity of interests among all their members, and these varying goals and needs can play havoc with communal tree growing. Conversations with villagers in Tanzania showed that they were intensely suspicious that any revenues obtained from the sale of wood from woodlots might be embezzled by members of the village government. According to Margaret Skutch, who carried out a study in the Morogoro area of Tanzania, the extent to which villagers are prepared to collaborate in village woodlot schemes is closely related to the degree of trust they have in the village leadership. [120]

Energy experts are fond of talking about the *fuelwood gap:* a given nation is using wood three or six times faster than trees are growing. The gap must be filled. Tanzania calculated this gap and in 1968 told villagers to plant five or six trees per person. The forestry service provided seedlings, but the trees were not planted. The government concluded that the villagers were irrational, and in 1982 launched an even more strident campaign under the slogan 'Forests are our wealth'. Results remain disappointing.

Melissa Leach compared fuelwood gathering and use in two Maasai villages in northern Tanzania in 1984. Enguike village is in the foothills and surrounded by forest reserves from which people gather wood. In theory they pay for permits to do this; in practice they don't. The second village, Meserani, is down on the drier plains and has very few trees around it. Foresters had visited both villages and told villagers to plant trees. The villagers had ignored them. [121]

The women of Meserani are suffering personal 'fuelwood gaps'. But these gaps are opening gradually, and the women's response has been gradual as well. They walk further for wood; they burn wood less for heat and light (Maasai huts get no outside light); they replace wood with dung, which is smokier and requires more tending; they cook less often recipes which require long simmering. These changes raise problems for the women, but women have bigger problems. There is not enough money to buy maize and beans, and the nearest water is two kilometres away. It is easier for them to cope with the fuelwood gap than with the food and water gap. To Leach's inquiries on fuelwood, one woman responded incredulously: "Are these the small and hopeless questions which brought you so far?"

There were many ironies in the situation. The women needed wood, but other problems — even *including* the problem of taking more time to gather wood — made tree-planting a low priority. Their personal responses to their personal fuelwood gap made it difficult for them to undertake the foresters' national solution to the national wood gap. A few villagers in Enguike, which did not have a fuelwood gap, had in fact planted trees for shade and windbreaks — without any encouragement from the foresters — because they had ample nearby water and fuelwood and so had the *time* to tend to the trees.

It is sometimes assumed that rural people do not know *how* to grow trees. So governments and voluntary agencies launch 'education' campaigns. Indeed, many governments and aid agencies consider that peasants are stupid and ignorant, and that once it is explained to them that they are damaging the environment, they will stop doing so. On the contrary, the African peasant is usually well aware of environmental bankruptcy; what he needs is practical help to escape from circumstances which force him to destroy the environment on which he knows he depends.

Most of Africa's farming communities already grow trees. In one mountain Tanzanian village, almost every family has a private tree plantation, and most individuals claim to have planted between 100 and 1,000 trees personally. And in Malawi, a 1982 survey showed that 40% of families had planted trees during the past five years, and some had planted up to 100, using seedlings which they grow themselves or collect from under nearby trees. In Kenya, many people plant trees for fruit, timber, shade and ornament, and seedlings are sold by the roadside in cans. But few people plant deliberately for fuelwood, expecting to obtain it from trees planted for other purposes.

The thorn tree *Acacia albida* is valued particularly highly in Senegal and other parts of the Sahel; it is either deliberately planted or left standing when land is cleared for agriculture. Its role in the farming system has been described as follows by FAO: [122]

"Its roots go mostly down rather than sideways, drawing up nutrients and using water that would otherwise be lost to local production. It provides shade for cattle in the dry season but sheds its leaves in the rainy season when agricultural crops are growing, thus providing them with humus and not competing with them for nutrients; and it produces poles, fuelwood and fodder for local needs."

Sometimes African farmers do not *want* to plant trees. In some places they harbour the tsetse flies that bring sleeping sickness to people and cattle.

Farmers may be afraid that trees will attract large colonies of seed-eating birds, which will damage the crops. Where landholdings are small, farmers may be worried that the competition of trees for water, light and soil nutrients will lead to an unacceptable reduction in crop yields.

> *Most schemes to encourage peasants to plant trees fail because the motive of the project is nowhere near the farmers' motives. One of the few successful schemes was the 'Johnny Appleseed' project of the World Bank and USAID in Niger, which established village tree nurseries where farmers would choose seedlings to plant themselves. In the first year, they overwhelmingly chose trees for shade, fruit and building poles, not for firewood. But in the second year, they collected very few trees, since they felt they had planted enough. They did not think it worthwhile to invest time and labour in planting trees outside their own land for firewood, as the Bank and USAID had hoped.*

Above all, it is becoming clear that the rural fuelwood problem cannot be separated from that of land-use in general. People with secure possession of the land they are farming are most of the way towards providing themselves with the fuel they need. They are in a position to accept outside help which provides them with seedlings and advice in growing them.

Wood for the cities

The fact that there is a commercial market for city fuelwood means that farmers who have a surplus of wood can in theory sell it. But this still does not necessarily mean that it is profitable for them to grow trees rather than other crops on their land.

The prices paid for fuelwood in the rural areas are usually very low. The urban dealers usually buy wood not from farmers, but from the poor, often landless, people who earn a precarious living scavenging or stealing wood wherever it can be found. These woodmen have little bargaining power against urban dealers or middlemen, and the price they are able to charge is usually well below a figure that would entice farmers to plant and harvest trees. Only when tree depletion has extended so far that transport costs rise above the costs of growing trees near the cities, does the planting of trees for fuelwood become economically attractive.

Most African governments maintain a cheap urban fuel policy, by keeping the selling price of wood from official forest reserves far below the economic costs of producing it. Where dealers pay fees for cutting forest wood, these usually bear no relation to the true costs of forestry plantations. In Niger, for example, the licence fee for cutting a cubic metre stack of wood is the equivalent of about eight US cents, less than 1% of the selling price in the market. If local tree growing is to be financially attractive, the licence fees for obtaining wood from the forests would have to be very much increased. But this is a step which governments find politically difficult: it would hurt the *Wabenzi,* the urban elite.

So there are few areas where growing trees for the commercial fuelwood market would be good business. The only major example of growing trees commercially for fuelwood was in Ethiopia around the turn of the century. At that time, there was a grave fuelwood shortage in the new capital city of Addis Ababa. The Emperor Menelik exempted land planted with trees from taxation, and as a result many landowners planted eucalyptus: gum trees. By 1920, large areas of gums had been established, and the fuelwood problem had disappeared. These plantations were maintained and, indeed, extended in area up to the 1960s. In recent years, however, they have been cut heavily, though Addis still has many stands of gums.

There have been few other comparable episodes of large-scale, private tree growing in Africa, although when British American Tobacco (BAT) shifted operations from Uganda to Kenya in the early 1970s, it insisted that peasants selling tobacco must also sell wood. So BAT provided forestry extension services.

In some countries, the forestry services have established fuelwood plantations, and there has always been a sale of lower grade timber for fuelwood in areas where forests are managed and logging is carried out. The World Bank estimates, however, that such supplies account for less than 5% of total fuelwood consumption in Africa.

The notion of large plantations specially established to supply the major cities has attracted a considerable amount of attention, notably from the donor agencies. It sounds logical, but such plantations have not yet made much economic sense. They are very expensive in labour and materials, for preparing the land, for fencing, fertilisers, planting, and protecting the trees.

One such 240-hectare drip-irrigated eucalyptus plantation was established with World Bank funding near Niamey in 1980. The objective was to produce trees — harvestable in three years — for fuelwood and building poles in Niamey. Each of the 264,000 trees got its own drip of water from a plastic hose. Recent reports indicate that the plantation is indeed producing wood and poles, but at a cost so high that the experiment will not be repeated. Fuel for pumping the water, spare parts, the continual clogging with sand of the small pipes, labour and the establishment of a parastatal marketing system all proved more expensive than estimated — and the project was established near the Niger River on prime rice growing land. The scheme was probably doomed from the start by its high-technology character, although some foresters felt it would have worked

Mark Edwards/Earthscan

World Bank-funded fuelwood plantation near Niamey, Niger. Providing individual drip irrigation for 264,000 eucalyptus trees proved too costly and unreliable. Big plantations have provided no answer to Africa's urban fuelwood needs.

if established on the edge of already-irrigated ricefields, with the trees pulling up surplus irrigation water from the water table.

Another World Bank funded 'peri-urban' tree plantation is producing wood near Bamako, Mali — unirrigated, but rainfall is higher there. It is working well thanks to the luck of a large forest reserve already in place and a talented project leader. Between Dakar and Thies in Senegal, natural forest was cut and bulldozed at a cost of $800 per hectare to make way for a 3,000-hectare unirrigated plantation of 'fast-growing' eucalyptus. But the new trees grew slower than the trees they replaced, and most have perished in the drought. [123]

The Bank seems now to have concluded that for most of the Sahel, big projects to grow trees for cities cannot yet overcome social, economical and technical difficulties. Tree growing tends to be slow and difficult in the drier areas without irrigation; in the semi-arid Sahel, it takes 10 years for an unirrigated eucalyptus to reach a size suitable for the cooking fire or for use as a post. Where such plantations are being considered, a judgement has to be made as to whether the land, labour, and financial resources might not be better used for agriculture. It may, indeed, be more economical to boost local food or cash crop production and import the necessary conventional fuels to meet the needs of urban consumers.

Mark Edwards/Earthscan

A cooking fire in Niger, the pot resting on a trivet made from a car part.
Unlike stoves, open fires are 'free', can be set up anywhere, burn wood of
any size and burn other fuels as well.

Improved stoves

Most people in the countryside cook on open fires, usually enclosed
between three or more stones or lumps of mud which act as pot supports:
the 'three-stone fire'. It is commonly alleged that such fires have efficiencies
of only 3-5% (amount of energy transferred from fuel to food) compared
with the 20% or more obtainable with a properly designed cooking stove.
So there have been numerous programmes to promote 'improved
cookstoves' throughout Africa. [124]

Most such efforts ignore the fact that the three-stone fire is well suited
to the circumstances in which it is used. Fuel aside, it costs no money.
It can be built quickly anywhere, indoors or out. It can use a variety of
fuels. Long pieces of wood do not have to be cut — an important point
when hardly anyone has a saw or even a sharp axe. The uncut wood can
simply be laid on the ground with its ends in the fire, to be pushed in when
more heat is required or pulled out when the fire is damped down or
extinguished.

Such fires *can* be used efficiently when the need arises. This has been
shown in the laboratory, and this is what happens in fuel-poor villages.

Where wood is abundant, people tend to use large quantities for cooking; they are indeed being 'inefficient' in energy terms. But where wood is scarce, they use much less.

Many organisations — private, UN, governmental — are trying to promote improved stoves in the African countryside. But it is hard to sell expensive metal stoves to 'save wood', where wood is available without cash payment and people rely on the three-stone fire. So some agencies are trying to design stoves which people can build themselves from local materials.

In Senegal, a stove was designed to be made by local people: the *Ban ak Suuf* stove, using the Wolof language words for the sand and clay it is made from. But these earth or mud stoves rapidly fall apart; after a year's use, the stove has usually crumbled to a state where it saves little if any energy compared to an open fire.

Efforts made to develop improved stoves for cities show more promise. Some urban people already use metal or ceramic stoves, and they pay for their fuel. An improved stove which will save fuel will be attractive to a consumer if its extra cost is paid for by obvious savings in wood or charcoal. Reports from the marketplaces of Niamey show that where a few years ago buyers were concerned with the burning properties of the wood, they are now more concerned with its size and shape. People are switching to stoves and seeking the short pieces which will fit into them.

An improved charcoal stove is now being widely adopted in Nairobi: a rare example of the successful transfer of appropriate technology from one developing country to another. In the 1920s, a new type of charcoal burning stove appeared in Thailand. Someone had the idea of fitting a ceramic charcoal stove inside an ordinary zinc bucket with an insulating layer of ash between the two. This double skin stove cut down on heat loss, and hence on fuel consumption, but was also safer to use because it reduced the risk of burns from a hot stove. This so-called 'Thai bucket' caught on and is now widely used in Thailand and other Asian countries.

A few years ago, a Kenyan version of the Thai bucket was developed by the Kenya Ministry of Energy, working with private pottery firms. It is said to reduce fuel consumption substantially and is now made by traditional craftsmen and sold commercially in the Nairobi markets.

In Niger, a new design of metal stove which encloses the pot and reduces energy consumption by 25%, compared with the traditional stove, has been designed; preparations are under way to have it made by local craftsmen. There are similar programmes in the Gambia, Sudan and other countries.

The main lesson from these efforts to promote new stoves is one that is being learned in other areas too: traditional methods are rarely irrational. Though they may seem so at first sight, the

*poor are not frivolous about the resources on which they
depend. This is not to say that technical innovations have no
place. But anything new will have to be carefully designed to fit
the needs, priorities and financial capabilities of the people for
whom it is intended.*

Innovators need to be more realistic in their expectations. There have
been some highly optimistic statements that improved stoves would solve
the problem of deforestation. A rallying call a few years ago said: "At
the moment 10,000 stoves have been built. To solve the problems of
deforestation we should have 100 million stoves within 20 years."

While better stoves may save energy, they will not of themselves prevent
deforestation, though they may help slow it. Population growth, the
conversion of land to agriculture, the reduction or elimination of fallow
periods, and the increasing numbers of grazing animals are all playing
their part in reducing the available wood resources. The cumulative effect
of these pressures is such that in many areas the wood would continue
to become scarcer even if fuelwood demand were to be eliminated
completely.

The real advantage of improved stoves is that they are safer and cleaner
than open fires, reducing the risk of children burning themselves, and
cutting out the smoke inside the hut which damages health and dirties
everything.

Chapter 7

Soil and fish: peasant farmers, peasant fishermen

"By using soil and water conservation,
we get rid of drought."
Slogan on a banner,
Tigray Region, Ethiopia

Given Africa's naturally fragile soils, and the concentration of rainfall in short fierce storms over a few months, erosion is hardly a recent development. But its acceleration in recent decades is now the key component in environmental bankruptcy.

Erosion has long been a problem where rich upland soils encouraged dense populations: in parts of Guinea, Nigeria, Rwanda, Burundi, Kenya, most of mountainous Lesotho, and above all in Ethiopia.

It is a rueful boast among Ethiopian agricultural experts that ancient Egyptian civilisation was based on bad agricultural practices in the Ethiopian highlands. Much of the silt which the Nile's annual floods deposited on Egyptian fields 4,000 years ago was washed down the Blue Nile from these rich volcanic regions. But those high rates have accelerated tremendously in recent years, due both to deforestation and to revolution; much of the soil is now retained by the Aswan High Dam.

Some 40% of Ethiopia was under forest at the turn of the century; 20% was still covered in the early 1960s. By 1984, government experts were quoting figures, based on satellite photographs, of 2-4%.

Less well documented have been the effects of the badly-needed land reforms following the 1974 coup which toppled Haile Selassie. The land of vast feudal estates, much of which was under-used or kept in fallow, was divided among the peasants, who naturally began to clear it and farm it hard.

Overall, the result is that Ethiopia now loses an estimated one billion tonnes of topsoil per year, according to USAID.

Just as Ethiopia's erosion is accelerating, so is soil loss across the continent: "The soils of Africa are a poor resource that is likely to deteriorate dramatically under pressure from increasing populations," wrote Ieuan Griffiths of Sussex University (UK). "Over much of the continent soil erosion is already a major problem. On a continent where the vast majority of people live directly off the land the consequences of further deterioration could be serious to the point of catastrophic." [125]

Erosion caused by land misuse — overcultivation, overgrazing, deforestation and bad irrigation — also affects the flat drylands of the Sahelian states, of Somalia, of northern Kenya, of southwestern Zimbabwe and of the South African bantustans. Soil erosion on the 10 volcanic islands which form the Republic of Cape Verde in the Atlantic west of Senegal is so spectacular as to lead to speculation that the country will have to be abandoned. [126]

> *Erosion is at last beginning to take its rightful place in people's minds as a threat to civilisation, to be ranked alongside plague and warfare. FAO director-general Edouard Saouma has called it "one of the most fearsome threats facing mankind". Lester Brown of Worldwatch Institute wrote in 1981: "Civilisation can survive the exhaustion of oil reserves, but not the continuing wholesale loss of topsoil".*

Colonial response

Erosion is a complex phenomenon. The shifting agriculture and rotational fallow systems which the colonialists saw practised when they first arrived in Africa already caused erosion, especially toward the end of a cropping period. This alarmed agronomists from nations of steady, year-round rainfall like Britain, France and Belgium, where erosion is often a sign of gross land mismanagement. In fact, much of the erosion colonialists saw was a problem of their own making, especially where peasants were crowded into small areas or forced to adopt inappropriate cropping systems.

"The colonial scare about soil erosion fitted with the view of shifting cultivation as backward, feckless and irresponsible", wrote Robert Chambers. [127] "Some colonial agricultural officers sought to impose order, discipline, straight lines, and control on what they saw as a primitive and chaotic system of cultivation which was destroying its environment."

On the pre-Independence Uluguru Land-use Scheme in Tanzania in the 1950s, farmers were forced to build bench terraces to protect land against erosion. They knew the work was useless and often chose infertile sites to avoid digging up fertile ground. After some years, official reports found that rice yields were often better on untreated land than on terraces. Later

Mark Edwards/Earthscan

Massive gulley erosion, Ethiopian Central Highlands. Such gulleys carry rainwater from the highlands, leaving 'drought' behind.

---

studies found that erosion in Uluguru was not caused by local cropping methods but by landslides, and the bench terraces the farmers were forced to build were in fact increasing the danger. [128]

"In Tanzania and Kenya, authoritarian soil conservation measures were so unpopular that they helped to generate and unite political organisations which then struggled for and won Independence. In the post-Independence decade it was scarcely then a matter of surprise that soil erosion was a non-subject," Chambers adds.

Hans Ruthenberg, in his massive study *Farming Systems in the Tropics,* makes two key points about the alleged 'backwardness' of shifting cultivation. [129] First, in terms of calories produced per hour of labour, it is far more *efficient* than the neat but labour-intensive rice terraces of Asia. Second, there are situations in which "soil mining (overcultivation so that both nutrients and soil structure is degraded) may be good economics, and optimum solutions in economic terms may be soil-mining solutions... The extreme conservationist tends to waste funds which are badly needed for more productive forms of capital development, and he may be as dangerous in terms of a stable world as the land miner. The disquieting aspect, in my opinion, is not that soil mining occurs, but the worldwide extent of the phenomenon and the speed of the mining process in most of the tropics''.

When there was much land and few people, techniques which led to soil erosion and loss of nutrients made some sense. The ground was regularly left to recover, while the vegetation bound and helped rebuild topsoil. It perhaps mattered little if some soil moved from one place to another.

In areas where this was not the case, where rich soils had spawned dense populations, African societies developed their own sophisticated soil conservation techniques with no help from white advisers. Ruthenberg lists 17 tribes and groups of tribes, from Benin, Togo, Nigeria and Cameroon in the west to Kenya, Tanzania and Uganda in the east, which traditionally practised some form of terracing. Several of these tribal areas support 100-150 people per square kilometre, compared to the sub-Sahara African average of 16. Many of these societies also used other soil conservation techniques such as irrigation, manuring and the stabling of livestock.

The social complexity and legal sophistication of the irrigation and furrowing systems of the Chagga people on the slopes of Tanzania's Mount Kilimanjaro have attracted the study not only of hoards of anthropologists, but of law students as well. The labour was based on community participation, and all farmers using the system had to belong to a board run by elders and take their turns at maintenance work.

How farming systems change

There is a spectrum of African agriculture running from 'natural' ground cover to plantations, according to Ruthenberg.

Clearing natural forest cover for shifting cultivation diminishes the total vegetation on the ground, but produces an edible crop. The 'next' step, from shifting cultivation to fallow cultivation, further reduces the total amount of vegetation produced, but because crops are taken more often, it increases food yields. The next shift — often under population pressure — from fallow cultivation to permanent cultivation with one crop per year, inter-cropped with beans, using traditional crop varieties and without fertiliser, increases the production of food but lowers the total production of vegetation still futher. With permanent cultivation, "the tendency is toward depleted soils, low yields and a very much reduced fallow-weed vegetation. Production occurs at a low-level equilibrium."

From this point, the introduction of improved varieties such as hybrid maize and fertilisers can increase both food production and total plant production. Double cropping takes this trend further. But many African farmers are trapped in the 'low-level equilibrium' of unimproved permanent cultivation. They are depleting their soil, getting low yields, earning little with which to improve either their soils or farming techniques, and are extremely vulnerable to any shock from outside: drought, war or pests. In fact, low-level equilibrium is the best they can hope for. In fragile areas like the Sahel and Ethiopia, that equilibrium is itself fragile, and slides easily into severe erosion and desertification.

Farmers trapped in permanent cultivation of poor land have few options. Their adjustments to growing land scarcity caused by population growth have been remarkably similar the world over. [130] They reduce fallow periods and concentrate cultivation on better soils responsive to cropping intensification; they make investments in land such as destumping, irrigation and terracing; they use manure more intensely; they switch from hand hoes to animal-drawn ploughs, and then to tractors.

These transitions occurred in much of Asia centuries ago under more gradual population pressure. They occurred in much of Africa long ago as well, and there is a slow transition to greater use of draught animals in parts of Nigeria and Zimbabwe today. But this scenario has little relevance for much of dryland Africa. True, farmers there do decrease fallow periods, but population growth and political and economic marginalisation are happening too rapidly to leave them with 'better soils' on which to concentrate labour. They instead expand cultivation to even less fertile, more vulnerable soils. They lack motivation and labour to irrigate, terrace and collect manure, and usually lack the manure to collect. Oxen are used for ploughing the volcanic soils of the Ethiopian highlands, but the short hoe dominates the Sahel from Chad to Mauritania, and attempts in a few countries such as Zambia to introduce animal-ploughing have not so far been very successful.

Political 'erosion'

> *Political forces must be included in any discussion of erosion in Africa: erosion is not only a technical problem, amenable to technical solutions. Erosion, like desertification, is more of a symptom than a cause.*

British environmentalist Edward Goldsmith has written that governments, bilateral and multilateral aid agencies fail to see environmental stress as *symptomatic* of a social and political crisis, based on unequal access to land, conflict between export-based cash crops and basic food security, as well as short-term asset stripping for a quick profit by those who make, or are beyond the control of, the laws. [131]

Randall Baker of the University of East Anglia (UK) argues that there is a correlation between vulnerable and degraded physical environments and politically marginalised and powerless people. "The erosion of their political power runs in parallel with that of the soil beneath their feet." [132]

Playwright George Bernard Shaw said that the main drawback to Christianity was that it had never been tried. Much the same might be said of technical solutions to soil erosion in Africa.

They are rarely tried, except in large aid schemes, because people kept outside the economic and political system lack both the means and the incentive to try them. But the technocratic approach persists, despite its ineffectiveness, because powerful people and organisations have a vested interest in it. The international agencies can and do talk generally about the perils of the world food situation and the growing amounts of food aid, "but they are powerless to point to the *real* solutions, as these are essentially political. Consequently, they adhere to the strictly neutral ground of technology." The scientists and aid technologists claim that they have the answers but are unable to apply them, says Baker.

The government of the severely eroded islands that make up Cape Verde have realised that technical solutions are not enough. All the usual techniques — terracing, tree-planting and check dams — are being used. But to inspire people to do the work, the government has handed over land once owned by the Ministry of Rural Development to the members of 65 cooperatives. The cooperatives have replaced the existing sugar cane with potatoes, tomatoes, carrots, onions and tree crops. They are given seedlings, fertilisers and pesticides, but must pay for them at cost price when their crops are marketed. And this brings up the most innovative part of the programme: the government is including marketing centres in what is essentially an anti-erosion project. Help with marketing may well have to become a part of anti-erosion projects across Africa. [133]

Two Niger villages

There are indeed technical methods of dealing with almost all the land degradation problems already discussed in this book. Many of them appear well suited for much of Africa, in that they require relatively little capital and relatively little expertise. They all tend to require a great deal of labour, which may or may not be available.

Moving sand dunes can be 'fixed' with latticework patterns of stalks or poles, among which fast-growing shrubs are planted. Gulley erosion can be controlled with check dams of stones and brush to slow the onrush of water. Hillsides can be protected by terraces which halt the downward slide of soil and water, putting the water into the ground where it can

Mark Edwards/Earthscan

Sand dunes threaten to engulf the stream bed which feeds the Niger village of Yegalalane. Villagers seem to have decided that the village — far from markets and far from security — is not worth saving.

---

benefit crops. On gentle slopes, contour lines can be 'dammed' with very low ridges of soil, vegetation or stones, again to conserve soil and water.

> *Why has the success rate of such efforts been so poor in Africa, when these efforts can be demonstrated to have worked in other parts of the world — and even in many parts of Africa?*

In 1982, Don Atkinson-Adams of the US voluntary relief organisation CARE showed me how he had helped to organise a technically effective scheme to keep a high sand dune from swallowing up a stream bed near the town of Bouza in Niger's Majia Valley. The stream bed was the only fertile agricultural land near the small village of Yegalalane. The dune was first anchored against the wind with a chessboard pattern of millet stalks. But the farmers had not donated the millet stalks. CARE had been forced to buy them at steep prices, despite the fact that the future of the settlement depended on their effectiveness in stopping the dune.

The spaces between the stalks had been planted with grass and shrubs, which required protection from sheep and goats. The village did not organise any volunteer guards; instead, CARE paid the guards a salary.

The money was due to run out in a few months. I asked Atkinson-Adams what he expected to happen then. He replied without hesitation: "The guarding will stop. The sheep and goats will eat the grass and shrubs and trample the millet stalks. The dune will take the valley."

How could the villagers be so apparently stupid, selfish and short-sighted? The answer is that even with that small stream bed in which to plant, the villagers' existence was so marginal, they grew so little and could market so little of what they grew, that they saw no logical reason for involving themselves in the hard labour of stopping the dune. It was easier to move elsewhere, into Bouza or Niamey. This was not a decision inspired by laziness, but a rational 'no' to exhortations to expend hard labour for marginal returns. Yet according to CARE, this project was "the foremost example of successful inland dune fixation in the entire Sahel".

In the same valley was another soil conservation project. Since 1975, CARE had very slowly overcome initial suspicion and apathy, and persuaded villagers to plant 250 km of tree windbreaks in lines across a flat, millet-growing plain. The hot, dessicating harmattan winds of the region blow regularly from one direction, so trees planted at a right angle to the wind can dramatically cut wind erosion. The wind not only dries the fields, but it carries off the the lighter, organic matter in the soil and leaves behind the heavier, infertile sand.

CARE had put $1 million into providing and planting the trees. Villagers had been convinced of the effectiveness of the shelter belts by 15% higher yields from 3,000 hectares of protected fields — an increase which took account of the land lost to agriculture in the tree belts themselves. This village was much nearer the main road and to markets than dune-threatened Yegalalane, so the increased yields had been converted into a yearly cash increase equivalent to $108,000, or a 10% rate of return on the investment of $1 million. The neem trees (an Indian species) were about ready for thinning in 1982, and the villagers were meeting to decide on ways to divide both the resulting fuelwood and proceeds from selling the wood, estimated at $80,000. This project had an air of hope about it.

Ethiopian terraces

The labour-intensive work of erosion control not only requires incentives; it also requires organisation. Terracing, tree-planting and gully damming demand a great deal of work — hundreds of work-days for every terrace.

Such work is inefficient on a farm-by-farm basis; it must be organised over a wider water catchment area. Terracing hillsides protects hill farms from erosion, but it also protects valley farms from flood and landslides, and provides them with a more regular water supply. And terracing and

Mark Edwards/Earthscan

Terraces dug by peasants in Ethiopia's Central Highlands, holding water after a rain. Soil scientists have the techniques to control erosion; but farmers hesitate to improve land when they are paid little for the crops grown on it.

tree-planting take land away from cropping, so some farmers suffer more than others. Such projects usually involve the reapportioning of land, which can take two or three years before the several months of digging begins.

About two-thirds of all Ethiopian farmland is on slopes of over 25°. Most of this land is found among the hills and gorges of the central highlands, which support more than 78% of the nation's population and 70% of its cattle. The highlands have already been virtually deforested. Government tree nurseries must get their seeds from the Coptic churchyards, where trees still grow because grazing and cultivation is traditionally forbidden, even in socialist Ethiopia.

Erosion in the highlands is not a subtle affair of gradually lowered yields, as in the wind erosion of southern Niger. Soil and boulders come tearing down the hills and spread nasty fan-shaped patterns of rubble across the valleys below.

Kebede Tatu is head of Ethiopia's Soil and Water Conservation Service. He is one of those rare government administrators — rare in any nation — who both has a university degree (from

*Uppsala University, Sweden) and who still gets out with the
farmers and gets his hands dirty. He says he does so because
"in most cases the peasant is more aware and understands the
complexities involved better than the policy-makers and the
administrators. It is very important to listen to the views of the
farmer." He becomes visibly upset when confronted with scenes
of thin people and thin cattle trapped in grassless valleys.*

Kebede claims that from 1977 to 1984, highland farmers, organised
through the Peasant Associations to which at least seven million Ethiopians
now belong, planted 500 million tree seedlings, and constructed 700,000
km of terraces — a length more than 17 times round the equator.

*In 1984 I saw these terraces all along the roadside on the main
north-south road through Wollo Region, and found them as
impressive a product of human physical labour as Egypt's
pyramids. Paul Vallely of* The Times *of London described "a
seemingly endless network of ditches cut into the sides of the
hills. It is as if contour lines were the invention of the farmer
rather than of the cartographer. It is the result of one of the
most massive anti-erosion programmes undertaken anywhere in
Africa."*

The peak of this effort coincided with the drought years, so many of
the seedlings have died, and there has been little water available for the
terraces to conserve. But where trees have grown among the terraces,
springs which have not flowed for years are now giving water. So far,
crop yields are not increasing, as there has been so little rain. As farmers
have to give up land to trees and terraces, there are fears that they will
lose their original enthusiasm.

This enthusiasm was first captured by the dramatic nature of the
erosion. Farmers can *remember* when the hills were forested; they
remember how fields once stayed in place; they can see the difference now.
They tell visitors how hard they have worked and how they hate to have
to let hungry oxen back onto slopes planted in seedlings — officially closed
to grazing — because drought and cattle have taken all other vegetation
in an area. (They were given food for this work by the UN's World Food
Programme in one of its biggest ever 'Food for Work' projects. Elsewhere,
food-for-work has not always been sufficient incentive for reforestation
work; peasants plant the trees, take the food and let them die to get paid
to plant more. But Ethiopian farmers seem convinced of the necessity to
reforest the slopes.)

Another sort of water conservation project, also motivated by
desperation, has been going on elsewhere in Ethiopia, in a part of Tigray

controlled by rebels. A female worker for a European relief agency (which does not publicise its activity in rebel territory for fear of jeopardising its work in government-controlled Ethiopia) walked into central Tigray carrying $303,850 in cash. Working closely with REST (Relief Society for Tigray) and local officials, she bought grain in villages which had surpluses (surprisingly near villages suffering from acute famine), hired donkeys and moved it to the sites of two food-for-work projects. All money and grain were strictly accounted for. Such was the confidence of REST in its rapport with the people that when a donkey fell ill, its grain load was left by the roadside to be fetched a few days later — in the midst of a famine.

The projects were various forms of 'water-harvesting', turning to the farmers' advantage the usually destructive runoff from bare mountains. Terraces and soil ridges are constructed at the base of a mountain on a gentle slope (3%), at right angles to the slope of the mountain, below a stone-faced ditch. During a flash flood, water drains at high velocity from the mountain into the stone-faced ditch which protects the terraces by breaking the momentum of the flood. From there, the water flows down the feeder canal and through the weir into the terraces on both sides.

This intensive work required spades, mattocks and other tools from Britain and about 1,000 person days per hectare. The local farmers seemed impressed by the demonstration projects. REST estimates an average family requires a minimum harvest of 1,600 kg of grain to survive. Farmer Cherkos Desalin in 1983 harvested 350 kg from his own hectare of land; in a good year he expected 2,000. But the land of the projects averaged yields of 3,200 kg/hectare, in some areas rising to 3,800. Cherkos pronounced himself convinced. Banners appeared at a Peoples' Congress meeting reading: "By using soil and water conservation, we get rid of drought".

The people of Wollo and of Tigray were motivated by desperation, but they were also organised — by the Ethiopian government on the one hand, and by REST, Tigray officials and foreign advisers on the other. Much of the Sahel — indeed, much of Africa — lacks such organisation, without which the necessary communal work cannot be done. Pockets of such communal organisation did exist all over Africa, and some remain. But colonialism, population pressure, new forms of land tenure combined with cash cropping, warfare and the flight to the cities have disrupted many such systems. In the case of the elaborate community irrigation projects of the Chagga on the slopes of Kilimanjaro, the recent introduction of piped water has led to laxity in the maintenance of the furrows, and shortages of land have forced people to cultivate ravines down to the rivers, removing trees in the catchment area and causing springs to dry up. [134]

Erosion is not a technical problem looking for solutions. It is a host of technical solutions looking for motivation, organisation and political will. And the key to its solution is the peasant.

PEASANTS AND RAINFED FOOD CROPS

> Government agricultural extension worker:
> "I don't believe you're going to get any apples off that tree this year."
>
> Farmer: "I reckon you're right, son. That's a pear tree."
>
> (Ancient joke, told, using different species, about government extension workers in many countries)

Among the evils of colonialism was its exploitation of Africa's small farmers. While providing them an unfair return for labour, it gave them little say in their affairs and little help in their pursuit of security. Has 'Independence' radically changed things for the farmer?

African peasants today have little or no political power. They are confined to poor land which they are forced to make poorer to survive; they grow crops or commodities for which they are underpaid; and they pay taxes but get little back in terms of government support.

Africa will continue to *de*-develop, both agriculturally and industrially, until these subsistence farmers are given a political and economic stake in their future. Unless this happens, most of the possible technical improvements in subsistence agriculture will not be tried. Neither farmers nor governments will have any incentive to do so.

The starting point

"The development of the production of cotton [in the Sahel] shows that the Sahelian peasant world is not frozen but is on the contrary able to evolve with startling rapidity", said a 1984 report published by the Club du Sahel, noting a more than fivefold increase in yields in less than 20 years. [135]

African farmers and herders have a deep and profound ecological knowledge, which they apply in getting a living from their lands. Virtually nowhere in Africa has their science been sufficiently studied.

The small farmer's expertise represents "the single largest knowledge resource not yet mobilised in the development enterprise... we simply cannot afford to ignore it any longer", wrote John Hatch. [136]

British colonial agricultural experts were forced to recognise this resource in West Africa after many of their own schemes came to grief. They noticed that the 'natives' were able to coax crops from the ground where Northern agricultural science said they should not grow. On the eve of World War Two, a team of British members of parliament and technical experts — calling itself the West Africa Commission — toured the region and issued a report calling for greater concentration on food crops, suggesting that the local farmers were excellent judges of soil type and potential and arguing that European researchers might learn a great deal from the practices of the local farmers. [137]

The report, published in 1943, disappeared in the chaos of the world war. The aftermath of war brought a new reliance on technology, with British tanks converted into tractors ploughing up large parts of Tanzania in the doomed groundnut scheme. Many of the young Northern tropical agriculturalists who helped to push the tractor into Africa after the war are now the senior advisers at the development banks and aid agencies.

Tanzanian President Julius Nyerere summarised the results in a 1983 speech: "While we had any foreign exchange, we bought tractors and combine harvesters for them [public commercial farms]. We taught our peasants to hanker after these machines. As few could afford to buy them, or had the means to maintain them if they did, our peasants went on working with the hand-hoe." He said that Tanzania was now beginning to concentrate on what it can do, moving from the hand-hoe to animal-drawn implements.

Tanzania also based its cropping on chemical fertilisers, building a fertiliser factory "heavily dependent on imported components", and even stopped teaching composting in schools as it was "old-fashioned". "The net result has been that in many places, nothing is done to refertilise our soil after it has been used, much less to improve its fertility", Nyerere added. "Our peasants can no longer 'move on' after their plot has lost its fertility; they just get less result from their sweat and — legitimately — complain that having told them to use fertiliser, we do not make it available at a price they can afford or when they need it."

To insist on the indigenous 'science' of the small farmer is not to revive the 18th century European ideal of the 'Noble Savage', or in the words of Robert Chambers, "to reincarnate him as the Rational Peasant whose actions are perfectly judged exercises in optimisation that even well-informed computers can only struggle to simulate". [138]

> *Peasants have much to learn from agricultural researchers, but so do researchers have much to learn from peasant farmers. Lines of communication have never been effectively opened in either direction; until they are, neither will benefit, with African agriculture and the environment on which it depends being the main losers. The scientist has attempted to impose inappropriate solutions from outside, with little knowledge of the small farmers' priorities or realities. The farmer has ignored such advice, and more often than not has been right in doing so.*

Integrated ignorance

In the mid-1970s, many Northern donors began to shift the emphasis of aid toward the rural poor, into 'Integrated Rural Development Projects' (IRDPs). The idea was that improving small farmers' yields was no good if they could not get their produce to market, and building roads was no good if there was nothing worth transporting. Projects had to be 'integrated', 'multi-sectoral' — trying to cover everything at about the same time: advice, chemicals, tools, roads, health, electricity and the like.

British aid expenditure on direct agricultural projects — many of them 'integrated' — jumped from £10 million in 1972 to £28 million in 1977 (at 1975 prices). But the projects simply did not work, or did not work anywhere near as well as expected. Enthusiasm waned. In 1981, Britain's aid to direct agricultural projects had fallen back to £10 million.

> *The donors' emphasis on the poor met considerable opposition from recipient governments. In fact, cynics in the development business claim that a gentlemen's agreement emerged in the mid-1980s, whereby the Northern donors agreed to stop talking about 'the poorest' if the Southern governments agreed to stop calling for a 'New International Economic Order'.*

But this does not explain why so many IRDPs failed, especially in Africa. In a remarkably frank analysis, John Morris and George Gwyer of the British Overseas Development Administration found that donors were trying to 'integrate' aid and advice with little understanding of the systems they were trying to 'integrate' into. [139]

Projects in Tanzania, Swaziland and Malawi were based on research into local farming methods — research which was being carried out *while* the projects were actually being implemented. In the Sudan, new patterns of agriculture were to be tested on 'development farms' before being implemented, but the tests were delayed and implementation proceeded without them. A Ghana project relied on research data and experience from elsewhere in Africa which proved "of questionable relevance to Northern Ghana".

Morris and Gwyer also found that there was very little testing of the proposed new crop technologies on smallholder farms. "This meant that the basis for achieving the productivity gains from the project was to some extent theoretical", they noted, with nice British understatement.

Project officials had not taken into account the increased labour which these new techniques required from the farmers and their families, nor the costs of fertiliser and other 'inputs' required. Given that the yields were disappointing, farmers had even less reason for spending money and labour. "For example, the increase in income per incremental man-day arising as a result of adopting the proposals being advocated in one project is now likely to be *negative* at present prices." (My emphasis: this means that extra effort meant less income per unit of labour, not more.)

Project management was often unconnected with existing institutions; the feelings of the local people had not been adequately assessed and there was generally insufficient feedback to project management, Morris and Gwyer wrote. The skills, needs, labour or social organisation of the smallholder were not taken into account.

Agricultural extension

Integrated projects were also based on getting into the field more 'agricultural extension workers': advisers on cropping techniques, soil conservation, seeds, fertiliser. Morris and Gwyer found, not surprisingly, that due to the "lack of demonstrably sound and financially attractive changes to offer the farmer", these extension workers did the farmers little or no good. But paying and housing the extension workers was costing so much, and the projects were earning so little, that the burden of the extension workers actually threatened the projects' budgets. Not only had the extension workers nothing to offer, they consumed a great deal of the aid meant for farmers and farming.

All over Africa, many extension workers fail to earn their keep because they lack any real knowledge which the farmer needs and can use. Often this lack stems from their ignorance of why farmers do what they do.

A study of Tanzanian smallholder coffee production [140] describes how in the Bukoba region coffee is grown inter-planted with bananas. This is due both to land shortages and poor soil. The bananas are planted in a permanent grove upon which fertility is built up by manuring and mulching with banana leaves and crop residues. When fertility is high, beans, coffee and other annual crops are planted among the bananas. "Nevertheless, for the past 40 years, the agricultural extension service has been encouraging farmers to plant pure-stand coffee and considering this practice the *sine qua non* of modern farming... It is scarcely surprising that the extension service has had minimal success."

In northern Uganda, farmers are officially advised to start planting cotton in mid-April. Tests show that yields fall off rapidly if planting is delayed for more than two months after this. Extension workers apparently do not realise that hailstorms hit northern Uganda at cotton harvest time. By delaying planting, farmers spread the hail risk. More important, by extending the season they can make time for a quick millet planting, both for food and with which to pay cotton workers.

In the Gambia, peanut farmers ignore advice that early planting saves weeding later. They plant late, so as not to compete for labour needed to grow millet. The late peanut crop does need more weeding, but there is nothing much else to do at that time of year anyhow, so this is a rational use of available labour.

Not only in Tanzania, but throughout Africa, farmers ignore 'expert' advice to replace intercropping with pure stands. Only recently has modern research caught up with them, showing that intercropping can give 60% higher gross returns per hectare than pure stands.

The last three examples are from the World Bank [141] which adds that African farmers all "respond rapidly to changing resource availability, constraints and incentives and balance available resources to meet multiple (often conflicting) objectives".

> *Extension advice has two somewhat contradictory failings: it is often wrong, and it is often unavailable. African governments spend little on it. In 1982, when the government of what was then Upper Volta was spending the equivalent of $8,000 per year on every soldier as opposed to $7 on every citizen, extension workers could not get petrol to drive out of the capital. In 1980, the travel budget of the Zambian Ministry of Agriculture could buy only one-fifth of the petrol it could buy in 1973, leaving agricultural staff essentially desk-bound, according to an International Labour Office report.* [142]

The farmer is a woman

Getting the results of research to African farmers means getting these results to women. "When one speaks today of 'the African farmer', one is talking about a woman", says Brian Walker, president of the International Institute for Environment and Development.

The role of women in Africa has always been hard. The Ugandan poet Okot p'Bitek described it in his *Song of Ocol:*

> *Woman of Africa*
> *Sweeper*
> *Smearing floors and walls*
> *With cow dung and black soil*
> *Cook, ayah, the baby on your back*
> *Washer of dishes,*
> *Planting, weeding, harvesting*
> *Store-keeper, builder*
> *Runner of errands,*
> *Cart, lorry, donkey...*
> *Woman of Africa*
> *What are you not?*

Today, the role of women is changing, rarely for the better, giving women even more work while denying them their traditional power.

First, men are forced to leave farms to find paid work in cities, work which often cannot be found. So women must labour on the farm, or go out to work on bigger farms to earn the cash the men are not sending home. Kenyan researcher Professor Philip Mbithi estimated that even when the man *is* on the farm, nearly half of his activities are not directly related to farm work: visiting, ceremonies, communal labour, travelling to market, hunting, attending political meetings and rallies. [143]

Second, environmental degradation can give women more work. As trees disappear, fuelwood sources move further from home. Women in northern Ghana may need a whole day to collect three days' supply of fuelwood, often walking eight kilometres with babies on their backs to the family 'bush farm' to collect the wood. In rural Kenya, some women spend 20-24 hours per week collecting firewood. In places where collecting 'free' wood has become exorbitant in terms of time and labour, women must work harder to earn more to buy firewood, charcoal or kerosene. Soil erosion may also mean that women have to work more land or land further from home to grow food for the family, and declining water resources means they must walk further to collect water.

Third, landholding and land-use patterns have been changing gradually in Africa throughout this century. Generally speaking, land is traditionally held by a clan or sub-clan, with a headman or council allocating the use of plots to individual farmers and families. Women rarely *owned* land under traditional systems, but had strong rights to *land-use*, rights which often remained in force after the death of the husband or even divorce.

The introduction of European legal systems and the advent of cash crops encouraged single ownership, most often in the name of the husband. In some traditional societies, women had themselves controlled fields on which they grew food for the family and from which they sold surpluses. One study of Kenyan land laws found that land registration dispossesses women of the security of tenure that they had in family holdings and vests it in men. [144]

Cash crops may encourage men to take over women's land rights. However when cash crops are introduced, women may lose rights to both cash and food that existed previously. Research around Africa has found that wives nearly universally oppose cash crops because they reduce the amount of land available for food. Women must spend more time cultivating their husbands' plots and less on their own. This would not matter so much if women were given a proportion of cash returns, but such money is usually considered part of male income.

So African women now have more of the responsibility of farming, but less power in the form of cash and control over land. And they get little help, because extension workers and researchers direct all their attention to the men who are officially in charge of the farms.

In Kenya, one researcher wrote that "training of rural women is often limited and where it is offered, the homemaker and domestic roles of women receive priority... Women managers are outside government communications networks where information about training is transmitted, and women operate under time and labour constraints which make absence from the farm difficult." [145]

In plainer language, women are never told about training schemes, and if they were, they would not have time to attend them. As women are more and more the farmers of Africa, then research and extension work which does not reach them will have little chance of improving African farming.

Crop research

African agricultural research has two failings: much has yet to be done, and much of what has been done has been the wrong sort of research. Africa can be divided very broadly into three foodcrop zones.

* The *sorghum* and *millet* zone (including pulses like chickpeas and cowpeas), stretching right across the Sudano-Sahelian region from Mauritania to Somalia.

* The *root crop* zone (cassava and yams), running through humid Africa from Guinea in the west through Zaire.
* The *maize* zone, dominating Kenya, Tanzania, Zambia and Angola down to the Cape.

All three of these types of crop have been grossly understudied, from an African point of view. "Until recently, tropical agricultural research was concentrated on export crops such as sugar, bananas, rubber, cotton, tea, coffee and oil palms", wrote the World Bank in 1982 [146] "Tropical research on sorghum, millet and maize started later and advanced more slowly. Outside the tropics, these cereals had been used primarily as animal feed and their taste was inferior; there was little incentive to improve them in tropical areas. Similarly, very little research had been done on pulses (such as chickpeas and cowpeas) and root crops such as cassava, because these were not grown in temperate areas. Whether modern scientific techniques and a high international and national research priority can make up this lost ground remains to be seen."

Two years later, in 1984, the World Bank appeared more pessimistic: "No major breakthrough has been achieved in genetic improvement of rainfed sorghum and millet, which account for 80% of the cultivated land in the Sahel and other areas of low rainfall. Nor can rapid progress be expected." [147]

Not only has international research ignored African food crops; much agricultural research in Africa concentrates on non-indigenous crops. It tries to get crops from elsewhere (wheat, Asian rice, potatoes) to adapt to African conditions, rather than raising yields of crops already well adapted to the continent. But there are three other ways in which African crop research often fails.

* It attempts to create varieties, of either local or exotic crops, with characteristics adapted to a type of *intensive farming* often unsuited to local conditions.
* It concentrates on the *technical aspects* of agronomy (yields, rates of growth, stem length, etc) at the expense of social and economic research to discover the acceptability of any innovation.
* And it fails to learn from local farming practices.

Much work has been spent on trying to grow improved Asian rice varieties along the Niger River. These have short stems, so that growth goes into grain and not stalk — provided water levels are carefully controlled. African rice copes with flooding by growing faster than the rivers rise. So African rice not only has greater survial potential than Asian rice, it does not require labour to control water levels. Its losses to birds like fire-finches are less; it fits in neatly with elaborate systems of fish-traps, and it is more glutinous than Asian rice, and thus is preferred by local women in making the traditional porridges. Yet researchers prefer Asian rice.

If a crop has merit, it will be taken up rapidly by farmers without a great effort by extension workers. A dry-seeded green bean was developed at Makerere University in Uganda in the 1960s. By 1979, it had spread as far as southwest Tanzania, where it was locally known as the *prostitute bean* because of its impressive good looks. This spread was totally outside government channels.

Hybrid maizes have spread throughout East and Central Africa, despite the fact that hybrids require new seeds every year. (This rapid spread provides another example of the peasant's ability to innovate. Hybrid maize was taken up by farmers in much of western Kenya faster than it had been adopted by US farmers 30 years earlier.) One popular variety is the fast- maturing 'Katumani' maize which is more resistant to drought than other types — but less resistant than sorghum and millet.

The plum tomato was introduced into northern Nigeria by tomato paste manufacturers. Local farmers soon realised they could get two and a half times as much for their tomatoes at local markets as the paste manufacturer, Cadbury-Schweppes, was paying them. By the mid-1970s, the tomato had spread throughout northern Nigeria and could be found in all marketplaces.

The system

The world's umbrella organisation for tropical agriculture is the Consultative Group on International Agricultural Research (CGIAR). The International Institute of Tropical Agriculture (IITA) in Ibadan, Nigeria, has responsibility within the system for yams and other crops of the lowland humid tropics. ILCA (International Livestock Centre for Africa) in Addis Ababa is responsible for livestock, and ILRAD (International Laboratory for Research on Animal Diseases) in Nairobi for livestock disease. Some institutes outside Africa concentrate on crops and climate areas of direct relevance to Africa. The International Crops Research Institute for the Semi-Arid Tropics (ICRISAT) in India concentrates on sorghum, millet and some of the legumes of crucial importance to the Sahel, and it runs some projects in semi-arid Africa. The International Rice Research Institute is in the Philippines, but advises on and helps to coordinate African rice research through IITA and the West African Rice Development Association (WARDA) in Liberia.

The CGIAR network grew from funding from the Rockerfeller and Ford Foundations, and by 1982 had a budget of $160 million a year from 33 major donors: governments, UN agencies and the World Bank. The

CGIAR's 13 institutes are designed to be centres of excellence, and are thus by definition 'elitist', often attracting the best African government scientists away from government laboratories and dampening the enthusiasm of national labs for engaging in agricultural research and thus competing with their 'betters'.

In an evaluation of the system's work, Paul Richards, a British anthropologist, finds that it has made some progress in spreading high-yielding varieties — cassava, rice, maize, sorghum and sweet potato — in West Africa. The institutes have begun to examine peasant systems of intercropping, minimum tillage and runoff agriculture. [148]

But he finds that by and large the institutes still tend to assume that biological and technological research problems can be separated from political and social issues. The research centres are also far removed from many of the farm communities whose aims they hope to meet, not only socially but in most cases geographically. Both these problems lead to the sort of inappropriate research described in the next section.

Governments are also distant from the real needs of the farmers. Robert Chambers found that though cassava was grown by over half the Zambian rural population and is a staple food, and in drought years a food of last resort, it did not even appear in Zambian agricultural production statistics. In 1980, there was only one research agronomist working on cassava in Zambia. [149]

Discussing research on African crops, scientists often stress the 'technical difficulties'. These are found mainly in the root crops, as it is very difficult to get them to propagate from seeds. But, speaking privately rather than officially, Northern scientists list other problems in conducting research in Africa. In the words of one international laboratory director who did not want to be named: "We can't do research work in Africa. Local people are not sufficiently qualified; governments will never spend the foreign exchange on purchasing the right equipment; there are no spares, no transport and no petrol. We avoid it wherever we can".

These problems can be overcome when the price is right. Scientists and governments have been willing to spend time, money and energy in Africa developing new strains of tea and coffee suitable for African conditions — but then these are export crops which earn dollars for African governments and supply commodities important to Northern economies and companies.

Researching what? For whom?

Even when research is done on 'peasant' food crops, it may be of the wrong sort.

Chambers found that much research on sorghum was going to improve its protein content (to make it a more efficient food for large-scale cattle ranches), rather than to improve its calorie content (which is what the people who eat it want).

Sorghum is drought resistant, but traditional varieties can take as long as nine months to mature, which makes it difficult to grow when rains are extremely variable throughout a year. Much work has therefore gone into producing sorghum varieties which mature more quickly.

In Ethiopia, peasants were offered a sorghum which matured in only three months. They would not plant it. In the highlands, farmers use sorghum stalks as a roofing material and both the leaves and stalks as fodder for livestock. The fast-growing sorghum did not have the right sort of stalks and leaves.

In describing this venture, Kebede Tatu, head of the Ethiopian Soil and Water Conservation Service, said: "We can't continue indefinitely. Science cannot keep coming up empty-handed. We cannot go in for classical research. We need sociologists to go out and see what the farmers are thinking." (His service had recently hired a sociologist).

Another common failure of reseachers is to undervalue drastically the labour of farmers, often because cheap labour is available to research stations.

In Burkina Faso, ICRISAT had a multi-disciplinary team — agronomists, economists and anthropologists — which prided itself on its close links with farmers. The team came up with a combination of cowpea and sorghum cropping which gave optimum yields on the research station and even did well when researchers managed plantings in farmers' fields. But on their own, farmers did not seem able to follow the researchers' instructions. Perhaps the 'stupid peasants' did not understand them, the scientists speculated.

A later analysis found that the new technique forced farmers to spend 25-50% more time weeding and — as cowpeas had to be planted in separate holes from the sorghum — 50% more time in planting. Improved yields hardly justified this increased labour. Peter Mation, an economist with the ICRISAT team, told this tale about himself and colleagues to emphasise the difficulties of ensuring that research, even that done in close cooperation with farmers, is truly relevant. [150]

There are a host of domesticated African plants which 'modern' research virtually ignores.

Fonio *(Digitaria exilis)* and iburu *(Digitaria iburua)* are two West African grains which can grow on poor soils, which require virtually no labour once planted and which are resistant to local pests and diseases. Fonio, which is important in dry areas of West Africa such as the Jos

Plateau, also goes by the name of 'hungry rice'. (These grains are of the same family as European and American 'crabgrass', a plant notoriously difficult to kill off.) Teff *(Eragrostis abyssinica),* a type of millet, is the most widely grown grain in Ethiopia, but is little cultivated elsewhere. It too has been little studied, but of all the common cereals in human diets, only wheat seems to have a higher protein content than teff.

> *Researchers tend to ignore such plants because research has ignored them in the past: there is little previous work with which to compare one's results; those results would not be of interest to one's peers or superiors or (perhaps most important) to one's funders. Scientists do like to break new ground — but only in areas that interest other scientists.*

Agroforestry

Not all agricultural research has to do with food crops. Given Africa's vast need for soil and watershed protection, and the fact that wood provides the domestic energy of nine in 10 rural Africans, much more research is needed on how to grow trees.

'Agroforestry' has become the word most widely used to describe the cultivation of trees on farms rather than in forests. The term is new, but deliberately growing trees as part of agriculture goes back into pre-history in much of Africa.

One of the best known examples of African agroforestry is practised by the Chagga tribe on the slopes of Mount Kilimanjaro. Their 'tree gardens' cover about 1,200 square kilometres with a dense population of about 500 people per square kilometre.

The Chagga gardens contain a multistorey arrangement of plants and trees. At the lowest level are food crops such as taro and beans, and grasses used for animal fodder; above these grow coffee and medicinal plants. The next zone up contains bananas, and standing above the rest are tall timber trees such as teak.

The system is constantly managed. At the right time of year, farmers cut away some of the higher foliage to let light onto the coffee to ensure better fruiting; they transplant trees and crops to ensure their better growth and development. They apply manure; and they grow plants which repel or eradicate certain pests. All the time, some plants are being cut and replaced as they become harvestable or reach the end of their useful lives.

Tree gardens have provided the Chagga with a stable agriculture for over a century. It is three-dimensional agriculture, not two-dimensional. But although the system still works well, it is coming under the same sorts of pressure as the Chagga irrigation system: the migration of young people to the cities leaves labour shortages and disrupts the traditional transmission of skills from one generation to another.

According to Peter Wood of the Nairobi-based International Council for Research in Agroforestry (ICRAF), agroforestry in Africa has traditionally been used to increase overall production per unit area; to reduce the incidence of diseases and pests; to enable planting to take account of soil variations; to exploit the different heights of various crops; to provide a continued and varying supply of food; to protect the soil against weeds and erosion; to even out the demand for labour during the year.

This potential is now attracting a good deal of research attention to agroforestry. But this enthusiasm should not obscure the fact that detailed information on agroforestry systems is still painfully limited. There is fairly good data on the effects of growing food crops between commercial tree species during the early years of a plantation. There is also extensive experience in some countries of using different types of commercial timber trees to provide shade for tea and coffee. But this detailed knowledge is a very small proportion of the theoretically possible combinations.

Producing appropriate *new* agroforestry systems will require a tremendous amount of time and labour. As John Raintree of ICRAF put it: "In agroforestry there is little scope at present for 'off the shelf' solutions. Our shelves, in fact, are practically empty, at least of scientifically understood and validated technologies."

As applies in so many other areas of difficulty in Africa, it is not that there is nothing which can be done. The potential of agroforestry is obviously immense. What is needed is the commitment of time, resources and political support.

A peasant-led 'Green Revolution'

In Niger, peasant farmers normally have only two weeks when the rains come to sow their crops. If they misjudge their timing, and sow before the rains have really started, or after the best rain has fallen, they will get little or no harvest. When one speaks of Africa's 'agricultural decision-makers', one is speaking of the peasants. Theirs are the life and death decisions.

Paul Richards' investigations of farming systems in West Africa have turned up a remarkable array of sophisticated techniques. The farmers use their own form of 'research and development' (R&D): trial plantings and quantitative 'input-output trials' (measurements of the amount of rice produced for amount of seed sown). A 1942 study of rice varieties used by Mende planters in three districts of Sierra Leone found 20 distinct varieties, some fast growing, some slow, and various types meant for different types of land and water. Knowledge of the varieties went so deep in the villages that children were given the job of separating out unwanted strains. [151]

To say that Northern researchers have been universally impressed by African peasant R&D would merely be patronising. The point is that this R&D has very often turned up solutions better than anything Northern science has to offer. This was discovered by colonial agronomists in West Africa, and is still being 'discovered' today. "Despite the publicity surrounding the Green Revolution's 'miracle rices', two of the most successful improved upland rices in Sierra Leone and Liberia, ROK 3 and LAC 23, are of local provenance", writes Richards; the varieties were selected by 'experts', but based on rices developed by local people.

More important is the evidence which shows how peasant farmers can incorporate 'high technology' inputs with techniques developed by local R&D. Richards recounts recent FAO fertiliser trials in Plateau State, Nigeria, which compared local farmers' own cultivation practices with 'improved' (that is, suggested from outside) cultivation practices. For monocrops of sorghum and of maize, the improved techniques proved best. But the best yields all round were obtained using fertiliser on intercroped stands — the farmers' usual practice. Where both plots used fertiliser, intercroppings of yams and maize achieved a value/cost ratio of 77.3 using farmers' cultivation practices, but a ratio of only 24.6 using 'improved' practices.

Peasant R&D is not limited to humid West Africa. British anthropologist Jeremy Swift's work with the FulBe pastoralists of Niger revealed that they left certain apparently fertile pastures alone, because they gave cattle night blindness. The herders associated the blindess with the lack of certain plants, an explanation which fits with the scientific explanation of vitamin A deficiency. The livestock extension service which had been working in the area for 50 years was unaware of the problem. The research team took some vitamin A to the camp of a herder whose cattle had night blindness. The herder did not object to the cattle being given the vitamin, but insisted that only half the cattle get the vitamin, so he himself could judge its efficiency against the untreated cows. [152]

African agricultural institutes are beginning to realise the need for getting their research out of the laboratories and test-plots and into the farmers' fields. But this will raise a host of problems. African higher education tends to train people to get off the farm and far away from 'ignorant' peasants. African agriculture extension workers will need to be retrained to see themselves as agents of these same peasants rather than as 'salesmen for the Green Revolution'. Researchers will have to come up with new techniques to allow them to get scientifically acceptable data in conditions not as 'controlled' in the laboratory. Not only will planting times and soil and moisture conditions vary, but the farmers will constantly modify the experiments.

Perhaps the best reason for radically altering present African agricultural research and development practices is that the 'input from the lab' approach has been tried for many years now and not worked well. Richards believes that 'people's science' is worth pursuing not out of admiration for the peasantry, 'but on the grounds that it is good science'.

One of Richards' associates asked a villager how the government could best help farmers. "You cannot turn a calf into a cow by plastering it with mud", he was told. The analogy is subtle but the meaning is clear: African agricultural change must be organic and come from within; slapped on solutions from outside do not work.

CONSERVING AFRICA FOR AFRICANS

"It is one thing to keep urban Americans from
farming Yellowstone, quite another to keep the
Maasai herders out of Kenya's
Amboseli Reserve."
Walter Lusigi, Kenyan ecologist

Much of the pressure for a more rational use of Africa's soil has been coming from wildlife conservationists. When the North thinks of conservation in Africa it tends to think in terms of wildlife, and when thinking of wildlife in terms of the big, spectacular species which conservationist literature describes as part of 'the common heritage of mankind': elephant, rhino, lion, gorilla and big antelopes.

But conservation is also about 'wild genetic resources' — the genetic material in wild plants and even in some wild animals which may improve breeds of domestic crop plants and animals, both in the North and in the South. And included among genetic resources are the unstudied, perhaps yet undiscovered, plants which have potential uses in medicines and in industrial chemicals.

The third major conservation challenge is the saving of the vast amount of human knowledge of African wildlife possessed by the people of Africa. Many African societies not only have a deep awareness of plants, animals and soils, but also of their inter-relationships and ecology.

But much of this knowledge is orally-transmitted, and is threatened as Africans leave the countryside for the cities and as 'bush culture' becomes less and less a part of daily survival techniques. Anthropological studies have shown that in some areas there is a big drop between one generation and the next in the number of plants which individuals can identify and for which they understand the uses. Among the Nupe of west-central Nigeria, older people are able to cite the names and uses of over 100 trees. But today only 14 species are commonly found in the farming areas, and young people are familiar only with these. The world is thus in danger of losing what US anthropologist Leslie Brownrigg has called "many person-centuries of human scientific research".

Indigenous libraries

In Latin America, the knowledge which indigenous or 'tribal' people have about the plants around them has attracted much attention and some study. It is easier in Latin America to distinguish between the indigenous people and the rest of the population. They tend to live in traditional hunting, gathering and small-farming societies, still relatively isolated from the dominant Latin population of the continent. Often this isolation is physical, in that they live deep in rainforests, a habitat which offers an overwhelming array of plant types and plant chemistry to be studied. Almost every rainforest tribe — and there are scores if not hundreds — has its own psychogenic drug used in ceremonies or healing. Most are unknown or unstudied by Western science.

Even in Asia, there is more general agreement about what constitutes a 'tribal' society: a group of culturally distinctive people living apart — both physically and in terms of survival strategies — from the larger national societies: the forest people ('tribals') of India and Bangladesh, and the mountain tribes of New Guinea, for instance.

But what is 'indigenous' in Africa? Is the successful Kikuyu plantation owner in his European-style suit and his Mercedes any less indigenous than the Mbuti pygmy in Zaire? Does indigenous mean 'isolated', so one is left with the people either missed by the great southern migration of the Bantu peoples, like the Mbuti, or those squeezed into inhospitable zones, like the San (bushmen) of the Kalahari? It may be only because of haziness of definition that the research into indigenous science which has at least begun in Latin America has hardly started in Africa.

Anthropologists studying the San people of the Kalahari have documented their dependence on wild plants, which constitute 80-90% of their food (most of the rest being wild animals), and their knowledge of where these plants are to be found, when they may be found, and their uses as foods, flavourings, medicines and arrow-poisons. But the chemists have yet to follow the anthropologists to study the properties of these plants, many of which are found only in the Kalahari. The Mbuti's knowledge of the Zaire forest plants — and of the animal species whose habits they know well enough to be able to hunt with nets — has likewise been praised but little studied.

Impressive books of useful plants do exist for parts of Africa, which could give the chemists a starting place. The huge study, *Useful plants of West Tropical Africa,* was first published by Kew Gardens, London, in 1936, and is only now being republished with substantial additions and changes. The original work contained some 4,600 species for West Africa alone. Other useful studies exist for Malawi (J. Williamson, 1972), for the edible plants of southern Africa (F.W. Fox and M.E. Norwood Young, 1982), and for the medicinal plants of East Africa (J.O. Kokwaro, 1976). In fact, a study by Raako Harjula of one Tanzanian herbalist, Mirau, showed that he regularly identified 130 plant species and compounded them into remedies for 187 human and animal complaints. [153]

There are studies which have yet to be done on the people themselves. The Maasai of Kenya and Tanzania (and other pastoralist tribes) exist on a high-cholesterol diet of milk and blood, yet their blood pressure does not rise significantly with age, as does that of most Europeans. Why? A research team from Tulane University (US) studied them to find out, but with little success.

Wildlife as food

Work is beginning to be done on the economic value of wildlife, both to African nations and to other nations which receive its benefits. Earthscan has published two books (*What's wildlife worth?* (1982) and *Genes from the wild* (1983), by Robert and Christine Prescott-Allen) which document the various economic benefits offered by wild plants and animals.

First, Africans *eat* a great deal of wild animal meat. About three-quarters of the population of Ghana depend heavily on wildlife for protein. In southern Nigeria game meat is eaten regularly by 80% of the population, and 70% of the rural population of Liberia eats some 'bushmeat' or makes money selling it. In fact monkey meat sells for more in Liberia than beef, and in Nigeria meat from giant rats commands three times the price of mutton. When fish is included under the 'wild meat' heading, eight African countries get more than 50% of their daily per capita supply of animal protein from the wild (Benin, Congo, Ghana, Liberia, Senegal, Sierra Leone, Togo and Zaire).

In discussing plants, distinctions between wild and domestic tend to be harder to make. First, there are many wild plants which are gathered and used, but not grown or cultivated in any way.

Second, there are 'protected' plants, which are not genetically different from wild plants, but which people encourage by replanting near settlements or by selectively destroying competing plants. These include the often revered baobab tree *(Adansonia digitata)*, a tree of the savannas whose leaves are used as a vegetable and in soups. The seeds of the shea-nut tree *(Butyrospermum parkii)* yield a white fat known as shea butter which is important as a food and a lighting oil throughout the Sahel. These trees are becoming scarcer as the people who value them diminish and they are cut for fuelwood. It is not only the isolated populations which rely on non-cropped plants for food. Studies by Ann Fleuret in Tanzania found that wild leafy plants comprised four-fifths of all leafy green vegetables eaten and were eaten at almost half the meals. [154]

Paula Williams, a fellow of the Institute of Current World Affairs studying human uses of forest resources in sub-Saharan Africa, reports that:

> Of 114 species of trees and shrubs analysed in the Sahel, 23 species had 'great importance' and 46 had 'limited importance' in human diets. But these plants are left out of economic reckoning, first because they are collected for 'free' by women, and second because most food studies tend to concentrate on staple foods, not extras.

According to Williams, if you ask a woman in Burkina Faso what she ate that day, she might reply "tao (the staple millet or sorghum porridge) and gumbo sauce". Closer questioning would show that she ate shea-nut fruits while at work in the fields and took some home to make the butter; that she made some beer fermented from the fruit of a local tree *(Sclerocarya birrea)*; that she used tamarind fruit, leaves and juice to make the tao more digestible and added fermented seeds of one of the locust trees *(Parkia biglobosa)* to the gumbo. [155]

Spices may do more than simply flavour food. Dr John Rivers of the London School of Hygiene and Tropical Medicine, working in Ethiopia during the 1972-73 drought, could not understand why poor and hungry people would continue to spend money on spices. He took some home for analysis, and found that the spices act as a powerful anti-bacterial agent, thus allowing the safe storage of meat before it was stewed.

Wildlife as medicine

The contents of herbalists' pouches are just beginning to be taken seriously by scientists, both African and Northern. This is first because 'traditional' medicine is the only type of medicine to which many Africans have access; and second, because many of these medicines have been found to be effective. Both Madagascar and Rwanda have taken traditional medicines as the starting point of their research and development into new drugs, and WHO is helping such bodies as the Pharmaceutical Society of Ghana and the University of Science and Technology at Kumasi, Ghana, to undertake similar work. It has been estimated that 95% of African traditional drugs come from plants. [156]

Such work is proving the worth of many 'new' drugs — new at least to Northern researchers. The plant *Elaeophorbia drupifera* is used in Ghana to treat guinea worm (mixed with palm nut oil so it will not poison the patient as well as the worm). Studies in Ghana have also turned up herbs effective in the treatment of post-natal bleeding, diabetes, infective hepatitis and urinary infections. [157]

This success should not be surprising, considering what Africa has already given the world in terms of widely-used medicines. Reserpine, used against hypertension, and ajmaline, used to maintain heart rhythm, both come from the serpentwood shrub *Rauvolfia,* which grows throughout Africa, as well as in the Caribbean and Asia. Both drugs are still obtained almost entirely from wild plants. Physostigmine, a muscle relaxant used in opthalmology, is obtained from the calabar bean *(Physostigma venenosum)* of West Africa.

African animals have yet to provide drugs, but they already provide species key to medical research. The chimpanzee is used for research into hepatitis B, and the African green monkey for the production of SV40 virus-free polio vaccine.

Wildlife as 'genetic resources'

Africa is the home of both the wild originals and of primative cultivated varieties ('cultivars') of many important world crop plants. Ethiopia alone is a 'centre of diversity' for such crops as wheat, barley, peas, lentils and flax, though none of these crops originated there. But wild *Coffea arabica,* which produces arabica coffee, occurs *only* in Ethiopia and southeastern Sudan. Crossed with cultivated coffee, it offers great potential for the improvement of coffee crops, but is so endangered by deforestation that it has been designated by the International Board for Plant Genetic Resources as one of three priority species for conservation in the wild.

The other two species are also African. The wild oil palm *(Elaesis guineensis)* actually seemed to be benefiting from habitat disturbance, as it is a tree of the forest edge which does not like shade. But recently the clearing of large tracts of land for urban expansion, industry and mono-crop plantations, along with the thinning of palm groves, have caused some experts to consider it endangered. Its loss would deny new genetic inputs to the palm oil plantations not only of Africa, but of Asia and Latin America as well. The third species is the *Olea laperrinei,* a close relative of the European olive *(O. europea)* found in the isolated mountains of

Sudan, Niger and southern Algeria and reported to be succumbing to drought, grazing, browsing and cutting. The young branches are a favourite source of fodder for cattle.

Wild and primitive African varieties have already improved key cultivated crops.

* Genes from the wild oil palm of Zaire, Ivory Coast and Nigeria have increased oil yields in Malaysia and Indonesia by more than 25%.
* Virtually all cultivars of extra long staple cotton in the Sudan are resistant to bacterial blight, thanks to genes from the wild cotton *Gossypium anomalum* found in several African countries from Cameroon to Namibia.
* Australian researchers collected wild samples of the perennial forage legume *Neonotonia wightii* from Kenya, Tanzania, South Africa and Malawi, took them home and developed the cultivars Tinaroo, Cooper, Clarence and Malawi, respectively. These have proved so successful on Australian ranges that they have been widely adopted not only in Africa, but in Latin America as well.

Examples like these have raised the question — very loudly in recent years in the halls of FAO — of who pays for the conservation of such plants. Must Zaire, Ivory Coast and Nigeria pay for the preservation of the wild oil palm, when its genes are more important economically to Malaysia and Indonesia? Do the plantation owners of those latter countries pay? Do transnational palm oil companies like Unilever pay? And how would such costs be estimated and collected and used?

In some cases Africa may directly benefit from such conservation (cotton and forage). In others, Africa gets no benefit. In still others, Africa stands to lose a great deal. The sweetener thaumatin was isolated from the West African plant *Thaumatococcus danielli*. Genetic engineering has allowed for the removal of the plant's 'sweetness' gene and its insertion into bacteria which can now produce the sweetener in factory vats anywhere in the world. The development threatens the growing of sugar on plantations, a key economic activity in South Africa, Mauritius, Egypt, Mozambique, Kenya, Swaziland and Zimbabwe.

The parks paradox

On no other continent do so many people live in such close proximity to wild animals, often large and dangerous wild animals. As Europeans moved into North and South America, they rapidly forced such beasts as the grizzly bear and the jaguar into remote habitats far from people.

Many of these habitats are now national parks, because they contain, in the form of majestic native wildlife, key elements of the nation's heritage.

Many African cultures have always lived among wildlife; wildlife is in a much more real sense part of their heritage, and hunting and gathering wild products a part of their everyday life. But national parks in Africa have followed the pattern of US national parks such as Yellowstone or Yosemite, where no economic activity or any hunting or fishing or gathering of wildlife is allowed. These 'rules' were developed in the United States and elaborated by the International Union for Conservation of Nature and Natural Resources (IUCN), based in Gland, Switzerland. They have been applied to Africa first by colonial administrators, then by Western-trained African conservationists, and are still the basis of most outside funding and support.

> *The result of applying such rules to African parks is the bizarre situation in which Africans are hired, trained and armed to guard African parks to keep out African people, for the benefit of both the protected animals and the foreigners who come to see them — and of course for the tourist revenue, which goes into government or hotel bank accounts, not to rural people.*

Africa's hundreds of national parks and game reserves have been established and run with almost all their attention on animals and tourism, and almost no attention on local Africans. The system has never worked particularly well, and pressures upon it are growing. "The idea of 'national parks' as it is presently conceived is an alien and unacceptable idea to the African population", according to Kenyan ecologist Walter Lusigi. "It is one thing to keep urban Americans from farming Yellowstone, quite another to keep the Maasai herders out of Kenya's Amboseli Reserve."

Most of the threats to Africa's parks come from government policies, or lack of them: pressure of people seeking land to farm, pasture for livestock and cash from poaching. Uganda's parks existed in name only during the Amin era. There were 30,000 elephants in Uganda in 1970, only 2,000 in 1980; in Kabalega Falls National Park elephants fell from 10,000 to less than 200. White rhino were declared extinct in Uganda in 1982, and the buffalo and hippo populations also suffered severe losses in Queen Elizabeth National Park.

The staffs of Boma National Park in the Sudan and Gorongosa in Mozambique have been put at risk by civil war. Tai National Park in Ivory Coast is being invaded by gold prospectors, and Mount Nimba Strict Nature Reserve in that country is being considered for iron ore mines. The waterfowl habitat in the Djoudj National Park in Senegal is threatened by a dam. Tanzania's Mkomazi Game Reserve is reportedly being turned into a cattle ranch, with six indigenous species lost already, and the

Barbara Cheney

A mother and two babies, southern Kenya. Smaller tusks in world trade show that younger elephants are being shot. No matter what one feels about wildlife, the inability of African governments to protect it shows their inability to control land and land use.

Ngorongoro Conservation Area in Tanzania is suffering neglect and underfunding. [158]

The success of the parks system can perhaps be judged by the fate of just one species: the African elephant. In 1983, 90,000 elephants were killed to produce 1,000 tonnes of ivory for world markets. About half were poached, and the rest were killed to control numbers or eliminate those which had become nuisances, according to IUCN consultant Peter Jackson. The average weight of each tusk in the trade has declined from about nine kilogrammes to six kg over the past eight years, meaning that the 'big tuskers' are disappearing and younger and younger elephants are being shot.

Africa will lose about half of its remaining million elephants over the next decade unless the slaughter is curbed. Elephants are declining both outside and inside the 360 parks and reserves in which they are found; only in Botswana, South Africa and Zimbabwe are populations stable or expanding.

People in parks

The general failure in Africa of parks developed on the American and European model has encouraged schemes to change their nature: to put the people back in the parks. Many such plans involve dividing parks into different zones. Fairly heavy land-use around the perimeter would give way to a 'buffer zone', or several zones graduated according to use, in which farming and herding were controlled. Other zones would be set aside for 'wildlife only'.

UNESCO's international Man and the Biosphere Programme (MAB) is looking into such systems. MAB is meant to improve the management of different types of ecosystems both in terms of human use and of the natural environment.

How this forward-looking goal can easily go wrong was shown in an in depth study of the Lufira Valley MAB reserve being established in southeastern Shaba province in Zaire by Brooke Grundfest Schoepf, formerly of the National University of Zaire. [159] In the 1950s the Lemba people were practising a complex system of agriculture and possessed a detailed ecological knowledge of the Lufira Valley — apparently a perfect situation for a MAB reserve. Yet Schoepf found that Zairese officials responsible for the MAB programme were unfamiliar with the local ecology and farming systems, and regarded the local people as lazy and intractable. Funds for ecological research from Belgium were going primarily to botanical ecology, with no study of the people or their agriculture.

When she wrote her report, the reserve was still being established. Plans called for a central zone in which all productive activities would be forbidden, a buffer zone in which people could carry out normal activities under MAB supervision but would be forbidden to introduce innovations harmful to the environment, and an outer, experimental zone in which "the inhabitants will be able to pursue their activities, but the introduction of new technologies will be regulated", wrote Schoepf, quoting official papers.

In fact, officials planned to impose rules in the outer area requiring farmers to plant larger maize fields. "Under the plan, peasants would be obliged to follow the directions of administrators who have never farmed, who have no knowledge of the local ecology, do not speak the local languages, and demonstrate no particular interest in the survival of the local people", according to Schoepf. The peasants were looking forward to increases in the familiar abuses of arbitrary fines and payments to officials. MAB, though, saw the peasants as "enemies of the environment", and large farms as "both powerful and progressive in their contributions to development".

Signs of hope

Schoepf's account shows how changes in national parks along 'progressive' lines may not necessarily be for the better, and may in fact combine the worst of both rigorous environmental protection with uninformed interference in farmers' fairly successful survival strategies. Experiments in Zimbabwe and Kenya are more hopeful.

Elephant poaching accelerated rapidly after Zimbabwe achieved Independence in 1980, as "black Zimbabweans living on the former Tribal Trust Lands, now Communal Lands, felt for the first time that they had a right to enjoy the wealth of the country", according to David Cummings of Zimbabwe's Department of National Parks and Wildlife. Yet poaching was not the only motive, as 90% of the animals were left to rot, "simply got rid of because they were associated with white rule", in the words of one warden. The government's initial response was to use the military to stop the poaching. [160]

In the Chizarira National Park and the Chirisa Safari Area west of Harare, the government undertook a novel anti-poaching scheme called 'Operation Windfall'. Elephants were uprooting trees and destroying crops outside the reserves, and wardens decided a cull of at least 1,500 was necessary. In most African nations, the revenues from hides and tusks go, at best, into the national coffers; more often, they go into the pockets of politicians. Operation Windfall earmarked this revenue for the local people.

Between early 1981 and June 1982, the equivalent of $960,000 was paid to two district councils, and used for local transport, schools and clinics. The culling employed 240 local people, and in 1980 paid $25,300 in wages. District councils also received all money paid by tourists for licences to hunt in the safari area. Much of the elephant meat was cut into strips, salted, dried and sold wholesale as 'biltong' in the capital at $2.00-2.50/kg. But under Operation Windfall, some 40,000 kg was sold locally at 60 cents/kg, providing protein for the rural population.

The programme was meant to give local people a stake in the survival of elephants — at least until they were culled. It was so successful that the parks department found it unnecessary to post wardens in the entire 1,320 sq km area.

In Kenya's Amboseli Game Reserve just north of Mount Kilimanjaro, Maasai herders lived in a kind of uneasy truce with wildlife, following the same migration routes to new pastures outside the reserve in the rainy seasons, and retreating to the Amboseli swamps during the dry season. But in the 1960s the interests of growing numbers of Maasai and their growing herds clashed with those of conservationists who wanted to turn the reserve into a national park.

Faced with the prospect of losing dry season water and grazing, the

Maasai retaliated by spearing wildlife. Over a 15-year period, the local rhino population fell from 150 down to eight in the late 1970s. The Maasai had a hard time pressing their case, for Amboseli had become Kenya's most profitable game area, earning the government 10 times more than the Maasai's herding. But the real question was not *what* the park earned, but *who* earned it, according to David Western, a Kenyan wildlife ecologist who has done research in the area for almost two decades. The Maasai were losing out to the wildlife, and getting nothing for their trouble.

Under a plan launched in 1977, the central region was established as a national park covering 390 sq km. The safety of wildlife when on its seasonal migration outside the park was secured by the payment of annual grazing fees to the Maasai. The park's administrative headquarters were moved outside the park, so the Maasai could also enjoy the social services it provided park staff. Visitor campsites were also moved outside the park, giving the Maasai direct tourist revenues. Piped water was provided for the Maasai herds outside the park during the dry season, and herders were given legal land titles in these areas.

The plan worked. Populations of rhino, whose numbers are decreasing elsewhere in Africa, doubled in Amboseli between 1977 and 1983. Numbers of elephants, buffalo and most migratory species have increased. The Maasai recognise that the park is theirs, and do not allow much poaching. Now the Maasai are among the wealthiest ranchers in the region. Snags remain. The water system has not worked as well as was hoped, and the Maasai are often forced to bring their herds inside the park. But a wildlife committee of local herders meets regularly with the park warden to discuss such difficulties.

"If the principles being tested in Amboseli do work, then there is hope that wildlife can avoid the hazards of confinement within parks by ranging more widely, and can benefit humans in the surrounding area at the same time", said Western.

Wildlife, especially the big grazing animals, are often the first to suffer from environmental bankruptcy, because they compete with people for the shrinking resources of marginal land. But it is no solution to protect Africa's game for the benefit of European tourists. Unless the local people support them, few African national parks will survive for very long. So multi-purpose use, putting the people back into parks, is essential in some form. As with sustainable agriculture, sustainable wildlife conservation depends on the African peasant and herdsman.

THE FISHERIES OF AFRICA

Peasant fishermen have been left out of the development of African fisheries in much the same way that peasant farmers have been left out of the development of Africa's agriculture.

Much of the seas around Africa are rich in fish, as are the lakes and rivers. Can fish do more to feed Africa? The answer is a hesitant 'yes', the problem greatly complicated by where the fish are and by who is catching them.

The richest areas are off the northwest and southwest coasts, where the same wind patterns that dry the Sahara and Namib deserts ashore cause an upwelling of nutrient-laden waters out to sea. There is therefore a poor match between the distribution of fish and of people. The fish lie off coasts where there are few people; the people live along coasts — especially the Gulf of Guinea and East Africa — which have relatively few fish. And the fish in Africa's lakes and rivers raise entirely different problems.

Northwest Africa

Offshore from central Morocco to Guinea lies one of the richest seas in the world. It attracts, as well as local 'peasant' fishermen, fleets from more than a dozen countries in Western and Eastern Europe, and from Asia. Total catches amount to more than three million tonnes, over 50% of which is taken by foreign vessels. The 'first sale' (before processing) value of the catch is about $1.4 billion.

This annual catch is probably close to the maximum the seas can sustain. Opportunities for expansion lie mainly with the smaller, less commercially attractive fish such as anchovy; most of the larger and more valuable species — hake, seabream, cuttlefish and octopus — are heavily fished or depleted. Some of the catch is consumed locally, but most is frozen and exported to Europe, Asia and other parts of Africa.

The fisheries of the Gulf of Guinea are moderately rich, though not rich enough to attract many long-range vessels. They support large local fisheries, and the catch goes mostly as fresh or dried fish for local use. There is a great variety of species, as in most other tropical waters. The more valuable species, such as shrimp, and the long-lived, such as groupers, are the most heavily fished. Taken as a whole, the stocks are fully exploited. There is little opportunity for expanding present catches significantly beyond the present catches of the countries in the arc from Guinea down to Zaire: between 800,000 and 900,000 tonnes a year.

The waters off northwest Africa, from the Straits of Gibraltar south to the Zaire (Congo) River, is the area of responsibility of the Fishery Committee for the Eastern Central Atlantic (CECAF), a regional fishery body set up by FAO. It has provided a forum in which the fishery problems of the region can be discussed by government officials and scientists from all interested countries. The coastal African states have successfully used information from CECAF in deciding on their policies, and in setting the quotas that can be taken by foreign fleets licensed to fish off their coasts.

Fish move into and out of the CECAF region in very odd ways indeed. Countries like Morocco, Senegal and Mauritania each export about 10,000 tonnes of fish a year, the bulk of it outside Africa. Meanwhile, the needs of nations like Nigeria, Ivory Coast and Togo mean that the CECAF region, one of the world's richest fisheries, *imports* more than one million tonnes of fish yearly. About 20% of the imports (by value) are canned. Various West European countries supply half the imports to the area, but the biggest single supplier is the Soviet Union, most of this in the form of frozen fish, most actually caught in the region or in African waters further south.

How can West African governments manage these fisheries and prevent overfishing, find ways by which the coastal states can get more benefit from the fisheries off their shores, and ensure that more of the fish are eaten in Africa?

There are both technical and political problems. Fish react in complex ways to heavy fishing. Some of the most valuable species, such as seabream, cuttlefish and octopus, have declined very severely, and are apparently being replaced by less valuable species. To the south of the main upwelling zone, the population of trigger fish *(Balistes carolinensis)*, which has little commercial value and was until recently relatively rare, has greatly increased. It now dominates the upper water layers in some areas, with a biomass approaching one million tonnes. The southern boundary of the large sardine stock, around southern Morocco in 1960, has moved south about as far as Senegal.

Some of these changes are clearly related less to fishing than to changes in ocean currents. A strengthening in upwelling of nutrient-laden waters means lower ocean temperatures but higher fisheries productivity. This change seems to be related to the spread of sardine, and its replacement by sardinella, a more typically warmwater species.

If governments are going to make the right decisions in trying to conserve the fish stocks, they will need the best scientific advice. Scientists, to give good advice, will need at least a basic minimum of data, including much better statistics on catches in the area.

But there is a long way to go before foreign-owned and foreign-operated fishing boats cease to take a large share of the total catch and more of the benefits go to the coastal states. Given the uncertainty of fishing, it is even possible that the coastal states should let the long-range foreign fleets continue to take the risks, rather than hastily constructing expensive African fishing fleets.

All the CECAF nations license foreign vessels, put local fishermen on board, extract licence fees and export taxes, impose quotas, and ensure that some of the catch is made available to local consumers and processors.

But there is no guarantee that CECAF can continue to operate effectively for very long. The basic funding for the CECAF office in Dakar comes from UNDP, which as a matter of principle only provides support for a limited time. That period is now coming to an end. Though various countries have offered support to specific CECAF activities, such as collection of statistics from the long-range vessels landing their catches in the Canary Islands, most of this support is also short-term. So far, FAO has not found a way of ensuring long-term support for the basic CECAF activities.

Southwest Africa

The resources and the fisheries in the area from Angola south to the Cape are very similar to those off northwest Africa. The Benguela current causes strong upwelling, which supports large stocks of anchovies, sardines and horse-mackerel, and slightly smaller stocks of hake and other bottom-living fish. Fishing is richest off the desert coasts of Namibia, exploited by fleets of long-range vessels, particularly from Spain and eastern Europe.

Local fisheries include large purse-seine fisheries catching sardine and anchovy, based in South Africa and Namibia (Walvis Bay); most of this catch is canned or converted into fish meal. Fisheries for direct human consumption, catching a variety of species, are based in Angola (mostly small boats working close to the shore) and South Africa. Foreign vessels account for over half the total catch of some 2.5 million tonnes.

This region is governed by the International Commission for the South East Atlantic Fisheries (ICSEAF), which includes South Africa and Angola, as well as the non-local fishery countries. (It must be the only international body in which South Africa and the Soviet Union are among the three or four most active participants!) ICSEAF is independent, financed by its members, and therefore does not have CECAF'S problems of long-term support. Like CECAF, it has been successful in compiling regular and detailed statistics of the fishery, and regularly reviewing the state of the fish stocks.

Most of the species are heavily fished, and like Peruvian anchovy and Norwegian herring, the sardine stocks off both South Africa and Namibia have collapsed. Namibian sardines, having provided annual catches of up to 1.5 million tonnes (1968), were down to only 50,000 tonnes in 1983, and even that was probably more than the stock could sustain. Man can bankrupt his environment at sea as well as on land.

The Law of the Sea treaty gives South Africa and Angola the responsibility for managing stocks for 200 miles off their coasts. South Africa, with a strong national fleet, has largely acted to follow up the scientific conclusions of ICSEAF, which imply a reduction in the amount of fishing. It has restricted the activities of foreign vessels, which now take only a few fish in South African waters. Angola has concentrated on its small-scale inshore fisheries. Most offshore fishing (particularly for horse-mackerel) is done by long-range vessels, and the local Angolan catch is still below pre-Independence levels.

Unfortunately, no government could implement a 200-mile fisheries zone off Namibia which would be recognised by all the fishing countries. (Namibia, formerly South West Africa, is administered by South Africa, whose authority is not recognised by the UN or by most other governments.) So except for much of the Walvis Bay sardine fishery, which takes place within 12 miles of the coast, management responsibility lies with ICSEAF, whose decisions have to be reached by consensus. Mesh size regulations and closed areas have been introduced, and a system of mutual inspection ensures that they are generally obeyed. Catch quotas are applied to the hake and horse-mackerel fishermen, but they have tended to be set at rather optimistic levels, and compliance is doubtful.

Foreign fishing off Namibia contributes nothing to its economy or the welfare of its people. These problems will be difficult to solve until there is a Namibian government able to institute an acceptable 200-mile limit, and thus regulate all fishing fleets.

Other seas

Off the east coast of Africa the resources range from moderate (Mozambique) to poor (Kenya, Tanzania, Ethiopia and Djibouti). They are fished mostly by peasant fisheries, and the total catch of these five countries is about 90,000 tonnes. Opportunities for expansion are limited, and the main fish supply for these countries comes from their lakes and rivers.

Somalia is an exception. There is some seasonal upwelling, again linked to near-desert conditions on shore, and the fish stocks are moderately rich, but since they are far from convenient ports have been ignored by most long-range fleets. Italian vessels have fished for high priced species, but the biggest opportunity for expanded production comes from the small surface-water species.

Perhaps as much as 500,000 tonnes could be taken annually from Somalia waters, compared with present catches of around 15,000 tonnes.

Efforts are being made to get some of this protein to hungry people ashore, and two Norwegian-built vessels will soon start pilot operations. But catching the fish may be the easiest problem to solve. Processing and distributing the catch, and making it acceptable to the nomadic and basically meat-eating population will be difficult. It may be that the fish stocks can contribute most to feeding Somalia in an indirect way, as a source of foreign exchange. Foreign vessels could be licenced, or a national fishery could produce fish or fishmeal for export.

Rivers and lakes

Africa's inland fisheries play key roles in feeding many of its people. They produce around 1.4 million tonnes yearly, more than the non-recreational inland catches of Europe and North and South America combined. Compared with marine fish, their distribution is also favourable, with large catches in some of the countries in the Sahel zone, especially Chad and Mali, where other food is scarce. Much of the fish come from the big lakes and permanent rivers, but very large catches are also taken at the end of seasonal floodings, as rivers like the Niger withdraw from extensive flood plains.

It is possible that, over the whole of Africa, inland catches might be as much as doubled. But much of this potential comes from stocks that are of little immediate economic interest, such as the small surface-water fish in Lake Tanganyika, or are too isolated for easy exploitation, such as those in the Okavango swamps of northern Botswana.

Most usable stocks are already being fully exploited. Much of the catch is marketed fresh, but there is a considerable trade in dried fish between African countries, sometimes over long distances. Much of the food value of these fish is lost due to insect infestation and other causes, before it reaches the consumer.

Humans have affected inland fish stocks in other ways besides overfishing. Large dams like the Kariba on the Zambezi on the Zambia/Zimbabwe border, and the Kainji in Nigeria on the River Niger, have produced huge lakes with substantial fish stocks. But there has also been significant loss in downstream fish production through changes in water regime, and the partial or complete eradication of strong seasonal flooding.

The transfer of various fish species from one body of water to another has had a patchy success. Introduction of small sardines into Lake Kariba and Lake Kivu on the Rwanda/Zaire border has led to some increases in catch. The introduction of the large Nile perch into Lake Kyoga in Uganda, from which it has spread into Lake Victoria, has seen a big change in the ecosystems. The perch have eaten the small species which could be caught in small nets and dried in the sun and which once fed the lakeside people. Many of the Nile perch, caught by wealthier people with big boats, are going to the seaside hotels on the Kenya coast. In Lake Kyoga their presence has resulted in a long-term dip in the total fish catch.

Diana East/Earthscan

Line fishing off Cape Verde. Some 70% of the marine catch off West Africa is taken by peasant fishermen in 108,000 such small boats and canoes. But peasant fishermen get less than 20% of the money governments spend on fisheries.

The Sahel droughts have directly affected fisheries. The floods of the Niger, Senegal and other rivers have stopped or been much reduced. Lake Chad is steadily drying up, and is now much smaller than a few decades ago. As a result the catches in Mali, though never known precisely, have dropped from around 100,000 tonnes in 1975 to only 33,000 tonnes in 1983. Catches in Chad have probably dropped by as much, though the government figures supplied to FAO have remained at 110,000 or 115,000 tonnes for the past 10 years.

Peasant fishermen

There are many parallels between the plight of the peasant fisherman and the peasant farmer. Both tend to get ignored while attention goes to large-scale, capital intensive producers. The operations of both are little studied and little understood. And in peasant fishing, as in peasant farming, the key role of women often goes unnoticed.

Peasant fishermen cannot replace modern trawlers because they cannot work as far out in deep and rough waters. But CECAF studies show that about 70% of the marine catch in the region is still taken by small-scale fishermen in about 108,000 canoes and small boats. Yet peasant fishermen get less than 20% of the funds allocated by governments to fisheries.

A study by the Canadian International Development Agency (CIDA) compared peasant fisheries to industrial fisheries. It found that peasant fisheries created employment, used modest local investment, exploited abundant resources, produced high-quality fresh fish for local markets, consumed little energy and caused little pollution. The industrial fisheries, on the other hand, created unemployment, relied on foreign investment, exploited poor offshore resources, produced fish for export, consumed much energy and caused substantial pollution.

But only Cameroon, Mauritania and Senegal have reserved any inshore areas specifically for canoe fishermen. CECAF programme leader George Everett called upon other governments to establish such zones — and to patrol them — and urged loan schemes to allow fishermen to purchase canoes, nets and motors. (He also recommended that the fishing communities be studied before changes were introduced.)

Given the expense and often the scarcity of petrol in many West African countries, fishermen often have trouble getting their outboard-motor canoes off the beach. CECAF has been helping fishermen switch — in some cases to switch back — to sail in Guinea Bissau, Sierra Leone, Equatorial Guinea and Cameroon. Meanwhile, FAO is looking at the possibilities of installing diesel engines to replace outboard motors in the big fishing canoes, or pirogues, of Senegal.

Women and fish

Women may be even more important to African small-scale fishing than they are to African small-scale farming. Few women actually go out in boats, but they take complete charge of processing, transporting and marketing the catch once it is landed. In Ghana and Togo, of approximately 100,000 people involved in shore-based fishing, 95,000 are women. [161] And because they handle the money — and perhaps also because male fishermen worldwide tend to be poor at managing money — women own most of the fishing boats and gear in West Africa.

Many peasant fisheries 'development' schemes have ignored women, and have quickly failed as a result. Ghana tried to establish a fish processing industry along the Cape Coast based on a male entrepreneur distribution system. It collapsed.

Diana East/Earthscan

Landing the catch on Santiago Island, Cape Verde. Men do the fishing in Africa, but women do most of the fisheries work after that: cleaning, curing, carrying and marketing.

But women virtually saved the peasant fishing industry in Ghana when the flat, leathery, bony and bitter-tasting triggerfish began to dominate catches. The women tried with no success various ways of curing the fish: salting, sun-drying and smoking. Finally they developed a quick-gutting and brining system, along with techniques for skinning and packing the fish.

> *Today brined, sun-dried triggerfish are sold through much of central Ghana, providing a cheap source of local protein, and the curing techniques are spreading to neighbouring nations.*

Chapter 8

Apartheid: institutionalised bankruptcy

"Apartheid is a killer and by far the most
dangerous on the South African veld.
It kills not only people but their land and
environment as well."
UN Environment Programme report on
apartheid and the environment, 1982

South Africa's system of apartheid is usually written about — quite rightly — in terms of its gross violations of human rights and human dignity. But apartheid also violates the physical environment of South Africa, and the environmental bankruptcy it is creating will ensure misery for generations to come — no matter when and how black South Africans take their rightful place in the country they already call Azania.

Racism is a problem in virtually every nation which contains more than one race. Most nations have tried to limit racial discrimination by establishing institutions and laws to give equal rights and opportunities to all races, even though in Africa there are few countries where tribal minorities are not in practice discriminated against in some way.

The key difference in South Africa is that it has established and violently maintains institutions and laws to limit the rights and opportunities of some races — the black, 'coloured' and Asian majority — to the benefit of one race — the white minority.

Environmental deterioration is also a problem in all nations. Most nations establish, or at least claim to be working toward, institutions and laws to control and limit such destructive land-use practices as overgrazing, overcultivation and deforestation. South Africa, through the larger apartheid strategy by which it attempts to apportion land along racial lines, institutionalises precisely these same destructive land-use practices: overgrazing, overcultivation and deforestation.

Apartheid holds up to the rest of Africa a peculiar distorting mirror. Previous chapters have shown how environmental bankruptcy affecting much of Africa stems from over-population, from agricultural labour shortages caused by a

Stan Winer/Christian Aid

KwaZulu landscape. Apartheid institutionalises not only racism, but also rural poverty and malnutrition, overgrazing, overcultivation and deforestation.

flight of labour to the cities, from farmers' inability to get reasonable returns for their agricultural labour, from a lack of political power in rural areas.

Apartheid systematically institutionalises all of these problems.

This section is not meant to be a complete study of apartheid — of its workings in the 'white' cities, mines and factories. It is meant to show the links between the moral bankruptcy of apartheid and the environmental bankruptcy of the 'homelands' or bantustans.

The system's surreal statistics

In 1980, South Africa had a population of 28.8 million: 20.9 million blacks (72.5%), 4.5 million whites (15.6%), 2.6 million coloureds (9%) and 821,000 Indians (2.9%). (More recent census results for the 'Republic of South Africa' excluded the people of 'homelands' to which the government claims to have granted a form of independence, an independence recognised by no other nation.)

The government has marked off 10 'homeland' areas which were supposed vaguely to coincide with 'original' tribal areas of various tribes. Four of these — Transkei, Bophuthatswana, Venda and Ciskei — are officially labelled as 'independent republics', and the remaining six as 'national states', with 'full internal self-government'. On a national level, this division of the land gives 86.3% of the total surface area to 15.6% of the population (white), and 13.7% of the land to 72.5% of the population (black). (This 13.7%, designated by the Native Land Act of 1913 and the Native Trust and Land Act of 1936 is a maximum amount; the full area has not yet been made available to blacks.)

Only about 10 million blacks live in their 'proper' homeland; 9.5 million live in 'white South Africa' and about 500,000 live on the 'wrong' homeland, suggesting that the government intends to one day move them to get the system right. A 1978 survey found that 57% of black men living in white areas had been born there and not in a 'homeland', that 80% had neither children nor parents living in a 'homeland' and that 60% had not visited a 'homeland' during the year before the survey was made.

Adding to the surrealism of the system is the fact that many of the homelands have been divided into separate blocks so as to exclude all industrial centres of any size, most transport lines, most mineral resources and all but the smallest white settlements. None has a port. Bophuthatswana, with a population of over 866,000, is divided into six separate blocks, one of them almost 320 km from its nearest neighbouring block.

"In short, it is difficult to see these areas, even after consolidation, as providing a satisfactory territorial basis for economically viable and truly independent nation states", according to Professor David Smith of Queen Mary College, London. [162] (The statistics above come from Professor Smith's report, which takes most of its figures from official South African sources.)

Given that South Africa's economy depends on cheap black labour for its survival, it is highly unlikely that the government intends for these 'homelands' at any time to become economically viable and truly independent nation states. Therein lies the inherent contradiction at the end of any discussion of apartheid. If 'separate development' works, if the 'homelands' do develop as economically independent nations, the South African economy will cease to function. Even the most glowing official descriptions of 'separate development' stop short of economic independence for the homelands.

"Once the process of emancipation has reached its conclusion, the Republic of South Africa will become a sovereign independent White nation state which will be associated with its Black neighbour states on the basis of political independence and economic interdependence". (From the government-sponsored Bantu Investment Corporation, quoted in Smith.)

It is small wonder that South Africa is institutionalising rural poverty and environmental collapse in the 'homelands'.

Origins and motives

Much of the thinking behind the agricultural development of the 'homelands' goes back to the 1955 report of the 'Commission for the Socio-Economic Development of the Bantu Areas within the Union of South Africa' under the chairmanship of Professor F.R. Tomlinson (and better known as the Tomlinson Commission). According to Dr Anthony Lemon of Oxford University (UK), [163] the commission believed that sound agriculture implied relatively large landholdings (44 hectare average) and heavy capital investment. This was reckoned to give each farming family practising mixed farming 120 Rand per year cash income. This figuring meant that the 'homelands' could support 1.8 million people.

As Lemon points out, "it has since been widely recognised that the incomes allowed by Tomlinson were unrealistically low if an African peasantry was to be held on the land". In 1956, the average income of an African in industry was 300 Rand. More important, there are 10.5 million people in the 'homelands' today — or about six times as many as the Tomlinson Commission reckoned the land could have supported *if* it had received the high investments Tomlinson recommended to support intensive farming.

But the government rejected the investment expenditures recommended by Tomlinson, and has forbidden white entrepreneurship and investment in the 'homelands'. So agriculture has not had the investment, especially in irrigation and cash crops, which the Tomlinson Commission envisaged in its scheme, and blacks have lacked the capital to industrialise the homelands to absorb excess labour.

The limiting of white investment in the 'homelands' does not apply to mines. The borders of the 'homelands' were drawn up to exclude mineral wealth, but since then deposits of coal, asbestos, chrome, platinum, iron and vanadium have been found. (The Ciskei and the Transkei, in fact, appear to be the only large 'homelands' without minerals.) In 1973, out of 112 prospecting licences issued for mineral exploration in the 'homelands', 110 went to white-controlled companies or individuals and two went to blacks. All of the 89 mining leases issued during that year went to whites or white-controlled companies. Almost none of the profits stay in the 'homelands'.

There are several hidden — or at least not officially discussed — benefits

Stan Winer/Christian Aid

At home on a 'homeland' (KwaZulu). Note erosion in background. The 'homelands' are not designed to develop separately. If they became truly independent and self-sufficient, the economy of the Republic of South Africa would collapse.

of the 'homeland' system for white South Africa. Employers of 'migrant' blacks from these 'independent' states need only pay wages high enough to cover the immediate needs of the worker. Employers need not consider any 'social security' payments, as social security is theoretically the responsibility of the 'homelands'. They need not consider support of the worker's wider family, as these theoretically have sources of income in the 'homelands'. The 'homelands' are not only a labour reserve, but "a mechanism for the supression of black living standards and a dumping ground for people the capitalist sector has no use for", according to British geographers John Soussan and Phil O'Keefe. [164] Parcelling blacks out among fragmented parcels of remote land also decreases the number of disaffected blacks within 'white South Africa', and makes the organisation of political dissent more difficult.

'Homeland' land

It is not true to say, as some anti-apartheid writers do, that the homelands contain the worst land in South Africa. One report published by the South

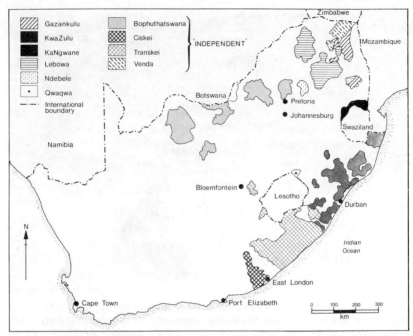

The 'homelands' of South Africa.

African Institute of Race Relations, for example, described these lands both as economically marginal land too mountainous, dry and remote to be productive and, in the same report, as the finest well-watered lands of the nation. [165]

Lemon quotes the official yearbook of South Africa (1974) to show that if 500 mm rainfall is taken as the minimum necessary for rainfed crops, then 76% of the 'homelands' are suited for this form of agriculture, as opposed to 35% of South Africa as a whole.

After all, Africans originally settled the general areas of the 'homelands' because it was some of the best land around. But they were mostly cattle herding people, interested in land for its ability to support livestock rather than crops, and requiring large areas of land, as do all pastoralists. Land squeezes began for them even before these areas became 'Bantu reserves', long before they became 'homelands'. There have been many decades of overgrazing.

"Confined as they were on the limited land areas of the reserves, the Bantus, who are essentially a pastoral people for whom cattle constitute a resource to be accumulated rather than consumed, greatly over-stocked the available pastures, thus exposing the soil to natural forces of erosion, which are particularly serious in the areas with heavy rainfall and mountainous terrain along the east where most of the densely populated reserves, e.g. the Ciskei, are located", according to a UN Environment Programme report on apartheid. [166]

Lemon describes the physical attributes of some of the larger, more populous 'homelands' as follows:

* *Bophuthatswana* — the largest in terms of area but an annual rainfall of only 254-500 mm; Malpopo and Limpopo riverbeds are dry ditches for much of the year; mostly cattle-grazing land; only 6.7% of land arable.
* *KwaZulu* — most populous and best watered; good irrigation potential from rivers; in many areas rainfall episodic and unreliable; large areas of rocky outcrops, shallow soils and steep hills; in parts soil erosion has reached the point where rehabilitation may be impossible; 14.8% arable land.
* *Transkei* — probably best agricultural potential; well-watered; several perennial rivers; extensive soil erosion; 18.7% arable land (highest figure after the tiny Qwaqwa 'homeland', with 20.3% arable land).
* *Ciskei* — variable climate; high fluctuation in perennial rivers; severe drought not uncommon; extensive soil erosion; 13.4% arable.
* *Lebowa* — rainfall from 350 mm in west to 710 mm in north; good irrigation potential; 15.9% arable.

Population, jobs and wages

As in the rural areas of other African nations, lack of opportunity in the 'homelands' encourages men to seek work in the cities. In 1980, the actual population density of the 'homelands' was 66 people per square kilometre, higher than any other continental African country except Rwanda. About 9.5 million blacks live permanently in 'white South Africa'. Another 1.3 million were listed in 1981 as 'migrant labour' from the 'homelands' to the 'white' areas. This figure had risen rapidly through the 1970s as the population of the 'homelands' increased by 66%, while the black population as a whole grew by 30%, according to Soussan.

In 1981, some 745,500 blacks were commuting across 'homeland frontiers' to work, most of them coming from Bophuthatswana into Pretoria and from KwaZulu into Durban. Daily commuters may travel up to 140 km every day, and weekly commuters up to 1,000 km each weekend, according to Soussan and O'Keefe. The income from migrant workers and frontier commuters represents about 70% of gross 'homeland' income, according to Smith.

Despite the fact that the South African economy depends on black labour, the black population is growing far more rapidly than the ailing South African economy can absorb it. Given present population growth rates, blacks will make up 77.6% of South Africa's total population in the year 2000 (72.5% in 1980), while whites will comprise 11.8% (15.6% in 1980). Yet given the current rate of growth in jobs, four out of every 10 blacks could be unemployed by the year 2000 — a situation which will put tremendous pressure on both South African cities and on life in the 'homelands'.

The growth of settlements in the homelands is dictated by the needs of the frontier commuters. Just as the capitals of colonial Africa tended to be sited on the edges of the colonies for accessibility to the controlling nations, unplanned 'cities' are springing up on the edges of the 'homelands' for ease of access to jobs across the frontiers. Officially, there are 800,000 'squatters' in the 'homelands'.

Professor J.B. Daniel of Rhodes University indicated how hard these factors make it to deal seriously with the 'homelands' as developing states. "Ciskei is an area which has come into existence primarily as a result of political decisions taken by Whites with little or no consultation with the Blacks who occupy the territory. The Ciskei may be described as a semi-selfgoverning homeland, presently considering a form of political independence; a territory with its extent still to be determined; with 68% of its people beyond its borders; and a third of its revenue received in the form of aid. In many respects the Ciskei is an anachronism." [167]

Agriculture on the 'homelands'

The odd combination of 'over-population' and labour scarcity is affecting the 'homelands' much as it is affecting parts of the Sahel. During the droughts of the early 1980s the 'homelands' were particularly hard hit.

"Apartheid is a killer and by far the most dangerous on the South African veld", said UNEP. "It kills not only people but their land and environment as well."

"Black farmers in the bantustans have seen their yields decline over the years", wrote Soussan and O'Keefe in 1983. "The loss of land to the white minority meant that a greater population of Africans was confined to smaller areas. This enforced over-population took its toll on the land. Within a few decades many sectors of the bantustans have become overgrazed and eroded. The problems have been worsened by the absence of many men as migrant labourers. Without their labour, black farming communities could not maintain the terraces which help prevent erosion and could not clear the veld to enable more nutritious grasses to grow. Demands for taxes and the legislative enforcement of bride prices exacerbated the problems by greatly increasing needs for cash, ...adding

Nancy Durrell-McKenna/Christian Aid

Train station in Soweto. Blacks commuting out of the 'homelands' may travel up to 140 km every day, and weekly commuters may cover up to 1,000 km each weekend.

to the incentives for young men to enter the white economy as migrant labourers.''

Among the reasons for land deterioration in the 'homelands', the UNEP report noted, were ''the extremely poor soils, ...the uneconomically small size of farm holdings, which average two hectares per family, thus ruling out any significant degree of mechanisation, and the lack of capital for fertiliser and other essential farming inputs, including soil conservation measures''.

Lemon found that maize yields in Bophuthatswana, which were among the highest yields of the 'homelands', were less than one-seventh of white farmers' yields in the Transvaal Highveld. The rapid population growth of the 'homelands' during the 1970s doubtless meant a sharp decline in per capita food production. Lemon also noted that only 2% of 'homeland' arable land was under cash crops and only 22,000 hectares (1973) of two million arable hectares (1.1%) was irrigated, despite the large irrigation potential to which he had pointed. Today only about 10% of the agricultural production of the 'homelands' is marketed; last century, South Africa's black areas were self-sufficient in food and were able to market their surpluses.

In Ciskei about 2% of the land is suitable for irrigation, and much of the 'government's' agricultural development funds have been put into irrigation schemes growing cash crops — cotton, tobacco, and beans, cabbages and broccoli which are sent to Port Elizabeth for freezing. Less than 500 irrigated plots are planned, when the Ciskei turns out 8,000 new job seekers each year. Meanwhile, little is being done for dryland agriculture. Some 47% of Ciskei land is moderately or seriously eroded and 39% of its pastures overgrazed, according to the 1980 report of the government's Ciskei Commission.

The white farmer's edge

White farmers in South Africa have long benefited from state support, credit, access to markets, extension and education. They have built up a system of intensive agribusiness based on chemical fertilisers, pesticides and irrigation. Yet according to Soussan and O'Keefe, this approach is producing "an increasingly fragile, barren environment which can only be maintained by greater and greater levels of input".

"While white farmers have extensive holdings and ready access to loans and various state subsidies, the Africans in the homelands have had to fend for themselves without any real assistance from state or private financial institutions", reported UNEP.

"Indeed, it would appear that sometimes black farmers are deliberately neglected by the government in order to prove their incompetence", adds UNEP. "Thus, for example, some of the white farms in the marginal areas of Bophuthatswana ...which have been recently transferred to Africans as part of the 'homelands' consolidation process have quickly deteriorated, and are now becoming veritable dust bowls, owing to lack of adequate support from the state and private financial institutions which made it possible for their former white owners to succeed."

The recent droughts also struck the white farmers, forcing them to milk the land harder in an attempt to keep yields up and pay for inputs. South Africa has traditionally exported maize, but had its third successive poor crop in 1984, with virtually no exports. In fact, ports built to cope with exports had to be adapted to handle large imports. With white South African agriculture facing this sort of pressure, the government will be even less likely to provide 'agricultural aid' to the 'homelands'.

White farmers have also been abandoning the countryside for the city, and one researcher estimated that by 1981 there were up to two million blacks living on farms abandoned by white farmers. The farms would hardly have been abandoned if they were fertile and profitable. (It should not be assumed that all blacks live either in 'homelands' or in cities. Estimates using 1980 census figures reckoned that of the 46% of blacks living outside 'homelands', 20.6% lived in rural areas. The government has been providing financial and other incentives to coax white farmers to reclaim rural 'white' lands.)

The fruits of apartheid

Statistics on the status of blacks in South Africa are notoriously unavailable and unreliable. Blacks are thought to be grossly under-counted in censuses. But the fruits of the 'homelands' policy can be seen in some of the health statistics which are available.

Among whites, 13 infants die in their first year for every 1,000 live births. Smith notes that there is no such figure available for blacks because many births and deaths are not recorded, "but a figure well in excess of 100 per 1,000 live births is likely". Soussan and O'Keefe have culled the following figures from studies published in South African medical journals: infant mortality for settled urban blacks, 82 per 1,000; for 'illegal' or 'unsettled' urban blacks, 107; for 'migrant worker' families, 227; and for families permanently restricted to 'homelands', 282 per 1,000 live births.

If this latter figure reflects the case accurately throughout the 'homelands', then child mortality is much higher there than in the poor black African nations: Burkina Faso (210), Sierra Leone (206). The 1984 *World Population Data Sheet* gives South Africa as a whole an infant mortality rate of 95, higher than such nations as Kenya (86) and Botswana (82) and about the same as Uganda (96). Yet South Africa — based on per capita GNP, a meaningless figure in a nation which keeps 85% of the population poor to keep 15% wealthy — is much richer than those black African nations. South Africa has a per capita GNP of $2,670, compared to Uganda's $230.

Robert Coles, a child psychiatrist who has been conducting research in South Africa for 10 years, offers the following grim conclusion: "Black infant mortality is 190 per 1,000 live births... Life expectancy is 15 years less than for whites; and 55% of black deaths occur between the ages of one and four, compared to 7% among whites." [168]

Adult blacks are not healthy either. In 1979-80 there were 17 reported cases of tuberculosis (mainly a disease of poverty) per 100,000 of the white population (which doctors and hospitals were told about) — and 1,000 among blacks. Blacks have poor if any access to modern health care; there are 300 black doctors, a ratio of one per 90,000 (WHO considers one to 10,000 too low), and few black hospitals; entire black communities must make do without any medical assistance at all.

But it remains the children who bear the brunt of the system. In South Africa, a black child dies from malnutrition every 20 minutes — some 30,000 deaths each year, according to Soussan and O'Keefe, who warn that these are probably underestimates. Over 30% of all black children are malnourished; in the 'homelands', this figure rises to over 75%.

Given increased population pressure in the 'homelands', given the decreasing ability of the land to support these numbers due to accelerated environmental degradation, given government policies which keep development capital out of the 'homelands', hunger can only get worse, and that fairly rapidly.

An old white South African expression says of the blacks: "When they don't eat, we don't sleep", indicating the white fear of rebellion by hungry, angry blacks. Yet the whites are now locked by apartheid into a system which forces blacks, especially the women and children, to go hungry. This can only harden political resolve for self-rule among the black population. In the next chapter, the links between environmental bankruptcy and bloody conflict in other parts of Africa are examined. Nowhere are these links more obvious than in the legislated environmental bankruptcy of the South African 'homelands'.

Chapter 9

Conflict, refugees and the environment

"The next war in our region will be over the
waters of the Nile, not politics."
Butros Butros Ghali, Egyptian Minister of State
for Foreign Affairs, 1985

In 1985, Africa was a continent in turmoil. Ten million people had fled their homes, some into famine centres, some into cities, many across national boundaries.

Most of these were 'environmental refugees', people fleeing land that could no longer support them. Others had fled wars, civil wars and government repression. But the connections between the wars of Africa and the 'droughts' of Africa were so tangled that it was impossible to tell who was fleeing what for which reasons.

Civil wars were degrading the environment in Ethiopia, Sudan, Chad, Angola and Mozambique — or at least were making sustainable agricultural development impossible. But then environmental degradation also fuelled conflict and instability across Africa, so it was impossible to tell cause from effect. To what extent were Tigrayans fighting against the Ethiopian government because that government was overseeing their region's decline into bare hills and barren ground? The environmental degradation of much of Africa threatened to stir conflict in the continent for generations to come.

Africa's environmental refugee crisis played havoc with the standard legalistic definitions of 'refugees' — political or economic — which had guided the UN's response over the past four decades. The definitions and coping mechanisms were born in Europe around the time of World War Two, when people needed to be fed and kept warm and legally protected until they could go home. But many of Africa's refugees will not be going home. In 1984 the UN High Commissioner for Refugees (UNHCR) for the first year ever spent more than 50% of its annual programmes budgets in Africa on 'durable solutions', and expected to spend almost 60% in 1985. Instead of keeping refugees alive until they could go home, they were spending money to help refugees settle and begin to make livings where they were. The very word 'refugee', given its meanings under

Mike Goldwater/Earthscan

Eritrea. The 23-year-old war these women are training for is older than most of them. Countries at war — Ethiopia, Sudan, Chad, Angola, Mozambique — have few resources available for environmental protection or agricultural development. And environmental degradation plays its part in causing wars and social unrest.

international law, was no longer applicable. The UNHCR was speaking of 'externally displaced persons in a refugee-like situation' and its budget lines had odd titles like 'UNHCR special programme of emergency relief assistance to persons of concern to UNHCR in Eastern Sudan'.

Five of the six nations on the UN's list of countries most seriously affected by hunger were also wracked by civil war. Or to put it another way, every African nation suffering from civil war also suffered from 'drought'.

* In 1985, Ethiopian troops had been fighting to subdue Eritrea for over 22 years, and had been fighting against insurgents in Tigray for over nine years. The three areas most deeply affected by the drought were Eritrea, Tigray and Wollo. Northern Wollo remained 'insecure' to relief operations because of the possibility of the fighting spilling over from Tigray at any moment. Nearly 300,000 'returnee' refugees had entered the southeastern region of Hararge from Djibouti and Somalia.

* In April 1985, the 16-year-old government of President Jaafar Nimeiri was peacefully overthrown by Defence Minister Abdul Rahman Swareddahab. The coup followed riots in Khartoum after Nimeiri devalued the currency and slashed subsidies on petrol, bread and other staples. Sudanese troops were fighting against the Sudan People's Liberation Movement of the Christian and animist peoples of the south. More than one million refugees had entered the Sudan from highland Ethiopia and from Chad.

* In 1985, Chad remained a curious semi-partitioned state; the government of President Habre in the capital, rebel forces under Goukouny Oueddeye in the north, with the extreme north effectively annexed by Libya, and increasing rebel activity in the south from a faction known as the 'Codos' (Commandos rouges). Some 60,000 Chadians had fled into western Sudan (the Sudanese government put the figure at 120,000), 40,000 into the Central African Republic and 8,000 into Cameroon.

* In 1985, Mozambique was "now no more than the FRELIMO government in Maputo", said one relief worker there. Though an overstatement, the activities of the Mozambique National Resistance continued, despite the alleged cessation of South African backing, to disrupt agriculture, relief efforts and marketing and to displace people. There were 12,190 Mozambican refugees in camps in eastern Zimbabwe, but this was only about one-fourth to one-third of the Mozambicans seeking refuge in that country. (Five years previously, thousands of Zimbabwean refugees had left Mozambique to return home after their nation won independence.)

* In 1985 in Angola, the struggles of the MPLA government in Luanda continued much as it had since independence in 1975, with dissident UNITA forces controlling much of the south and a very small pocket of FNLA resistance in the far north. There were at least 25,000 Angolan refugees in Zaire's Shaba province. (In 1977-79, Angola had taken in Shaba refugees during the two wars in that province.)

Was the correlation between conflict and famine merely a coincidence? British geographer Phil O'Keefe maintains, somewhat ironically: "The only early warning system you need of famine is lists of which governments are spending disproportionate amounts of their GNP on military activities; look at Ethiopia, Sudan, Chad, Angola and Mozambique". The year 1984 saw massive amounts of grain shipped to Africa, but it was also the first year in history that the value of arms imported by Africa outstripped the value of imported grain.

Other nations bore out this correlation less dramatically. The Somali government of General Mohammed Siyad Barre faced increasing opposition from the Somali National Movement in the north, and the northern capital of Hargeisa was under a state of emergency for much of 1984. The Ethiopian-backed 'Somali Democratic Salvation Front' also remained active. In early 1984, Somalia was said to hold 700,000 refugees, though unofficial estimates were as high as double this. Yet during that year, Somalia received 70,000 more refugees.

Mauritania suffered a coup in December 1984 which gave the Military Committee for National Salvation a new leader in the form of Colonel Maaoya Sid'Ahmed Ould Taya. Mauritania had broken its neutrality in the western Sahara struggle, and the new government quickly returned to that neutral position.

Zimbabwe was riven by tribalism, the Shona aligned with the ruling ZANU party of Robert Mugabe and the Ndebele tied to the ZAPU opposition party of Joshua Nkomo. There were charges of scores of political assassinations among the Ndebele/ZAPU faction, and of mass killings in Matabeleland by the government's notorious North Korean-trained Fifth Brigade.

All these nations were also on the UN list of the 20 'drought afflicted' nations. The relationship between military conflict and drought/famine is complex. In Chapter Two we showed how drought is connected with misuse of the soil and with poor agricultural practices. Obviously a government fighting militarily for its life is going to put a fairly low priority on tree-planting, terracing and on sound agriculture in general. Its capacities will be devoted to war, not land reclamation.

Much has been written about how warfare damages the environment, not so much through the 'desertifying' activities of shells, bombs and tracked vehicles, but because war rules out care of the environment. Would the present famine in Ethiopia have been less severe if the government had devoted much more of its attention and resources to organising the peasants to plant trees? And if the government had not been spending more on military activities than it was earning on all of its exports (1981: military spending, $378 million; exports, $374 million)? One suspects so.

But war and environmental degradation are linked in both directions. War damages the environment; but environmental degradation can also add to the pressures from which conflict emerges. This is often less obvious in the open spaces of Africa, more obvious in a densely-settled nation like El Salvador where the erosion of topsoils caused by inequitable landholding offers peasants yet another motive to take up arms against the government.

Ethiopia in the early 1970s was, like El Salvador, a nation characterised by landlords holding huge estates. The owners under-farmed them to keep grain prices high, while peasant plots averaged less than a hectare each. Most peasants lived in feudal conditions similar to those of European peasants during the Middle Ages.

When the 'Sahel' drought struck Ethiopia in 1972-73, these peasants died in their scores of thousands. Emperor Haile Selassie attempted to cover up the seriousness of the drought, and was overthrown in a military coup in 1974. The coup brought in the Provisional Military Government of Socialist Ethiopia — the Derg — and led to the bizarre swop in which the United States switched its support from Ethiopia to Somalia and the Soviet Union dropped Somalia to back Ethiopia. The coup may have been caused by the famine, but the famine was not caused by the drought. According to a report commissioned by the post-revolutionary Ethiopian Relief and Rehabilitation Commission: "The primary cause of the famine was not a drought of unprecedented severity, but a combination of long-continued bad land-use and steadily increased human and stock populations over decades, rendering a greater number of people vulnerable when drought struck".

So the big power tension in the Horn of Africa, considered of global strategic importance because of its 'gateway' position as regards the Suez Canal and Middle Eastern oil, has a part of its origin in Ethiopian highland landholding patterns and erosion rates.

The Sudanese government's practice of renting out rich Nile-side estates to 'suitcase farmers' while giving little support to peasant dryland agriculture was described in Chapter Four. These agricultural policies had two effects: they left the over 16 million Sudanese who live on the land vulnerable to drought, and they earned very little foreign income.

In early 1985, Nimeiri's government was pressured by a US withdrawal of aid, by the International Monetary Fund and other creditors to make the usual sort of belt-tightening reforms. The Sudanese pound was devalued from 1.3 to 2.5 to the dollar, and bread and petrol prices were raised by about 60%. In riots in late March, some 2,600 people were arrested and several killed. Early demonstrations were staged by the poor and hungry, whom the government described as 'vagabonds', but the demonstrations were joined by doctors, teachers, bankers and judges — who were angry at finally being forced to pay heavily for government policies which had in fact favoured them and other urban elites at the expense of the small farmers.

The governor of Khartoum province, Babiker Ali al-Thom, told journalists that 690,000 'alien elements' from remote areas had sneaked into the capital. He said the government was carrying out plans to rid Khartoum of the unemployed and others who joined the riots and to remove 'squatters' as "a prelude to deporting them to production sites in various provinces".

In fact, those 'alien elements' were mostly Sudanese drought victims from the west, and there were precious few 'production sites' in the provinces to which to send them. But the fact that dryland farmers have always been regarded as 'alien elements' by Khartoum officials was one of the root causes of the Sudan crisis which led the army to overthrow Nimeiri in April 1985.

Sean Sprague/Earthscan

Mathare Valley shanty town, Nairobi, is being filled by farmers whose land has eroded from beneath them, or who have otherwise been forced in from the countryside. It is "a pool of hopelessness" — and of anger.

Traditionally, African populations have reacted to political pressure, and to land pressure, by moving on. But Africa's open spaces are closing up, due to population growth and misuse of the land (two other phenomena which are at the same time causes and effects, one of another). Environmental degradation is bound to fuel more riots, wars and revolutions in the future. Many future coup d'états may in fact be coup d'environnements.

The Nairobi riots

One of the best examples of the way environmental pressure can cause bloodshed was provided by an abortive coup and a riot which was small by international media standards.

In May 1982, the UN Environment Programme celebrated in Nairobi the 10th anniversary of the UN Conference on the Human Environment in Stockholm, and Kenyan president Daniel arap Moi was among the heads of state who spoke on environmental issues. During the meeting, visiting journalists had been touring villages just north of the capital, witnessing the severe gulley erosion resulting from farms having been divided into smaller and smaller parcels among offspring and then over-farmed. Many reporters had also visited Nairobi's shanty towns. Landlessness is growing in Kenya, and more people were estimated to be landless in the early 1980s (890,000) than at Independence (500,000). Many of these landless have little option but to build a shanty near Nairobi and seek work.

But Moi's speech ignored these nearby environmental problems. He concentrated instead on the 'threat to the world environment' posed by nuclear weapons. Many of those listening thought at the time that Moi's own government was much more immediately threatened by erosion and the world's fastest growing population rate than by nuclear war.

In August of that same year, air force officers launched an ill-organised and unsuccessful coup. But they did manage to take over the radio station briefly and announce the fall of the government. The shanty towns erupted into rioting and looting. Officially, 160 people were killed — though unofficial estimates were much higher, with some reports of hundreds of bodies in the streets. "The peripheral slums of Nairobi from which people demonstrated their anger in 1982 are ...a pool of hopelessness", wrote Randall Baker of the University of East Anglia (UK). "Soil erosion and urban crime, in these circumstances, are related phenomena with the same underlying cause." [169]

Environmental refugees

There were said to be 10 million refugees in the world in 1984. But in 1984, there were 10 million uprooted people in Africa, people seeking refuge in relief camps or with relatives or in cities. Even before the famines, the number of refugees in Africa was increasing. However, according to a statement by the UN High Commissioner for Refugees in 1984, there has been no significant political event in Africa in the past two years to explain the major new refugee movements.

The vast majority were environmental rather than war refugees. Interviews in the famine camps along the eastern Sudanese border with those coming in from Tigray and Eritrea suggest most fled hunger rather than fighting. One man held up a handful of sand and let it flow between his fingers. "This is why we left. Our land is like this", he said. His face showed he was not unaware that his place of refuge in the Sudan was just as much a wasteland.

Chad had similarly faced 17 years of internal fighting and a decade of drought, but the level of fighting appeared low and localised in late 1984. Most of the thousands who crossed into Sudan and the thousands who went in to the Central African Republic did so in search of food.

Further west, people were also fleeing both into cities and across borders. French geographer Jean Copans had estimated that in the 1968-73 drought, 20% of the Mauritanian population moved into towns and into abject poverty, while 5% of the Mali population did the same. In the current drought, Mauritanians were moving both into towns and into Mali. "Whole villages are being abandoned. [Mauritanian nomads] have literally swamped Mali with their cattle, in search of water and pastures," while others were moving as far as Burkina Faso and Niger, none of which countries could afford to host them, according to *Africa* magazine. In Mali itself, the northern population also flocked into towns. This movement, coupled with serious inflation and an increase in government austerity, put pressure on one of the region's most well-entrenched governments. "Contrary to predictions, however, there were still no overt protests against [President Moussa] Traore's 17-year-old military regime", wrote Kaye Whiteman. [170]

The Ivory Coast gets the bulk of Sahelian international refugees, both those escaping rural poverty and those seeking opportunities in this relatively prosperous nation. There are an estimated two million recent immigrants into the Ivory Coast, according to Howard French, writing in the *International Herald Tribune,* an influx eased both by that nation's 'open door' immigration policy and the strong cross-border links which the northern Mande people have with Mali, and the Senoufo with Burkina Faso. Yet there has been a recent resurgence of anti-foreign sentiment, which makes foreigners fear that they may be forced out of the country under whatever government follows that of 79-year-old President Houphouet-Boigny.

Many of the people flocking from Africa's countryside into the cities even in years of normal rainfall are also environmental refugees, fleeing an environment of poverty, drawn by hope of food and jobs in the cities.

Not all make for shanties in the capital. It is a widely held misapprehension that Africa's biggest cities are growing fastest. In Tanzania, between the census years of 1967 and 1978, the 'intermediate' cities of Mbeya, Shinyanga, Mwanza, Tabora and Singida all had higher growth rates than Dar es Salaam, according to David Satterthwaite of the International Institute for Environment and Development.

But the economic livelihoods of these smaller, 'regional' cities depend more than the capitals on a healthy agricultural life in the surrounding countryside. These cities need farmers with money to buy goods and services, and they need farmers producing surpluses to be processed and packed and shipped from them. The development of these intermediate cities would take a large burden off the capitals, but they cannot develop in the face of declining production and purchasing power in the countryside.

Nomads versus farmers... and versus nomads

Desertification of the grasslands increases the conflict both between competing groups of pastoralists and between pastoralists and settled farmers. These clashes are rarely reported in the press, as they rarely happen near big cities or in front of outside observers. It is a chronic rather than acute form of conflict.

African pastoralists have raided one another since long before recorded history. Much of it was almost ritualistic, part of young men's rites of passage into adulthood. Also, as control of grazing land has long been the key to survival, pastoralists traditionally go armed and use force when their grazing lands are threatened. The Tuareg of the southern edges of the Sahara were as much a military tribe as a pastoral tribe, and controlled a military empire. But such conflicts have become less ritualistic and bloodier, as land has become scarcer and herders switched from swords and spears to rifles.

During the droughts of the early 1970s, Nyamatong cattle herders moved out of the Omo River region in southwest Ethiopia and seized the lands of the Toposa herders in Sudan. The Toposa moved onto the lands of the Larim people and into a valley of northern Kenya used by several pastoralist tribes. The reverberations of this movement are still going on across the various national borders.

Ethiopia plans to move large numbers of Amharic people down from the central highlands into the southwest. Ethiopia has a long history of moving Amharic people into the lands of non-Amharic peoples. But this scheme threatens to stir the resentment of the cattle-herding Oromo people, and may further increase tension in the Ethiopia/Sudan/Kenya border region.

About four-fifths of Kenya is semi-arid or arid. The population of this area has doubled over the past 20 years, and will double again over the next 20, according to experts at the Integrated Project on Arid Lands (IPAL) run by UNESCO east of Lake Turkana. Jostling among tribes — as well as plain banditry — has resulted in a relentless series of armed clashes which kill or wound about one herder per week on the project. The IPAL staff were seriously considering hiring armed guards to protect the men taking cattle and camels to distant pasture. There were reports that large numbers of ethnic Somali were killed by Kenyan security forces in northeastern Kenya in 1984, according to William Tordoff of the University of Manchester (UK). [171] Desertification is partly responsible for the increased raiding, but the raiding encourages herders to keep too

Mark Edwards/Earthscan

Afar nomad camp, Ethiopian Central Highlands. Many nomads carry guns the way Englishmen carry umbrellas. During the drought they have used them more and more to enforce claims on scarce grazing land.

many animals on 'safe' pastures, a practice which accelerates desertification.

Also in 1984, the Kenyan government had to restrict movement of people and animals along the border with Uganda between West Pokot and Karamoja to stop cattle rustling. And the government admitted that 57 Degodia tribesmen had been killed when police and army units intervened to stop inter-tribal feuding over grazing and water rights.

The Karamojong of northeast Uganda are a traditionally fierce cattle-herding and cattle-raiding people, who are estimated to have lost 300,000 of their 450,000-strong herds to drought and increased raiding in the first five years of the 1980s. Some of the Karamojong became armed with automatic rifles when one clan raided a government armoury in the confusion at the end of the Amin era, and this upset the balance of power among the clans. In 1984, a group raided cattle on the farm of the just deceased Ugandan Army chief of staff, and killed about 100 local militiamen pursuing them, according to Glenn Frankel of the *Washington Post*. But the Kenyan and Ugandan governments launched a dual operation against the raiders when they fled into Kenya, using Kenyan helicopters and Ugandan soldiers. Somewhere between several dozen and several hundred Karamojong were killed, many of their cattle slaughtered by the military and their fields left unplanted. The Karamojong in early 1985 existed amid a barren landscape on emergency relief from abroad.

The pastoralist-versus-farmer problem is an under-reported part of the political violence of Zimbabwe. The Shona, associated with the ruling ZANU party, are mainly farmers. The government resettlement programme to get black Africans off the old 'reserve' lands and onto some of the land owned by white farmers is said by the Ndebele people (who tend to rely more on cattle and are aligned with opposition ZAPU) to be geared to farmers rather than herders. Disparity between the peoples has been heightened by the fact that the pastures of Matabeleland in the south have been particularly hard hit by drought. In September 1982, some 90,000 Shona squatted on farmland in the eastern province of Manicaland; the government left them alone. When the rains in the south failed in October 1982, many Ndebele went looking for fresh pasture, and thousands squatted on farms bought for resettlement. The result, according to newspaper reports, was attacks on the squatters by the army's 'Fifth Brigade'.

It is not, however, as if herders always invade the farmlands. In fact, across Africa there are probably more cases of farmers slowly infiltrating traditional grazing land — land that was traditionally reserved for grazing precisely because it could not support annual crops. Studies of changing land-use patterns in Kenya have found far more examples of spontaneous settlement by farmers of grazing land, than of changes in the opposite direction.

Shared rivers

"The next war in our region will be over the waters of the Nile, not politics", said Butros Butros Ghali, Egypt's Minister of State for Foreign Affairs, in 1985. "Washington doesn't take this seriously because everything for the United States relates to Israel, oil and the Middle East. They're aware of the African dimension of our problem, but it's simply not a priority."

The 'African dimension' refers to the fact that the Nile is an 'African' river with a basin touching on nine other African nations: Ethiopia, Sudan, Kenya, Uganda, Central African Republic, Zaire, Rwanda, Burundi and Tanzania. Egypt's population of 47 million will grow to 66 million by the year 2000, and the Nile is virtually its only source of water. The Aswan High Dam and the Nile have saved Egypt during the present drought, but have also made Egyptians more than normally aware of how vulnerable they are. If the drought were to continue for another year, electricity generation would be affected. After two more drought years there would be no electricity generation and one-third of the area now irrigated would be waterless, according to Joyce Starr, director of the Near East programme at the Center for Strategic and International Studies in Washington, who interviewed Mr Butros Ghali. [172]

All nine of these 'upstream' nations are ambitious to increase their own land under irrigation, and these nations have been slow to enter into water use planning negotiations with Egypt. In fact, Ethiopia fired an ominous diplomatic warning shot on the issue when its delegate to the 1977 UN World Water Conference stressed "the sovereign right of any riparian state, in the absence of an international agreement, to proceed unilaterally with the development of water resources within its territory".

Egypt may in the near future need the water stored in Lake Tana on the Blue Nile in Ethiopia and in the small lakes of the Victoria Nile in Uganda. Using this water might involve letting the levels of these lakes rise, flooding lake-side villages. Neither Ethiopia nor Uganda has water development treaties with Egypt. Ethiopia is already contemplating irrigation projects which would reduce the discharge of the Blue Nile into Sudan and Egypt by four billion cubic metres a year. The fertile valleys of Ethiopia's Blue Nile are a target resettlement area for drought victims of the highlands.

Egypt has also made clear its position on protecting its access to Nile waters. Former president Anwar Sadat said in 1978: "We depend upon the Nile 100% in our life. We shall never hesitate, because it is a matter of life or death".

It would be ironic if Africa's next war were over the Nile, for it is Africa's only international river which has been internationally managed, and that fairly successfully. (Africa has 12 river basins shared by four or more countries; these rivers are governed by 34 treaties. Europe has four rivers shared by four or more countries, governed by 175 treaties.) Egypt and the Sudan have managed to share out the water for decades. In fact, Egypt would be in a better position if work had not been disrupted on the joint Sudan-Egypt 240-kilometre Jonglei Canal to provide the river with an evaporation-saving short-cut through the world's biggest swamp. But separatists in southern Sudan stopped work on the canal in 1984 when they kidnapped (and later released) the canal's chief engineer, claiming that Egypt planned to steal Sudan's water.

Egypt has also been wasteful of Nile water, allowing anyone who can afford the price of a pump to take any amount of water desired out of the national canal system, according to Starr. But the strength of Egyptian feelings about 'water rights' cannot be overstated. Starr quotes Butros Ghali: "Our problem cannot be solved according to classical formulas. Without political imagination, Egypt will become a new Bangladesh fraught with drought and famine — but with one difference. This Bangladesh will be on the beaches of the Mediterranean — only one half-hour by jet from the rich people of the North."

The other great rivers of Africa have created little tension because they have been little used. The Zaire (Congo) is entirely contained within humid tropics (and mostly in one country, Zaire, though its basin includes nine), and will not be much used for irrigation. Other African rivers have much to offer irrigation and have basins in several countries: Niger (10 states), Zambezi (8), Volta (6). Lake Chad's basin includes six nations and is important to the agricultural futures of Chad and Niger especially. But recently major river basin development schemes have got under way on the Senegal, Niger, Gambia and Casamance (Senegal), all with USAID funding. Senegal, Mali and Mauritania are all involved in Senegal River development.

Major development schemes are not a prerequisite to riverine conflict. The Beli River, which flows along the borders of Mali and Burkina Faso, became the subject of a dispute between the two countries in 1974, after settlers began to move permanently into the Dori district and use the pools there, traditionally watering holes used by herders moving between the two nations. Both states laid claim to the region, and in 1974 there were armed clashes. In 1975, Mali claimed that Burkina Faso forces had raided two villages and killed two people. But by 1979, the two nations began to fear that their dispute was attracting the interest of outside powers, and set up a joint commission which resolved the matter.

Not all of Africa's water disputes are about above-ground water. There is a vast sandstone aquifer which stretches beneath Libya, Egypt, Chad and Sudan. In 1977, international management of this aquifer was among the transnational projects recommended by the UN Conference on Desertification; even then, there were fears for both the quality and quantity of the water. Pumping and other discharges were by 1976 seven times higher than the estimated recharge rate, and the practice of pumping salt water down oil wells to increase yields was increasing the salinity of the aquifer.

There has never been any 'international management', and in August 1984, Libya's Colonel Gadafy pressed a button in Sarir, eastern Libya, which sent a 'river' of water streaming out of the sand towards the Mediterranean, to water crops along the way. This $11 billion artificial river involves a 1,900-km pipeline and has aroused fears in Egypt and the Sudan that it will rapidly deplete the aquifer. In his speech inaugurating the project, Gadafy called Egypt a she-goat enslaved by Israel and the United States, and urged the Sudanese to overthrow their government.

Inter-state tension, refugees, revolutions, civil wars, urban riots and rural unrest are clearly connected to environmental bankruptcy; to deforestation and overgrazing, to soil erosion and landlessness, to drought and hunger and migration to the cities as well as to disputed rivers and underground aquifers. The UN, foreign aid agencies and African governments must tackle the environmental causes of violence if they wish to move towards a peaceful continent.

Chapter 10

Aid, development and the future

"In a sense, we're talking about a kind of
recolonisation — about sending smart white boys
in to tell them how to run their countries."
— unnamed Northern aid official,
Financial Times 3 April, 1985

The thousands of speeches made about Africa in early 1985 all had in common two phrases: 'no quick fix' and 'no easy answers'. The common realisation that Africa was in for a long troubled future stemmed not only from the depth of the crisis under discussion, but from the common understanding that there do not exist any 'models of development' which can be applied to Africa.

"We have to realise that, from the time when our still young nations attained independence, Africa has been searching for a model of development", said Niger President Seyni Kountché. "Extrapolations from the experience of other countries, or direct transplants, are often seized on because they seem to provide easy answers. In either case, an essential factor is neglected: the traditions and customs, so powerful in Africa, on which we have forged our civilisation."

Previous African development models appear to have failed dismally — even tragically, given two major famines in little more than a decade. But these models are clung to, partly because there is little better at hand, often because they match the adherents' ideologies, and finally because it can always be argued that they were never given a proper chance.

The 'take-off' model of the late-1960s held that if enough money could be pumped into key sectors of a given economy, the entire economy would be accelerated to such a speed that development would take off. Both events and countless academic studies have shown this to be a naive assumption. But today Northern governments committed to free market approaches are still seeking 'growth areas' into which to pump aid.

The 'import substitution/primary exports' model has also been found wanting and has "more or less run its course", according to economist

John Loxley at the University of Manitoba (Canada). [173] This theory argues that African states will export commodities such as coffee or copper, and use the money to develop industry to manufacture products which at present they import. But in practice, African industries have tended to rely on imports rather than produce substitutes for imports, and the commodity exports have fared badly in the world marketplace.

Africans, especially the poor, seem to have been poorly served by all ideologies. "From the point of view of basic needs, ideologically speaking, Marxist, Capitalist, Socialist and mixed economic models in Africa have suffered broadly the same defects, experienced the same failures, and have misfired in moving the mass of their people forward in much the same way", said Brian Walker, president of the International Institute for Environment and Development. "The poor of Tanzania, Kenya, Angola or of South Africa face approximately the same bleak, uncompromising future. The African poverty trap, in a word, treats competing doctrinaire ideologies with much the same contempt."

Organisations which presumed to advise Africa in the past have now become more hesitant. As recently as 1981, the World Bank was optimistic enough to speak of 'accelerated development' in Africa, and its report by that name made export crop production the key to African prosperity. By 1984, the Bank was willing to settle for 'sustained development', and its report by that name offered advice along the lines of 'belt-tightening' policy reforms in government activities and expenditure, and improvements in government and financial institutions. It called for governments and donors to support 'basic programmes' in population control, education and training, agricultural technologies, health and environmental management.

The World Bank plays an odd role in Africa, and indeed in the world. It disperses public funds on projects, but it does not publicly evaluate those projects. It does not evaluate them at all until they are 'complete', and then makes the evaluation public only if the recipient nations agree. Few African nations favour such public judgements. So the World Bank, funded by taxpayers' money from many countries, but overwhelmingly from the US and other western states, is far less open to outside criticism and evaluation than most national aid agencies.

The Bank, among all its public analyses of the African crisis, has not analysed its own role in that crisis. The Bank has "advised countries to diversify agricultural production without adequately forecasting the decline in prices that would inevitably follow widespread acceptance of that advice", according to Loxley. "Thus, as the output of tea and tobacco has increased significantly over the past 10 years stimulated by IBRD/IDA (the World Bank and its soft-loan affiliate, the International Development Agency) programmes, world prices have in consequence fallen." Loxley goes on to point out the inconsistencies of the 'accelerated development' report, prepared under the supervision of Elliot Berg:

> "It projects that world prices of five out of nine of Africa's major food exports are likely to decline in the 1980s even before implementation of its proposals for promoting agricultural exports, and while it admits that Africa's 'dependence on exports of slowly growing primary products is a disadvantage', it then glibly asserts that 'exports can be diversified' and that 'Africa's share of world trade in most commodities could be increased with relatively small effects in prices'."

Loxley finds that the Bank has actively participated in creating an industrial structure in Africa which is highly dependent on imported inputs and on scarce technical and managerial skills, and in advising African nations on agricultural planning and crop pricing. But he cannot find any evaluation by the Bank of its own record in these areas.

African organisations have done no better at finding realistic ways forward. In 1981 the Organisation of African Unity published the 'Lagos Plan of Action for the Economic Development of Africa 1980-2000'. It stressed increased investment in food production and improvement in marketing and support services. In industry, it called for more processing of raw materials and the establishment of capital goods industries. It proclaimed the 1980s 'Industrial Development Decade in Africa'. It called for closer economic and investment links between African nations to make Africa less reliant on the world economy. But it was a horribly general statement: no details, no ways and means.

The political and economic scholars of African development stress not solutions but the gaps in their knowledge. The unofficial markets in which so much of Africa's trade takes place have been little studied; the effects of price incentives on crop production are not understood. The actual workings of African government agencies have not been analysed. Scholars continue to argue over whether capitalism has had a profound or a superficial effect on rural economies, and over whether Africa suffers from too much or too little integration into the world economy.

Officials are becoming surprisingly humble in their admission of their own and their organisations' ignorance. In the words of World Bank senior vice president Ernest Stern: "We have not always designed our projects to fit the agro-climatic conditions of Africa and the social, cultural and political frameworks of African countries. This is evidenced by the percentage of poorly performing projects in the agricultural portfolio and by the fact that we, and everyone else, are still unclear about what can be done in agriculture in Africa."

Mark Edwards/Earthscan

Afar nomads, their cattle killed by drought, Ethiopian Highlands. If Northern aid is to be aimed more toward 'growth areas' and private enterprise, how will such people be helped?

Conditionality and aid

At precisely the same time that agency officials and academics are admitting their own ignorance, there is a growing insistence on tying long-term development aid to sweeping political changes recommended by donors. It is called conditionality, and it is unprecedented.

"In a sense, we are talking about a kind of recolonisation — about sending smart white boys in to tell them how to run their countries", said one unnamed Northern aid official, quoted in *The Financial Times* of London. And the newspaper found that "increasing numbers of African governments are being forced by desperate economic hardships to swallow their pride and accept the ex-colonialists' prescriptions. Some are even embracing new policies with gusto, apparently convinced that the white man's medicine can be adapted and Africanised to serve their countries' needs."

New policies are obviously required, and an OAU heads of government meeting in early 1985 acknowledged the need for domestic reform. UN and World Bank experts spoke of a "growing professional consensus as to what needs to be done". The called-for reforms were a broad package: cutting government expenditures, especially on personnel and on food subsidies; cutting out parastatals; more reliance on private enterprise; devaluation of over-valued currencies; better government accounting.

The previous chapter described how in 1985 Sudan devalued its currency and let bread and petrol prices rise by 60%, and the coup which followed the reforms. In 1984, Zaire's President Mobutu Sese Seko devalued his nation's almost worthless currency by 500%, cut government spending, liberalised trade, removed price controls and increased prices paid to farmers. Prices rose quickly, but the government managed to hold inflation at 30% a year. The government was not threatened, but then Mobutu rules by what Amnesty International has described as "a significant incidence of brutality, extortion and harassment of the population by law enforcement officers". The police states of Africa may have an easier time living with the 'new consensus' than the more democratic regimes. Zaire and the Sudan also had an advantage in their special client relationship with the United States, which has allotted half of its total aid for sub-Saharan Africa in 1985 to just five nations: Zaire, Sudan, Somalia, Kenya and Liberia.

There were two particularly worrying aspects to the new conditions — besides, of course, the somewhat spotted historical record of 'smart white boys' in Africa. First, private enterprise works relatively well in the North, where it is guided and directed by a huge body of law and tradition. Africa lacks these traditions, laws and enforcement ability. The private traders who buy the grain in the Sahel run perhaps the most efficient operation in the region. But their activities often leave farmers poor and hungry.

'Privatisation' is no more a magic answer for Africa than is socialism or communism.

It is equally clear that parastatals are inefficient. Maybe a new mix is needed and the mix will be got right. Looking at present trends, the World Bank [174] sees hope in the number of countries in which food prices paid to farmers have risen significantly (Mali, Niger, Liberia, Ivory Coast) and those which have eliminated parastatal control of food crop marketing (Sudan, Uganda, Zaire) and where government intervention in such marketing is being reduced (Zambia, Somalia, Senegal, Madagascar, Ivory Coast).

A second and perhaps more profound problem is that the idea of 'conditions' suggests a deal between donor and recipient nations, a quid pro quo. And there were worries that the donors would be unable or unwilling to keep up their side of the bargain.

The World Bank and UN agencies have a certain amount of carrot-and-stick leverage with African governments. But they have none with the donor governments from which the aid must ultimately flow, according to David Ward of the London-based World Development Movement. "The danger, therefore, is that African governments will swallow the bitter pill of domestic reform whilst the donors continue to give relatively diminishing volumes of aid in the old traditional, poorly coordinated and inappropriate manner."

African leaders may draw their own lessons from Nimeiri's fate. The United States froze aid in late 1984 to force him to undertake reforms. He did. In April he flew to Washington, where President Reagan praised the "difficult steps" he had taken, and where a US official described him as "a good friend of the United States who continues to have our support". While he was away, he was toppled in a coup; the United States quickly recognised the new government. The episode will not encourage other leaders to follow Nimeiri's 'difficult steps'.

It was not so much that the donors' good will was in doubt, but in the middle of the African famine, it was becoming obvious that there would be new constraints on aid in the future, certainly on the sort of 'basic programmes' needed — more research into smallholders and their food crops; family planning and health; environmental protection and restoration; and more appropriate education and training.

Aid after the drought

The 'constraints' come in several different forms. First, the public sector belt-tightening recommended by the Bank itself requires a great deal of aid. The 'structural adjustment' of governments and economies must be paid for. Large proportions of the aid asked for in recent Bank consultative group meetings for Ghana, Senegal, Zambia and Madagascar were for these sorts of 'adjustments'.

Second, relief of the drought/famine crisis was consuming a great deal of aid in the form of emergency relief. This was saving lives, but taking both money and effort away from development aid. World Bank officials privately admit that the crisis is having a disastrous effect on many of its women-oriented, health and environment programmes. In early 1985, the UN was trying to raise $1.6 billion worth of food, medicine and equipment just to tide Africa over until the next harvest.

Third, Africa's longer-term crisis is reflected both in falling production and declines in the 'features of modern society': transport, energy, hospitals, telecommunications. Much of the aid going to Africa will have to rehabilitate this decrepit infrastructure. About half of the proposed International Development Agency (IDA) lending to Ghana in 1985 was for 'high-priority' rehabilitation projects in the urban, transport, energy and agricultural sectors. Zambia was busy rehabilitating railways, fertiliser production and its oil refinery. Madagascar was concerned about highway rehabilitation. The bulk of lending to Senegal over 1985-87 was to go to rehabilitation projects in water supply, irrigation, power and telecommunications. It is not that such rehabilitation is necessarily wrong or wasteful — and it is perhaps better than the usual emphasis on new projects — but it is not a direct help to the rural majorities. The Bank in early 1985 was trying to raise $2 billion for a special fund for Africa; much of this would go to structural adjustments and rehabilitation.

Fourth, donors such as the US and Britain are shifting away from basic programmes, toward goals more in line with their own government ideologies. Jack Shepherd, a specialist on US foreign policy at the Carnegie Endowment for International Peace, offers the following bleak assessment of US aid to Africa: cutbacks on multilateral aid in favour of bilateral aid which the US can control; an end to contributions to IDA; more military aid and more politically-motivated aid; and increased conditionality. The US is playing down multilateral aid in favour of its own 'Economics Policy Initiative' (EPI), which has offered $500 million over 1985-89 to those nations willing to undertake "more dynamic, growth-oriented economic policies". [175]

"Opponents of the EPI, some Africans among them, argue that its funding is inadequate and that its provisions violate nations' sovereignty. Economic policy that is acceptable to American Republicans may not be acceptable to Africans. Opponents also ask whether the United States will turn its back on hungry nations that cannot or don't wish to change their economic policies or that don't agree with our definition of internal economic reform."

Weighing in, southern Sudan. Development aid is going to 'restructure' African economies and governments, to rehabilitate decrepit railways and communications systems, to feed famine victims. Programmes for mothers and children are being cut.

Wendy Wallace/Earthscan

There is a project in Mali which demonstrates what happens when aid goes only to the 'dynamic and growth-oriented'. The Mali Sud II Rural Development Project — funded by the World Bank, the International Fund for Agricultural Development and the governments of Mali and France — is working with village associations to increase yields of cotton, millet, maize, legumes and livestock, by getting credit, seeds, fertilisers and pesticides to farmers. But about 500-600 of the 4,500 villages in the area are deemed 'too poor' to be eligible for credit or help. The villagers have little food, little money, and many are simply abandoning their homes. It is a bit like the 'triage' system used by army medics during World War One, when they separated the wounded into those who would improve without help, those who would benefit from treatment, and those beyond all help. Is this the new face of Northern development aid?

Finally, there is the problem of food aid. There has been a growing realisation over the past decade that Northern food surpluses given or sold at concessionary rates to African governments tend to depress local farm prices and drive local foods 'out of fashion' in cities. The food aid rarely reaches poor or hungry people. The European Community (in a working paper), the British House of Lords, the World Council of Churches and 75 Canadian development NGOs have all issued statements calling for the abolition of food aid except in emergencies.

Africa's food emergency has set back progress — if progress was being made — towards a more rational food aid system. With 30 million people in dire need of emergency food aid, debates over the efficacy of food aid in general appeared tactless at best. Food aid had already become 'institutionalised' in many African nations before the drought. But around the world, many nations can date their seemingly permanent dependence on such aid from an 'emergency'. Food aid to Haiti has not stopped since Hurricane Hazel in 1954; Guatemala has received much greater amounts of non-disaster food aid after its 1976 earthquake than before. The 1968-73 Sahel drought increased the 'regular' food aid to those countries.

It is impossible to predict what global politics, the world economy and changing fashions in development aid hold in store for Africa after the droughts and famines subside. But there is depressing evidence that there may be less, not more, aid available.

So just as the skills and resourcefulness of peasant farmers are beginning to be appreciated, just as it is becoming clear that Africa cannot develop without them, there may be less aid available to back up their efforts, less aid to get practical research applied to their real needs, less aid to protect their lands and to guard the health and nutrition of their families. Is there hope for Africa?

AFRICA: IS THERE HOPE?

"If the hungry could eat words,
Africa would recover."
— BBC Television commentary, 1985

It would be cynical to conclude that there *must* be hope for Africa, just because there is so little else available.

And it would be naive, in the face of the previous catalogue of resource over-use and misuse, leading inexorably towards continent-wide environmental bankruptcy, to conclude that there *must* be hope for Africa because of its vast resources of under-used soil and water and human ingenuity.

Disaster itself can often be a powerful force for political and economic change. But this effect is usually overstated, as governments and relief agencies talk of building a model society after a catastrophe, like a phoenix rising from the ashes. "Unfortunately, the record of success in producing the phoenix has not been overly noteworthy", writes US disaster consultant Frederick Cuny. [176] There were certainly no model societies established in the Sahel after the 1968-73 drought; and in fact the urban steel and concrete phoenix nests hastily constructed after that disaster left rural people even more vulnerable than before, as events later proved.

But there is a powerful feeling today that the depth of the continent's crisis must bring Africa and the rest of the world to its senses. "For nearly two decades, Africa's post-independence dream of political liberation has gradually been turning into a nightmare of economic collapse. The present famine may be that nightmare's cathartic climax — the impending mortal blow which suddenly jolts a whole continent awake", wrote British journalist Anatole Kaletsky. [177]

And despite the new emphasis on conditionality, it is hard to imagine Africa turning its affairs entirely over to foreign 'experts':

> "Now there is much less awe in Africa about the foreign expert who flits from one capital to another dispensing economic cures from his briefcase. More and more, Africans are learning that many of these people are no experts at all. Back in their home countries they would probably not be allowed to tinker with the workings of a small-scale farm, let alone an entire nation", wrote Hilary Ng'weno, editor in chief of the *Weekly Review,* Nairobi. [178]

It is also hard to imagine African farmers continuing to put up with economic and development strategies which rely on their labour while leaving them poor, hungry and desperately vulnerable to future droughts.

Some government leaders are promising change. According to Niger President Seyni Kountché: "Our conviction is that, despite the errors of the past, it is still possible for Africa to become self-sufficient in food production. But there is a prerequisite: Africa must conceive of an authentic development strategy which takes into account our experiences, our failures and our successes. We must abolish policies which marginalise the bulk of our labouring people."

Some aid agencies are promising change. In a searing confession of Swedish aid failures, of a sort that could not be imagined from any aid agency only a few years ago, Goesta Edgren, under-secretary of state in the Swedish Foreign Ministry responsible for development, said in early 1985: "As a result of an inappropriate choice of technology, the Swedish rural water programmes in Tanzania and Kenya have reached what must be termed a dead end. After 15 years of quite considerable investment in piped water and mechanised pumping equipment, hardly more than 10% of our installations are still in use."

He went on to explain how donors had made African agriculture more vulnerable to 'external shocks' by increasing reliance on sensitive hybrids which require more water and imported inputs. He found an increasing awareness among both donors and African policy-makers that "training, research and extension work must devote more attention to developing the management of multiple crop systems, using the small farm unit rather than one particular crop as the focus of analysis".

Some academics found cause for optimism even in the combination of disaster and inappropriate agriculture. "Governments stricken with falling revenues become more disposed to listen", wrote Jonathan Barker, a political scientist at the University of Toronto. "Partly under the impacts of new forms of agricultural organisation such as contract farming, collective villages, large, centrally managed schemes and partly as a result of the expectation of significant government services and price-setting action, peasant farmers are likely to become more involved in politics. Over the long run, that is the likelihood.... Africa's multiple crises mean that there is hope for change." [179]

Anthropologist Paul Richards goes so far as to hope that the budget deficits and external debt problems of agricultural ministries and governments might even force state institutions to move away from the big fixes toward closer cooperation with peasant farmers. [180] But this is all hope and promises. Is there any evidence that governments are willing to gamble on the abilities of small farmers? Are African farmers and villagers themselves forming the sorts of groups and organisations they will need to communicate both with their governments and among themselves?

The Zimbabwe model

In early 1985, Zimbabwe was still listed by the UN as one of 20 drought-stricken African countries in dire need of food aid. In fact, Zimbabwe farmers surprised even their own Ministry of Agriculture, which had predicted maize import needs of 600,000 tonnes, by producing enough to return Zimbabwe to its pre-Independence food self-sufficiency. There was even hope of exports.

It was not the 3,000 large-scale, commercial farmers (still mainly European) who were responsible for this surprise, but the peasants who farm more than 41% of the land. Their contribution to maize production had never exceeded 7.5%, but in 1984-85 it was expected to top 35%, a record, according to James Travers of *Southam News Services*.

Though surprised by the result, the government took full credit for it. Since Independence in 1980, maize collection depots have been moved from the railheads closer to the farmers to lower transport costs. The number of small farmers with access to credit has increased from 3,000 to nearly 70,000; maize prices have been kept high enough to give the farmers incentives to produce, and fertiliser prices have been kept down.

Before Independence, Zimbabwean smallholders on communal lands who had completed courses in practical training in basic agriculture were given Master Farmer certificates. These Master Farmers, now numbering about 100,000, formed themselves into self-help groups to coordinate problems with supplies and credit. The National Farmers' Association was formed in 1980 to coordinate this action nationally.

Zimbabwe had advantages. In the Sahel, people in the cities eat wheat and rice while rural people grow and eat millet and sorghum. In Zimbabwe, maize is both a food and a cash crop, in that it is still a staple among the urban dwellers.

Zimbabwe Minister of Agriculture Denis Norman maintains that "no agricultural industry anywhere in the world will operate unless one has back-up services and structures. You've got to have a fairly organised research system, extension services and financial arrangements. This is where we have the advantage over most Third World countries, and particularly the rest of Africa, because our systems work." (There were, of course, reports that the dominant Shona tribe was getting the best of these extension and credit services.)

Though the markets of Africa are little understood, Zimbabwe offers evidence that peasants can produce surpluses if offered incentives. But then that has already been proven by peasant success with cotton and palm products in West Africa and coffee in Kenya. Robert Bates of the California Institute of Technology even argues that African countries which have done relatively well agriculturally, such as Kenya and Ivory Coast, are those in which farmers have gained political power and used it to enact policies which favoured agriculture. [181]

If governments do try to work more effectively with the farmers, the farmers themselves will need to establish effective organisations to speak for them.

Getting organised

The Mossi Plateau of Burkina Faso is grossly overcultivated and, given current farming practices, over-populated. But its villages do have a tradition of farming cooperative work parties for big village projects. In 1977, Bernard Lédéa Ouedraogo forged this tradition into an organisation called 'Se Servir de la Saison Séche en Savanne et au Sahel' ('Making Use of the Dry Season in the Savanna and the Sahel'), or 'Six S's' for short.

By 1985, it had grown into 1,200 village groups, 700 in Burkina Faso,

Diana East/Earthscan

Santiago Island, Cape Verde. Women move huge stones to build hillside terraces, which must stand up to strong — but very rare — rains. The people of Cape Verde have struggled against drought since Independence in 1975.

300 in Senegal and 200 in Togo. The organisation runs 'schools' to teach village group leaders new techniques, and can provide finances based on word-of-mouth agreements and discussions. It also stops handing out funds if it finds they are being badly used. (It has received financial backing from West German and Swiss groups.) The larger organisation leaves it up to the local body to obtain the specific advice and materials it needs. Village groups under Six S's have undertaken small irrigation and drainage, erosion control and reforestation projects. They have established fruit tree nurseries and built village grain storage facilities. All efforts are based on the slogan 'development without destruction', and they use this guideline: 'The peasant: what he is, what he knows, how he lives and what he needs'.

Zimbabwe's ORAP (Organisation of Rural Associations for Progress) is an Ndebele association of local groups based in Bulawayo. Founded in 1981, by 1985 it numbered 300 groups and employed six field workers. It grew out of women's clubs, but now includes many men, this despite one woman member's opinion that "Men are always slow in taking things up. They want to wait and see. When there is progress, they come."

There has been progress and the men have come, to such an extent that one male member admitted that "at least now with ORAP men are not spending all their time in beer drinking; they are beginning to work". The work of ORAP groups is divided between service projects (water, sanitation, food storage) and income-generating projects (sewing, carpentry, building, baking), with training and education as well. Originally, groups were given $500 from a central fund for their activities, but to increase self-sufficiency, grants were stopped for income-generating activities and loans are made instead. ORAP is funded by international non-governmental organisations such as Oxfam, Oxfam-America and others.

The recent three-year drought in Matabeleland encouraged ORAP groups to try to figure out why they were so vulnerable. After much discussion, they blamed it on the switch from traditional, drought-resistant crops to hybrid maize, on their need to sell food for cash quickly after harvests, and on the lack of pest-free storage facilities. So ORAP is now basing its activities on a four-point strategy: switching back to traditional seeds and fertilisers; quantity and variety in food production; better village food storage; and improved water storage and irrigation. They have also organised transport to move food from where it is to where it is needed in drought areas. Typical group names in the Sindebele language reflect ORAP's self-help goals: *Siyazenzela* ('We're doing it ourselves') and *Vusanani* ('Support each other to get up'). [182]

In the Casamance area of Senegal, women's gardening groups have become a major force for development. Gardening is traditionally 'women's work' in this region, as is controlling the household accounts; the men raise cattle, clear land and work on cash crops. Government attempts to start gardening groups in the late 1960s failed amidst a glut of tomatoes and potatoes on the local markets. Women tried again during the drought of the early 1970s, in an attempt to earn money to buy grain. Famine relief aid wiped out these groups, as they became dependent on gift food. The current resurgence is a happy combination of village trends and government trends, according to Soon Young Yoon of UNICEF, which supplied some groups with simple tools.

The gardening, using water from wells, is work for the dry season when everyone is not out planting rice. Women pay a membership fee of $2.50 to give the groups a capital fund and another payment each year after produce is sold. The groups are part of a pyramid structure, from village to ward council to departmental council to regional council. This allows communication and coordination with the government body PIDAC (Integrated Project for Agricultural Development in Casamance), which provides some technical advice, seeds and insecticides. But locally the groups are democratic; their strength "is in their local support and there is little indication that they intend to surrender much power to any centralised organisation", writes Soon. But some groups, totalling 10,000 members have gathered under a 'federation' to run a truck to market the produce.

Groups vary from nine to 900 members, and men are joining, perhaps because there are no comparable men's cooperative groups which have so dramatically increased income. But despite male membership, the groups are still called 'women's gardening groups'. Organisation varies from village to village. In some, each woman has her own garden. In the village of Dianky, each woman works her own plot, but there is a communal two hectare plot, the profits of which go into a common fund. Women are assigned rows; if a woman does not tend her row, the other women say nothing, but put her empty basket on her row at harvest time. The meaning is clear: she either fills it from her row or from her own garden.

Women feel that these group gardening schemes have both raised income and improved family nutrition and health. But they also provide a structure by which local people can work with the government in coordinating rural development projects. They are linked with reforestation and other projects which both protect the environment and decrease women's work.

Senegal has the general reputation of backing big projects at the expense of peasant agriculture, but comparing the results of big Senegal River dam programmes with the relative success of some peasant initiatives, former President Leopold Senghor said: "It's the peasants, yet again, who've proved cleverer than anyone else. When you ask them what they want they don't hesitate for a second, they ask for small-scale projects. From time immemorial they've had to battle against drought. They need help, they don't need people to think for them." [183]

There are other examples of grassroots development around Africa, along with many examples of failures. Most of the 'farmers' cooperatives' in Africa have not worked well because they were formed by central governments, and have not been adapted to local conditions. They are too centralised, unwieldy and complex to be run by their own members. But some are better than others; most are more or less democratic, and all could become the basis for putting farmers in touch with governments. The same can be said for many farmers unions. The Union des Producteurs Agricoles in Tunisia effectively promotes farmers' interests and has considerable influence with the government. But such unions are dominated by the big farmers.

Despite their protestations, many governments are frightened of farmers' organisations which become too well-organised or self-reliant. Tanzania has promoted the slogan 'Education for Self-Reliance' — and then fairly consistently stamped out any organisations which became too self-reliant.

*In the 1960s, several villages in the Songea area of southwest
Tanzania founded the Ruvuma Development Association. The
RDA operated on the basis that small industry and agriculture
had to be developed side-by-side. By 1969, the RDA had
established a grain mill, a sawmill, a mechanical workshop and
had other equipment and vehicles. It was receiving funding and
actually hiring expatriates from abroad to give technical help. It
was a showplace visited twice by President Nyerere. But the
government became worried that the RDA was a form of
socialism which did not depend on a strong central party. In
1969 the government disbanded the RDA, confiscated its assets
(mills, equipment, etc) and dispersed the school's teachers to the
far corners of Tanzania.*

Africa provides many examples of government fear and even jealousy
of successful small farmer and village organisations. Any *non*-
governmental organisations tend to be seen as actually or potentially *anti*-
government. But any plan to bring peasants more actively into national
life will involve a certain amount of decentralisation of government power.
Contrariwise, when even the most centralised and authoritarian
governments 'organise the peasants' for any purpose, this usually has the
side-effect — often undesired by the government — of improving peasant
solidarity.

*The Ethiopian military regime set up the vast network of
Peasant Associations to control the rural populations better,
and to undertake major works like terracing and tree-planting.
Several government officials in Wollo Region told me in May
1984 how forceful and demanding representatives of these
associations were becoming on the subject of rural reforms. The
officials spoke with a combination of pride and trepidation.*

Getting aid in

Donors often stress the lack of 'absorptive capacity' for aid in African
countries: there are not enough skilled people to administer the money,
to turn the money into effective action, and to keep track of the results.

The World Bank suspects that donors often cannot get their aid
absorbed because they are pushing the wrong sort of aid — "most
obviously, support for new projects rather than for operating and
maintaining existing activities". [184] The Bank seemed to be implying
that if donors looked more carefully at what is going on rather than

F. Botts/FAO

Ethiopian 'Peasant Association' members digging erosion control terraces. Even when military regimes organise peasants for work, the organisation gives its members a voice with which to communicate with the government.

concentrating on what *they* want to do, they might find ways in which their aid can be absorbed.

> *The village-level, people-based, grassroots agricultural development organisations beginning to appear in Africa may provide new, effective, points of absorption for donors.*

The main bodies involved in this sort of aid are the non-governmental organisations (NGOs): both those based in Africa, such as Six S's and ORAP, and those development and relief oriented NGOs based in the North, such as Oxfam and CARE. The African crisis, while it has highlighted the failures of the government and multilateral aid agencies, has also highlighted the success of the NGO approach.

"Dollar for dollar, the small bodies help more people than the big donors", wrote *The Economist* (UK), in a leader article. "More lives are saved by paying to train a barefoot 'doctor' or to help meet the running

Mark Edwards/Earthscan

The CARE-sponsored windbreaks in Majia Valley, Niger. The project has increased cereal yields and provided fuelwood. CARE started it, the farmers took it over and are running it. Governments and Northern aid agencies have much to learn from the approach of the non-governmental organisations.

costs of a village health organisation than building — for all to see — a hospital.'' [185]

"If Africa is to feed itself it needs to break away from the structure of past development finance, so that funds, expertise and technology reach it on a human scale through non-government organisations working with the private sector either completely outside the framework of government or in collaboration with small local agencies'', wrote the *The Times* of London in a leader. [186]

In recounting the dismal failure of the UN's 1977 Plan of Action to halt desertification, just about the only good news which UNEP had to offer in 1984 was the success rate of the NGOs. Its report said:

"In some respects, NGOs have been the most effective agencies in the campaign against desertification. Dozens of them around the world have become involved, above all in field projects such as tree-planting and soil and water conservation... Their high record of success is related to the small-scale and local direction of their projects and the requirements for local community participation, as well as their flexibility in operation and their ability to learn from other mistakes. The dominance of field activities gives these actions an impact out of proportion to the money invested."

How have these NGO workers, often without farming experience themselves, often low on agricultural skills and on cash, succeeded when highly-paid, well-funded Northern consultants with PhDs in tropical agriculture have failed?

Most of the answers are found in UNEP's short description above: 'small-scale', 'local direction of projects', 'community participation', 'flexibility', 'ability to learn from their mistakes'. (That description also effectively points out the failings of the foreign agencies and national governments: overbearing, inflexible and unable to learn from their mistakes.)

The introduction to this book described how Northern government aid agencies, and African governments, fail to support the small farmers and to protect the land upon which they live because they cannot see immediate political or economic reasons for doing so. Helping people of little political power to grow crops of little economic value is not part of either's brief.

But most NGOs work not from political or economic but from humanitarian motivation. This starting point means that they also base their projects on community participation and on local direction, that they listen and learn. It is not so much because of their 'humanitarianism' that they succeed, but their humanitarianism guides them into certain methods of operation which happen to be the most effective ways of motivating people and spreading new ideas.

So agencies and governments, to avoid past errors, are either going to have to work more *through* NGOs and small local organisations, or work more *like* them — or maybe do both.

East African development scholar Goran Hyden doubts that governments can ever themselves reach the African small farmers, because any development of these small production systems must be more closely associated with the day-to-day operations of these systems than a government bureaucrat can ever be. But he adds:

"There is plenty of room to manoeuvre here provided government leaders realise and accept that much of what governments now do in a terribly unreliable and inefficient manner can be carried out much better by NGOs and voluntary community efforts (of education, health, marketing, etc). I believe an increasing number of people in prominent positions around Africa are beginning to accept this point, which isn't revolutionary, yet fundamental for the future of development on the continent." [187]

These ideals of 'local direction' and reliance on local knowledge and resources seem at first glance a poor foundation on which to base technical improvements. How can peasant agriculture improve if improvements must be based on peasant knowledge? In fact, projects based on, and building from local knowledge are the *only* way technical change can come about. Local farmers know enough to know what is better, to seize on it and use it. CARE brought windbreak technology to Niger's Majia Valley and explained it. The villagers took it and made it work.

But for this to happen more often, there will have to be a complete turn around in agricultural extension. Now the extension workers see themselves as selling outside solutions to peasants. They will have to come to see themselves as taking the peasants' problems to the researchers. They will have to become agents of the farmers, rather than of the governments.

"A priority for a number of early extension workers in the United States was to communicate farmers' needs to researchers, not to disseminate scientific findings to potential users", wrote Paul Richards. Such "extension workers were truly 'agents' (professionals charged with the representation of their clients' interests), rather than the 'educators', 'communicators', even 'salesmen', they have since become". [188]

Asking the right questions

Given the number of rural development projects which have failed to realise even a small part of their goals, how can one judge small projects which are likely to have any success? US geographer Ben Wisner has formulated a 'check list'; if the answers to his 10 questions are by and large positive, then the given project has the potential to do more good than harm: [189]

1. Is the project oriented toward the needs of the people to be involved in it?
2. Is the focus of the project on women or on a definable group of 'rural disadvantaged'?
3. Is the control local? (The answer here must almost always be a compromise, as donors will demand some control of how the money is used, and one always assumes a certain amount of potential or immediate national government control.)

4.   Does the project make use of local human resources: knowledge, skills, cultural values and forms of organisation?
5.   Is the project based on local material resources — materials, energy and land?
6.   Is the project sustainable in the long term? (The answer will depend, of course, on what is meant by the long term, but also on the answers to the previous five questions.)
7.   Is the external aid provided in sensibly limited amounts and in such a fashion that the people being helped do not become dependent on it?
8.   Are new group alliances being formed through the project? (Casamance and ORAP both formed new links between men and women for mutual support. Projects which increase differences between rich and poor or between, say, pastoralist and settled farmer — as in the case of many big dam projects — divide rather than bring together rural groups.)
9.   Is regional coordination sufficient, or is there potential conflict with large-scale regional plans? (Big 'food for work' programmes often overwhelm local projects bent on helping people to become food self-sufficient.)
10.   Finally, is the project resulting in a shift of power in favour of the disadvantaged group? (Wisner says "this effect is as rare as it is essential to long-term sustainability and reproducibility" of the project. Obviously, such a shift may conflict with vested interests of locally powerful people or even with the interests of the national government, as the Ruvuma Development Association did in Tanzania.)

This seems an awfully idealistic check-list. But experience has shown that where the answers to one or two of these questions are a resounding 'no', projects fail — or at least fail in terms of improving many people's lives over the long term. Swedish water aid was need-oriented, but the technology was based on foreign knowledge and skills (Question Four) and foreign materials (Question Five). The 'integrated rural projects' also failed because they were not based on local skills and knowledge. Even obviously need-oriented 'Mother-Child Health' programmes fail because mothers come to rely on the imported food provided, feeling that it is all their children need, and stop feeding local produce to the children. Studies around Africa have found that often children only gain weight when such aid *stops.*

Africa's hope lies in the well-being of its farmers. Its farmers would perhaps be better off if world commodity prices were higher, if oil were much cheaper, if interest rates were lower, if there were a New International Economic Order (assuming it were fairer than the present one). But in the meantime, perhaps the best the farmers themselves can hope for is to be a little less vulnerable to drought, to be able to produce a little more food, to be a little healthier. And their best hope for this lies in the spread across the continent of farmer-based rural development efforts, locally led, sustainable, spreadable.

The closing pages of this book examine a few such efforts in the areas of environmental degradation, to show that there is hope for Africa and that the hope lies largely in the hands of Africans — with a bit of the right sort of help from outside.

Soil and water

The terracing of Wollo Region and the water spreading projects in Tigray Region in Ethiopia show the sort of things that can be done when conditions are right, as does the anti-erosion work in Cape Verde.

Israel has developed a number of simple, cheap anti-desertification techniques in the Negev Desert. Oxfam workers took those to northern Burkina Faso in the early 1980s. All the techniques revolved around focusing scarce water on places where things had been planted. Scooping a shallow bowl in the soil only a few metres across, only a few centimetres deep, produces a 'micro-catchment' area. If a tree is planted in the middle of that bowl, the rainfall on the entire small area is directed to the base of the seedling.

Oxfam hoped to get a lot of fuelwood trees grown in this manner, and showed the villagers how. The villagers were impressed, but also planted trees for fodder, fruits and nuts, and suggested some shrubs good for fuelwood which the Oxfam foresters knew nothing about. Villagers then decided that food crops were even more important than trees, and began to adapt the water-focusing for millet crops.

The best technique for cereal crops was 'contour damming'. Building very long, very small ridges — only a few centimetres high — at right angles to the slope stops rainwater runoff and puts water into the soil. These are hardly 'dams'; they are low rows of soil and stones or even sticks and stalks. Such flimsy ridges are enough, because the land is really very flat, with very slight slopes. But this means that the contour lines cannot be detected by the human eye, and if dams do not go along the contours, water will be concentrated on one part of them and will break through.

Oxfam worker Peter Wright showed the villagers how to use a long piece of clear plastic hose filled with water as a surveying tool. The ends of the hose are secured to poles held upright. When the height of the water levels above the ground are equal, the two poles are on the same contour line. Farmers can mark the contour and run their ridge along it. Oxfam helped other farmers visit contour dam fields and talk to farmers using them. Word got around, and now the practice is widespread in northern Burkina Faso and is spreading in Mali. Its potential for the rest of the Sahel is immeasurable.

A completely different approach to getting the most from rainfall is developing in Mali, where farmers in 16 villages have been issued with single side band (SSB) radio receivers. The project itself is complicated. FAO and the Swiss government are helping fund the Regional Centre for Agrometeorology and Hydrology (AGRHYMET) in Niamey and the Mali government's own Telecommunications Administration Network. Despite this complexity, from the farmers point of view the project consisted of the SSB receivers and the chance to experiment for themselves. They were not told what to do.

AGRHYMET analysed local weather, humidity and soil moisture, and radioed advice on when to plant, weed, thin crops and root out diseased millet stalks. Moisture is crucial to all these operations. Weeding, for instance, should be done when soil is dry and not before a big rain. Farmers were asked to cultivate half of their fields traditionally and half following the radioed advice, which included not only weather advice but recommendations on seeds and fertiliser. As an *experiment,* the operation was a bit of a failure. The farmers all abandoned their traditional techniques when they saw the results of the areas grown by radioed advice, according to IUCN consultant Peter Freeman. [190] Here again is an innovative, relatively cheap partnership between new technology and small farmers which could help much of the Sahel, perhaps much of Africa.

Livestock and rangelands

Rangeland control projects have not worked in Africa because these controls have had little to do with the goals of the herders. Livestock projects will doubtless fail until governments adapt their goals to those of the herders, rather than expecting herders to tend their herds according to centralised government policies. The Oxfam herd rebuilding efforts in Niger (Chapter Five) worked because they were based on pastoralist customs. This experiment is being duplicated elsewhere in Africa, especially northern Kenya.

Sheep and goats are particular villains in the desertification story because they strip the ground so closely. The local Catholic diocese in Kitui District east of Nairobi is attacking both poverty and desertification by getting bigger and better sheep and goats to farmers. The diocese, with the help of Ministry of Agriculture extension workers and funding from international NGOs, runs a ranch holding about 800 high-quality animals. Farmers come in and take courses on livestock raising, management and marketing. Their farms are then visited by government experts attached to the diocese ranch, and the farmers get advice specific to them. They can buy studs — billy goats and rams — at reasonable prices or even, upon approval of their village council, at a subsidy which they are expected to repay. There is no other source of reasonably priced quality animals in the region. Most of the people in the area are subsistence farmers, and most of the area is suitable only for stock raising. So sheep and goats are key to subsisting.

Getting fatter, higher quality animals to the farmers can actually improve rangelands because such animals use food more efficiently. And they bring a better price at market, so farmers do not need vast herds of skin-and-bone animals; they can do better with fewer.

> But GASP (Goat and Sheep Project) is a trick in a way, because the diocese is also using it to attract farmers and farm families to literacy classes, women's groups and more general dryland agricultural workshops, where farmers can exchange ideas and listen to extension workers. GASP also tries to attract local extension workers in with the farmers, to improve cooperation and understanding between the two. It is estimated that GASP has reached, in one way or another, about 30,000-40,000 people. 'Development' is being carried in on the backs of fatter sheep and goats.

Trees

The tree-planting in Ethiopia's Wollo Region and CARE's windbreaks in Niger show that once *animateurs* (project leaders) and farmers are on the same wavelength about *why* trees should be planted and which trees should be planted, trees do get into the ground. Africa is far behind Asia in agro-forestry, because it is far behind Asia in intensified agriculture. But there are promising agro-forestry projects in Africa, the success or failure of which can only be judged after about another decade. However, areas like the Sahel still await research packages which show farmers how to use trees on their farms.

African NGOs have had more success than governments in planting trees. The Six S's group in the Sahel is planting trees, as are Kenyan NGOs such as the National Council of Women and the National Christian Council of Kenya, which have been working with the Forest Department to publicise tree-planting, purchase seedlings, develop nurseries and distribute seedlings throughout the community. These Kenyan groups have done so well that representatives of Senegal's CONGAD (NGO Council in Support of Development) have visited Kenya's NGOs to get advice. It may be that Africa's non-governmental organisations find it easier to cooperate than do Africa's governmental organisations.

Tanzania's tree-planting programme has been disappointing, but schoolchildren in Dodoma, Arusha and Singida regions have established tree plantations of up to 10 hectares in degraded areas. Such work is a neat way of teaching the children that Africa's roots do lie in Africa's soil.

The future

A few soil conservation projects here, a few goats and sheep there and a few trees dotted about the landscape. There are many other examples, but they do not add up to an impressive collection. If they did, Africa would not be in the state it is in now.

These few have been chosen to show what can be done, and even how things can be done. The African famine shows why things must no longer be done in the same old ways.

Northern governments wanting to help Africa can always find scope for their 'big fixes' — the biggest fix of all would be a rewriting of Africa's debt so it bears some relationship to any possibility of repayment. Africa may continue to need food relief for some time to come, and it certainly will need help in affording commercial energy for a longer time.

But the direction of Africa's agriculture can no longer come from Washington, Paris and London. It cannot even be run from Lagos, Harare and Nairobi. It must be run largely by the farmers, and by their organisations, with the help and support of the aid agencies and the governments and the research stations. This help and support must come in many small packages, rather than a few big dams and big plantations. And these packages must be delivered with great humility by people who work closely with the farmers, people who do not mind when the packages are shaken up and rearranged and perhaps used in a way that the deliverers had not quite intended.

It might all work. African governments might be ready to take advice from the North on how to handle their money and bureaucracies — the North is good at this. And they might be ready to take advice from farmers on how to get crops grown — the farmers are good at this. Or at least, they have proved better than anyone else.

Mark Edwards/Earthscan

Learning for the future — in the midst of famine. Korem relief camp, Wollo Region, Ethiopia.

This book has tried to describe the environmental bankruptcy which is spreading insidiously across Africa, which has made Africans so vulnerable to the terrible famines of 1984 and 1985, triggered by the drought. Bankrupt environments lead to bankrupt economies and bankrupt nations, and could ultimately lead to a bankrupt continent. But environmental bankruptcy is man-made, caused by unwise governments and foolish aid and development policies.

Environmental bankruptcy has not been caused by the stupid African peasant, as so many of these governments and aid agencies and their experts like to think. On the contrary, it is the African peasant who best understands how and why he or she has been forced to damage the environment on which they depend, and it is he or she who is the key to rebuilding their continent.

To ground Africa's future in an environmental reality which is maintainable, to produce development that is sustainable, will require a great deal of common sense: common sense from the South; common sense from the North. What is increasingly apparent in the African crisis is that common sense is a very rare gift.

References

1. World Bank, (1): *Toward Sustained Development in Sub-Saharan Africa: a Joint Program of Action,* Washington DC: World Bank, 1984.
2. Lamb, David: *The Africans,* London: The Bodley Head, 1982.
3. Dumont, René: *Stranglehold on Africa,* London: André Deutsch, 1983.
   4. Hobson, Sarah: 'Dam the river; damn the peasant', London: Earthscan, Earthscan feature, 29 March 1985.
5. Brown, Lester: *State of the World: 1985,* New York and London: W.W. Norton & Co., 1984.
6. World Bank, (1), op. cit.
7. The Independent Group on British Aid: *Aid is not enough: Britain and the world's poor,* London: Independent Group on British Aid, 1984.
8. Brown, L., op. cit.
9. Sen, Amartya: *Poverty and Famines: an Essay on Entitlement and Deprivation,* Oxford: Clarendon Press, 1981.
10. Cutler, Peter: 'Famine forecasting; prices and peasant behaviour in Northern Ethiopia', London: International Disasters Institute, in *Disasters,* 8/1/1984.
11. Nicholson, Sharon: *The Sahel: a climatic perspective,* Paris: CILSS/Club du Sahel, 1982.
12. Daniel, H.: *Man and Climatic Variability,* Geneva: World Meteorological Organisation, 1980.
13. Hare, K.: 'Recent climatic experiences in arid and semi-arid lands', Nairobi: United Nations Environmental Programme, in *Desertification Control Bulletin,* No. 10, May 1984.
14. Griffiths, I.: *An Atlas of African Affairs,* London and New York: Methuen, 1984.
15. World Bank, (1), op. cit.
16. Twose, Nigel, (1): *Cultivating Hunger,* Oxford: Oxfam, Oxfam Report, 1984.
17. Griffiths, I., op. cit.
18. Giffith-Jones, S. and Herbold Green, R.: 'African external debt and development: a review and analysis', unpublished study done for the African Center for Monetary Studies (Dakar, Senegal), and the UN Conference for Trade and Development (UNCTAD), 1984.
19. World Bank, (1), op. cit.
20. Overseas Development Institute: *Africa's economic crisis,* London: ODI, Briefing Document No. 2, September 1982.
21. Griffiths, I., op. cit.
22. Derman, W.: 'USAID in the Sahel: Development and Poverty', in Barker, Jonathan, ed.: *The Politics of Agriculture in Tropical Africa,* London and Beverly Hills: Sage Publications, 1984.
23. Freeman, L.: 'CIDA and agriculture in East and Central Africa', in Barker, J. op. cit.
24. Giffith-Jones, S. and Herbold Green, R., op. cit.
25. Giri, Jaques,: 'Retrospective de l'économie Sahelienne'. Paris: Club du Sahel, 1984.
26. Higgins, G.M., Kassam, A. K., Naiken, L., Fisher, G. and Shah, M.M.: *Potential*

228

   population supporting capacities of lands in the developing world, Rome: Food and Agriculture Organization, 1982.

27. Retel-Laurentin, Anne: 'Tackling the scourge of infertility',. London: International Planned Parenthood Federation, in *People,* Vol. 8, No. 1, 1981.

28. ODI: *Africa's food crisis,* London: ODI, Briefing Document No. 1, May 1984.

29. Dumont, R., op. cit.

30. Earthscan: *Urban land and shelter for the poor,* London: Earthscan, Briefing Document No. 35, April, 1983.

31. Lamb, David, op. cit.

32. O'Keefe, Phil: 'Women, food and the flight to the cities', London: Earthscan, Earthscan feature, 5 October 1984.

33. World Bank, (2): *World Development Report 1984,* Washington DC: World Bank, 1984.

34. Giri, J., op. cit.

35. World Bank, (2), op. cit.

36. Population Reference Bureau: '1984 World Population Data Sheet', Washington DC: Population Reference Bureau, 1984.

37. United Nations Children's Fund, (1): *The State of the World's Children: 1985,* London: Oxford University Press, 1985.

38. UNICEF, (2): *The State of the World's Children: 1984,* London: Oxford University Press, 1984.

39. UNICEF, (1), op. cit.

40. Scotney, N.: 'Water and the Community', in *World Health Forum,* Geneva: World Health Organization, Vol. 5, No. 3., 1984.

41. UNICEF, (1), op. cit.

42. World Bank, (3): *Health Sector Policy Paper,* Washington DC: World Bank, 1980.

43. UNICEF, (1), op. cit.

44. Banerji, Debabar: 'Primary health care: selective or comprehensive?', in *World Health Forum,* Geneva: WHO, Vol. 5, No. 4, 1984.

45. World Health Organization: *World Health Statistics Annual,* Geneva: WHO, 1980.

46. Evans, J.R. et. al.: 'Health Care in the Developing World', *New England Journal of Medicine,* Boston: Massachusetts Medical Society, Vol. 305, November 1981.

47. Evans, J.R., op. cit.

48. Klouda, A.: 'Prevention is more costly than cure: health problems for Tanzania, 1971-81', in Morley David., Rohde, J., and Williams, G., eds.: *Practising Health for All,* Oxford, New York and Toronto: Oxford University Press, 1983.

49. Klouda, A., op. cit.

50. Morrow, R., 'A primary health care strategy for Ghana', in Morley, D., et al., op. cit.

51. World Bank, (4), *Zimbabwe: Population, Health and Nutrition Sector Review,* Washington DC: World Bank, 1983, Report No. 4214 ZIM.

52. Dregne, H.E.: *Evaluation of the Implementation of the Plan of Action to Combat Desertification,* Nairobi: UNEP, 1983.

53. FAO: *How development strategies benefit the rural poor,* Rome: FAO, 1984.

54. Mabbutt, J.A.: *Assessment of the Status and Trends of Desertification,* Nairobi: UNEP, 1983.

55. Marnham, Patrick: *Fantastic Invasion,* London: Jonathan Cape, 1980.

56. Carton, B. and Karhausen, G.: *La Revue Nouvelle,* Brussels: Tome LXXXI, Numéro 1, 1985.

57. Griffths, I., op. cit.

58. Ruthenberg, Hans: *Farming Systems in the Tropics,* Oxford: Clarendon Press, 1980.

59. Tinker, Jon: 'Sudan challenges the sand dragon', London: *New Scientist,* Vol. 773, No. 1040, 1977.

60. Tinker, J., op. cit.

61. Commonwealth Secretariat: *The Debt Crisis and the World Economy,* London:

Commonwealth Secretariat, 1984.
62. Twose, N., (1), op. cit.
63. World Bank, (1), op. cit.
64. Brown, L., op. cit.
65. Grainger, Alan: *Desertification: how people make deserts, how people can stop and why they don't,* London: Earthscan, 1982.
66. Madeley, John: 'Sudan: famine in the breadbasket', London: Earthscan, Earthscan feature, 1 February 1985.
67. Freeman, L., in Barker, J., op. cit.
68. Dinham, Barbara and Hines, Colin, *Agribusiness in Africa,* London: Earth Resources Research, 1983.
69. Twose, N., (1), op. cit.
70. Dinham, B., and Hines, C., op. cit.
71. Pingali, P. and Binswanger H.: 'Population density and farming systems: the changing locus of innovations and technical change', Washington DC: World Bank, World Bank Discussion Paper (ARU24), 1984.
72. Chambers, Robert: Rural Development: Putting the Last First, London: Longman, 1983.
73. Twose, N., (1), op. cit.
74. Twose, Nigel, (2): 'Why the poor suffer most: drought in the Sahel', Oxford: Oxfam, Oxfam Report, 1984.
75. Vallely, P., London: *The Times,* 1 March 1985.
76. Economist Intelligence Unit: *World Commodity Outlook 1985,* London: EIU, 1985.
77. Grainger, A., op. cit.
78. Goldsmith, E. and Hildyard, N.: *The Social and Environmental Effects of Large Dams,* Wadebridge, UK: Wadebridge Ecological Centre, 1984.
79. Beadle, L C.: *The inland waters of tropical Africa,* London: Longman, 1974.
80. Griffiths, I., op. cit.
81. Ibid.
82. Dinham, B., and Hines, C., op. cit.
83. Goldsmith, E., and Hildyard, N., op. cit.
84. Sandford, S.: *Management of Pastoral Development in the Third World,* New York: John Wiley and Sons, 1983.
85. Sollad, A.: 'Livestock production in Mauritania', in *Food and Agriculture Sector Assessment,* Washington DC: Development Alternatives Inc., 1983.
86. Hurault, J.: 'Surpatrage et transformation du mileu physique', Paris: IGN, 1975.
87. Grainger, A., op. cit.
88. Lamb, Robert: 'How to make deserts', London: Earthscan, Earthscan Feature, 29 October 1982.
89. Lusigi, W.J., and Glaser, G.: 'Combating desertification and rehabilitating degraded production systems in Northern Kenya: the IPAL Project', in Di Castri et. al., eds.: *Ecology in Practice,* Vol. 1, (Ecosystem Management), Paris and Dublin: United Nations Educational, Scientific and Cultural Organisation and Tycooly Press, 1984.
90. Sandford, S., op. cit.
91. Sollad, A., op. cit.
92. Sandford, S., op. cit.
93. Grainger, A., op. cit.
94. Goldsmidt, W.: 'The failure of pastoral economic development programs in Africa', in Galaty, J.G., ed.: *The Future of Pastoral Peoples,* Ottawa: IDRC, 1981.
95. Oxby, Clare: *Group Ranches in Africa,* Rome: FAO, 1981.
96. Western, D.: 'The environment and ecology of pastoralists in arid savannahs', *Development and Change* 13: 183-211.
97. Linear, M., pers. com.
98. Blench, Roger: 'Pastoral labour and stock alienation in the sub-humid and arid zones

230

of West Africa', London: ODI, Pastoral Development Network, Paper 19e, 1985.
99. Dinham, B. and Hines, C., op. cit.
100. Malik, A.: Speech delivered at 3rd World National Parks Conference, Bali, Indonesia, 1982.
101. Myers, Norman: *Conversion of Tropical Moist Forests,* Washington DC: US National Academy of Sciences, 1980.
102. Lanley, J: *Tropical Forest Resources,* Rome: FAO Forestry Paper No. 30, 1982.
103. Caufield, C.: *Tropical Moist Forests,* London: Earthscan, 1982.
104. Sanchez, P.: *Properties and Management of Soils in the Tropics,* New York: John Wiley and Sons, 1976.
105. Grinnell, H.R.: 'A study of agrisilviculture potential in West Africa', Ottawa: IDRC, 1975.
106. Eckholm, Erik: *Down to Earth: Environment and Human Needs,* London: Pluto Press, and New York: W.W. Norton, 1982.
107. FAO: *Tropical Forest Resources,* Rome: FAO Forestry Paper No. 30, 1982.
108. Myers, N., op cit.
109. FAO: *Tropical Forest Resources Project.* Rome: FAO, 1981.
110. *New Scientist,* London: 21 February 1985.
111. Hopkins, Brian: *Forest and Savanna,* London: Heineman, 1974.
112. Foley, G., and Barnard, G.: *Farm and Community Forestry,* London: Earthscan, Earthscan Technical Report, 1984.
113. Foley, G.: 'Realities in rural energy planning', *Revue de l'energie,* Paris: les éditions techniques es economiques, August/September 1983.
114. Foley, G., and Barnard, G.: *Biomass Gasification for Developing Countries,* London: Earthscan, Earthscan Technical Report No. 1, 1983.
115. United States Agency for International Development: *Energy, Forestry & Natural Resources Activities in the Africa Region,* Washington DC: USAID, 1984.
116. Weber, F.: 'Review of CILSS Forestry Sector Programme', Washington DC: USAID, 1982.
117. Weber, F.: 'Village Woodlot Firewood Production', Dakar, Senegal: AFRICARE, 1981; Joint AFRICARE, USAID and PC Evaluation.
118. FAO: 'Projet d'Evaluation des Ressources Forestières Tropicales', in Les Ressources Forestièrs de l'Afrique Tropicale, Rome: FAO, 1981.
119. Hoskins, M.W.: 'Benefits foregone as a major issue for FLCD success', Washington DC: USAID; Paper proposed for the Community Forestry Seminar, Washington, 1982.
120. Skutch, M.: 'Why people don't plant trees: village case studies, Tanzania', Washington DC: Resources for the Future, 1983.
121. Leach, Melissa: pers. com., 1985.
122. FAO: 'Forestry and Rural Development', Rome: FAO Forestry Paper No 26., 1981.
123. Freeman, Peter: pers. com. 1985.
124. Foley, G., Moss, P., and Timberlake, L.: *Stoves and Trees,* London: Earthscan, 1984.
125. Griffiths, I., op. cit.
126. Special correspondent, 'Saving the soil for food', in *International Agricultural Development,* Reading, UK: J. Madeley, January/February 1985.
127. Chambers, R., op. cit.
128. Fuglesang, Andreas: 'The myth of people's ignorance', in *Development Dialogue,* Uppsala, Sweden: The Dag Hammarskjöld Foundation, 1984, 1-2.
129. Ruthenberg, H., op. cit.
130. Pingali, P., and Binswanger, H., op. cit.
131. Baker, R., 'Protecting the environment against the poor', *The Ecologist,* Vol. 14, No. 2.
132. Baker, R., op. cit.
133. Special correspondent, op. cit.

134. Sheridan, David: *Cropland or wasteland,* London: Earthscan, Earthscan Briefing Document No 38, 1984.
135. Giri, J., op. cit.
136. Hatch, J.K.: 'The Corn Farmers of Motupe: a Study of Traditional Farming Practices in Northern Coastal Peru', Madison, Wisconsin: Land Tenure Center, University of Wisconsin-Madison, USA, 1976.
137. Richards P.: *Indigenous Agricultural Revolution: ecology and food production in West Africa,* London: Hutchinson, 1985.
138. Chambers, R., op. cit.
139. Morris, J., and Gwyer, G.: 'UK experience with identifying and implementing poverty-related aid projects', in *Development Policy Review,* Vol. 1, 1983.
140. Andrew Coulson, quoting Raikes, P., in *Tanzania: a Political Economy,* Oxford: Clarendon Press, 1982.
141. World Bank, (5): *World Development Review,* 1982, Washington DC: World Bank, 1982.
142. International Labour Organization: 'Zambia, basic needs in an economy under pressure', Geneva: ILO, 1981.
143. Wisner, Ben, quoting P. Mbithi, pers. com. 1985.
144. Wisner, B., quoting S.B.O. Gutti, op. cit.
145. Wisner, B., quoting K.A. Staudt, op. cit.
146. World Bank, (5), op. cit.
147. World Bank, (1), op. cit.
148. Richards, P., op. cit.
149. Chambers, R., op. cit.
150. IDRC: *The IDRC Reports,* Ottawa: IDRC, Vol 13, No 4, 1985.
151. Richards, P., op. cit.
152. Chambers, R., op. cit.
153. Harjula, R.: 'Mirau and his practice: a study of the ethno-medicinal repertoire of a Tanzanian herbalist', London, Tri-Med, 1980.
154. Fleuret, A: 'The role of wild foliage plants in the diet: a case study from Lushoto, Tanzania', in *Ecology of Food and Nutrition,* Vol. 8, 1979.
155. Williams, Paula: pers. comm.
156. Prescott-Allen, Robert and Christine, *What's wildlife worth?,* London: Earthscan, 1983.
157. Prescott-Allen, R. and C., op. cit.
158. McCloskey, Michael, 1984. 'World Parks', *Sierra,* San Francisco: The Sierra Club, November-December, 1984.
159. Schoepf, B G.: 'Man and the Biosphere in Zaire', in Barker, J., op. cit.
160. Side, Dominique: 'How to stop poachers', London: Earthscan, Earthscan Feature, 10 September 1982.
161. Brownell, W. and Lopez, J.: *Development Forum,* Vol XII, No 5, June 1984.
162. Smith, D: 'Update: apartheid in South Africa', London: Queen Mary College, 1984.
163. Lemon, Anthony: *Apartheid: a Geography of Separation,* Farnborough, UK: Saxon House, 1976.
164. O'Keefe, P., and Soussan, J.: pers. comm., 1985.
165. Lemon, A., op. cit.
166. Boateng, E.A.: 'The environmental impacts of the apartheid and bantustan policies of South Africa', Nairobi: UNEP, 1981.
167. Daniel, J.B.McI.: 'Agricultural development in the Ciskei: review and assesment', in the *South African Geographical Journal,* 1980.
168. Coles, Robert: 'Blacks in South Africa need outside medical help', Paris: *International Herald Tribune,* 20 February, 1985.
169. Baker, R., op. cit.
170. Whiteman, K., in Hodson, H.V., ed.: *Annual Review,* London: Longman, 1984.

171. Tordoff, W., in Hodson, H.V., op. cit.
172. Starr, J. 'Egypt is African and its principal problem is water', Paris: *International Herald Tribune,* 22 February 1985.
173. Loxley, J.: 'The World Bank and the Model of Accumulation' in Barker, J., op. cit.
174. World Bank, (1), op. cit.
175. Shepherd, J.: 'When foreign aid fails', in *The Atlantic Monthly,* April 1985.
176. Cuny, F.: *Disasters and Development,* London: Oxford University Press, 1983.
177. Kaletsky, A., London: *Financial Times,* 3 April 1985.
178. Ng'weno, H., New York: *Newsweek,* 19 November 1984.
179. Barjer, J., in Barker, J., ed., op.cit.
180. Richards, P.: *Indigenous Agricultural Revolution: Ecology and Food Production in West Africa,* London: Hutchinson, 1985.
181. Bates, R. in Berry, S.S.: 'The food crisis and agrarian change in Africa', *African Studies Review,* 1980-81.
182. Chavunduka, D.M., et al.: 'The story of ORAP in Zimbabwe's Rural Development', manuscript, Bulawayo, Zimbabwe: Organisation of Rural Associations for Progress, 1985.
183. Dumont, R., op. cit.
184. World Bank, (1), op. cit.
185. *The Economist,* London: Vol 294, No. 7385, 16 March 1985.
186. *The Times,* London: 1 April 1985.
187. Hunter, G., ed.: 'Enlisting the Small Farmer: the Range of Requirements', London: ODI, 1982.
188. Richards, P., op cit.
189. Wisner, Ben, op. cit.
190. Freeman, Peter, 1985, pers. com.

Further Reading

BARKER, Jonathan ed. *The Politics of Agriculture in Tropical Africa.* London: Sage Publications, 1984.

BATES, Robert and Loftie, Michael eds. *Agricultural Development in Africa: issues of public policy.* New York: Praeger, 1980.

BLAIKIE, Piers. *The Political Economy of Soil Erosion in Developing Countries.* London: Longman, 1985.

CHAMBERS, Robert. *Rural Development: Putting the Poor First.* London: Longman, 1983.

DINHAM, Barbara and Hines, Colin. *Agribusiness in Africa.* London: Earth Resources Research, 1983.

ECKHOLM, Erik. *Down to Earth.* London: Pluto Press and New York: W.W. Norton, 1982.

GRAINGER, Alan. *Desertification: how people make deserts, how people can stop and why they don't.* London: Earthscan, 1982.

GRIFFITHS, Ieuan. *An Atlas of African Affairs.* London and New York: Methuen, 1984.

LIPTON, Michael. *Why Poor People Stay Poor: Urban Bias in World Development.* London: Temple Smith, 1977.

RICHARDS, Paul. *Indigenous Agricultural Revolution: Ecology and Food Production in West Africa.* London: Hutchinson, 1985.

RUTHENBERG, Hans. *Farming Systems in the Tropics.* Oxford: Clarendon Press, 1980.

SANDFORD, Stephen. *Management of Pastoral Development in the Third World.* New York: John Wiley and Sons, 1983.

TIMBERLAKE, Lloyd and Tinker, Jon. *Environment and Conflict: links between ecological decay, environmental bankruptcy and political and military instability.* London: Earthscan, Earthscan briefing document No. 40, 1984.

WIJKMAN, Anders and Timberlake, Lloyd. *Natural disasters: Acts of God or acts of Man?* London: Earthscan, 1984.

WORLD BANK. *Accelerated Development in Sub-Saharan Africa: an Agenda for Action.* Washington DC: World Bank, 1981.

WORLD BANK. *Toward Sustained Development in Sub-Saharan Africa: a Joint Program of Action.* Washington DC: World Bank, 1984.

EARTHSCAN PAPERBACKS

A Village in a Million by Sumi Krishna Chauhan   1979
£2.00/$5.00

Mud, mud — The potential of earth-based materials for Third World housing by Anil Agarwal   1981   £2.50/$5.50   Also in French & Spanish

Water, Sanitation, Health — for All? Prospects for the International Drinking Water Supply and Sanitation Decade, 1981- 90 by Anil Agarwal, James Kimondo, Gloria Moreno and Jon Tinker   1981
£3.00/$5.50

Carbon Dioxide, Climate and Man by John Gribbin   1981
£2.50/$5.50

Fuel Alcohol: Energy and Environment in a Hungry World by Bill Kovarik   1982   £3.00/$5.50

Stockholm Plus Ten: Promises, Promises? The decade since the 1972 UN Environment Conference by Robin Clarke and Lloyd Timberlake   1982   £3.00/$5.50

Tropical Moist Forests: The Resource, The People, The Threat by Catherine Caufield   1982   £3.00/$5.50   Also in French & Spanish

What's Wildlife Worth? by Robert and Christine ̄ ;cott-Allen   1982   £3.00/$5.50   Also in Spanish

Desertification — how people make deserts, how people can stop and why they don't by Alan Grainger   1982   £3.00/$5.50   Also in French

Gasifiers: fuel for siege economies by Gerald Foley, Geoffrey Barnard and Lloyd Timberlake   1983   £3.00/$5.50

Genes from the wild — using wild genetic resources for food and raw materials by Robert and Christine Prescott-Allen   1983
£3.00/$5.50

A million villages, a million Decades? The World Water and Sanitation Decade from two South Indian villages — Guruvarajapalayam and Vellakal by Sumi Krishna Chauhan and K. Gopalakrishnan   1983   £3.00/$5.50

Who puts the water in the taps? Community participation in Third World drinking water, sanitation and health by Sumi Krishna Chauhan with Zhang Bihua, K. Gopalakrishnan, Lala Rukh Hussain, Ajoa Yeboah-Afari and Francisco Leal   1984   £3.00/$5.50

Stoves and trees by Gerald Foley, Patricia Moss and Lloyd Timberlake   1984   £3.50/$5.50

Fuelwood: the energy crisis that won't go away by Erik Eckholm, Gerald Foley, Geoffrey Barnard and Lloyd Timberlake   1984   £3.50/$5.50

Natural disasters: Acts of God or acts of Man? Anders Wijkman and Lloyd Timberlake   1984   £3.50/$5.50

Urban land and shelter for the poor by Patrick McAuslan   1985   £3.50/$5.50

Desertification
— how people make deserts, how people can stop and why they don't

by Alan Grainger

A decade ago the Sahel drought killed thousands of people and millions of animals. It focused world attention on the dangers and causes of desertification, and moved the United Nations to call a major conference in 1977 which concluded that desertification was caused by human inaction.

But despite all efforts, the Sahel once again faces famine. Far too little is being done either there or in the 100 or so other nations affected by desertification to keep good land from going bad.

Desertification examines the reasons: overcultivation, overgrazing, deforestation and bad irrigation. The rich nations, the poor nations and the international agencies know what needs to be done to stop cropland and pastures turning to desert. Why, then, is so little being done?

Natural disasters: Acts of God or acts of Man?

by Anders Wijkman and Lloyd Timberlake

Droughts, famines, floods, hurricanes, earthquakes, volcanoes... six times more people died from natural disasters each year in the 1970s than in the 1960s. But the number of disasters went up by only 50%. Why?

This book shows how people are changing their environment to make it more *prone* to disasters, and to make themselves more *vulnerable*. It shows that disasters mainly hit poor people in poor countries. The average Japanese disaster kills 63 people. In Peru, the average death toll is 2,900. In 1974, a hurricane killed over 4,000 people in Honduras. A similar hurricane in Darwin, Australia, killed only 49.

Natural disasters: Acts of God or acts of Man? shows how misleading the term 'natural disaster' can be. Forces of nature such as earthquakes, cyclones and extreme variations in weather can trigger disasters, but in many Third World countries it is environmental degradation, poverty and rapid population growth which turn a natural hazard into a major disaster.

This book questions whether the rich nation's usual response to disaster — fast, short-lived emergency assistance —is any longer adequate. Today, most major disasters are 'development' gone wrong, development which puts millions of poor people on the margins of existence. Disaster relief alone is like bandaging a rapidly growing wound. The appropriate response must include an element of true development — development which reduces rather than increases vulnerability to disasters.

* * * To be published July 1985 * * *

Acid earth
The global threat of acid pollution

Acid rain is not just about rain. It comes as snow, fog, mist and on the wind in clouds of dust and gas. It leaves dead forests, sterile soils, polluted rivers, crop losses and corrodes buildings. It has become perhaps the most pressing and most universal environmental threat of the century.

Acid earth, the first global review of acid pollution, overturns the view that acid rain is solely a West European or North American phenomenon. It describes causes and effects, political implications and the controls already available. And country case studies from every continent confirm the alarming breadth of the crisis. Acid pollution is reported in Zambia and South Africa, Malaysia and Venezuela, and even in the Arctic, where haze has turned experimental filters black. Winds carry acid across borders, creating international tension.

Acid earth argues that the causes of acid pollution are now well understood, and the methods of controlling it are widely available. There is little excuse for not beginning to de-acidify the earth.

Price: £3.95/$5.50

All Earthscan publications are available from:

Earthscan
3 Endsleigh Street
London WC1H ODD, UK

Earthscan Washington
1717 Massachusetts Avenue NW
Washington DC 20036, USA